OFFICE WARFARE

ALSO BY MARILYN MOATS KENNEDY:

Office Politics
Career Knockouts
Salary Strategies
Powerbase

OFFICE WARFARE

Strategies for Getting Ahead

in the Aggressive 80s

MARILYN MOATS KENNEDY

Macmillan Publishing Company

New York

Macmillan Publishing Company
866 Third Avenue, New York, N. Y. 10022
Collier Macmillan Canada, Inc.

Library of Congress Cataloging in Publication Data
Kennedy, Marilyn Moats, 1943–
   Office warfare.
   1. Success in business.   2. Organizational behavior.
3. Industrial sociology.   I. Title.
HF5386.K2784   1985   650.1′4   85-2906
ISBN 0-02-562010-X

Macmillan books are available at special discounts for bulk purchases for sales promotions, premiums, fund-raising, or educational use. Special editions or book excerpts can also be created to specification. For details, contact:

Special Sales Director
Macmillan Publishing Company
866 Third Avenue
New York, New York 10022

10 9 8 7 6 5 4 3 2 1

Designed by Jack Meserole

Printed in the United States of America

For the millions of working people
who've been victimized in the political wars.
Here's your chance to fight back!

Contents

Acknowledgments

Everyone who helped on this book should have had hazardous-duty pay! It was a battle. Getting people to talk about whom they've done in isn't easy. They don't like to talk about plots that went awry or plots that backfired. Therefore, we have protected everybody's identity. There isn't a real name used anywhere in the book—even of those who were successful! Some of their colleagues might see possibilities for new wars that we'd be guilty of igniting. All have been privately thanked.

Patricia O'Keefe came in halfway through the project and did great service in editing. Janet Shlaes worked throughout in research and editing. Donna Reimer virtually ran Career Strategies while I worked on the book. All three of these women were indispensable.

My husband, Daniel, and daughter, Anne Evelyn, suffered neglect with better grace than anyone has a right to expect. They deserve to be recognized for that.

The Northwestern University, Wilmette, and Evanston libraries were extremely helpful. The librarians answered our questions with enthusiasm.

My agent, Jane Jordan Browne, and my editor at Macmillan, Arlene Friedman, were always ready with suggestions, which we used.

Introduction

Want to develop unbeatable potential as a victim of office warfare? Just keep playing politics the way you did in the 1970s. Ignore what's changed and you're setting yourself up. Look at the recent past and you'll see why.

Remember the 1960s? Despite the Vietnam War the economy was in reasonable shape and jobs weren't that difficult to get. High school and college seniors looked forward to, and received, a variety of job offers. At prestigious colleges high grade-point averages meant competition for talent—even for English and history majors, much less accountants and engineers! The *Fortune* 500 companies courted and recruited the best talent they could find, while selling their stability, progressiveness, prestige, and long-term advancement opportunities. "Dropping out" for a few years to find oneself was not a problem—it even had a cachet of radical chic. After all, there were plenty of jobs "out there." Taking time out only meant postponing your job offers, not reducing them.

The 1970s changed all that. Suddenly recruiters were an endangered species. On some campuses they came for "courtesy" interviews, which backfired. Instead of building company goodwill, they enraged students, who discovered there were no jobs. College graduates ceased protesting to become as sober-sided (some said dull) as their parents had been in the 1950s. Getting any job replaced getting the "right" job as entry-level workers vied for positions that people ten years older wouldn't have considered.

White males especially felt the heat as more and more women seriously pursued careers. The sixties male knew that while many female peers might start as serious career women, most would drop out to become housewives and mothers. The seventies male couldn't count on that. While the seventies male might want a spouse whose dowry was an income that matched his, he certainly didn't want her as a competitor in his office. He discovered, to his continuing dismay, that he had no choice. She was not only there, but appeared to have settled in for the long run.

You can see this reflected in the civil rights laws. In 1974 Congress declared maternity a disability to be dealt with by employers as any other temporary medical condition. A woman's job might be held until she returned from maternity leave. Ten years before, maternity was a permanent condition, not a temporary disability. Women were expected to leave their jobs.

The 1980s brought to fruition the changes started in the 1960s, but without that era's prosperity. A lowered inflation rate, so prized by politicians and economists in theory, put tremendous pressure on workers to improve productivity, to take jobs more seriously, and, most important, to compete strenuously. The era of plenty had ended. What was left was a stagnant economy with a growth rate so low that there was no upward thrust to assist new workers. New jobs weren't being created at the same rate as in prior years. If someone missed a promotion, he or she couldn't count on another opportunity in twelve to eighteen months as had previously been the case. It now might literally take years before an opening occurred, especially among *Fortune* 500 companies.

The new, almost hysterical, emphasis on productivity had, and has, but one objective. Each worker must produce a greater amount of high-quality work for the same or less pay! Regardless of what a company says, bottom line, loyalty is out, increased turnover is in. How else to flat-line the salary curve? If people stay in the same job more than three years, they become very expensive help.

Many could be replaced by a less expensive beginner. Hence, the need for planned turnover.

But then how would new jobs be created? If each person produced more, the number of jobs would contract, not expand. If twelve workers did the work of fifteen, the company would be stronger, but what happens to the three displaced workers? Most people, neutral to positive on the productivity issue, failed to draw the obvious conclusion. They didn't see that the promotion they wanted wouldn't occur unless one of two things happened. Either the company's growth rate had to greatly exceed the national average, or the occupant of the coveted job had to leave or move up. It was an entirely new ball game. All of those people who, in the past, had taken the view that productivity was the patriotic way began to reconsider. It was only patriotic as long as it didn't negatively impact their careers.

One of the most profound events, in terms of its effect on the long-term prospects of professionals and managers, didn't even happen to them. Do you remember when Lee Iacocca, president of the Chrysler Corporation, convinced the United Auto Workers to agree to a pay cut in order to save the company? If you're a professional, you probably approved. You thought that union people were unproductive and overpaid. White-collar workers at Chrysler also took cuts and layoffs but that was easily explained. The company was in desperate trouble and they saw the problem through management's eyes. However, did you see the domino effect coming? Did you know that, inevitably, it had to reach you? Many people, because they didn't belong to a union, missed the message.

The message was obscured because professionals and managers believed their interests were identical with top management's. Never had so many people so miscalculated exactly where they stood! As we will see, top management did not, and does not, agree. They tend to see everyone beneath them as "labor." Not since the Depression had workers been asked to take pay cuts. What Chrysler did was force its workers to "buy" a piece of the company. The workers were going to pay for its rehabilitation whether they chose to or not. They were going to become "shadow" owners.

The Chrysler scenario electrified top management people everywhere. Eventually your top management, if they haven't already, may look at you and say, "How much is your job with this company worth to you? Are you willing to take a five or ten percent salary cut?" At the very least, management in many companies is systematically getting rid of the annual across-the-board salary raise, which is the same thing. Since you don't consider yourself overpaid (neither did the UAW), you need to look at your job and your relationship with your present company (or any future employer) in a whole new way. In 1985 it's clear that owners, managers, and workers are changing their relationships. They may not be perfectly aware of the changes but by now most of the players know the script has changed. From our point of view, this change is important because it alters the internal politics of the company. Understanding these changes will alter your career planning as well as how you approach and participate in company politics.

Organizational politics is changing dramatically. The old mindset was a fairly gentlemanly one (except for the few buffoons who actually plotted and stabbed backs). "The politics here is murder," they'd say. People laughed ruefully and commiserated with each other. The new game is deadly serious. People everywhere are thinking and strategizing about the political process. It's a matter of survival. If the productivity movement works—and most experts think its impact will be felt to some degree everywhere—people will continue to work hard for the same, and inevitably less, money. As this change occurs, politics will become the key to advancement. Many people would argue that politics was always key and that there is no change. However, there is a change in degree. Many jobs are going to be eliminated and people are going to be outplaced, de-hired, severed—any word you care to use. It's no longer just a matter of jockeying for power, influence with the boss, or promotions. The issue is survival and politics is key there, too.

Several years ago Peter Drucker began talking about the oversupply of middle managers. That was most un-grateful of him, since the people most likely to buy his books are the very people whose ranks he advised top man-agement to thin. He was, however, pointing out both the obvious and the inevitable. Since managers work through others, in order to be more productive each has to manage more people. Thus some managers would become unnec-essary and unemployed.

Where does that leave us now? All of these changes, most unlikely to be reversed as long as Japan, Inc., and Germany, Inc., stay on course, mean that politics will be the principal means of deciding who moves up, who stays, and who goes. Hence, the title *Office Warfare*. That de-scribes the present situation precisely. People who would never before have been aggressive toward a peer or boss are up in arms. They're going to play hardball, however reluctantly, in order to survive. How office warfare occurs, and what to do about it, are the subjects of this book.

OFFICE WARFARE

Chapter 1. Who Started the War? Old Political Styles

The Political Watershed

In 1985 it's clear that 1979 was a watershed year in American history. Of course, very few people realized it at the time. Before 1979 office politics could often be joked about. It was taken very seriously by only a minority of workers, probably not more than 10 or 15 percent. At least half the people believed you could opt out, just duck all the push and shove. Someone would say ruefully, "Gee, there's a lot of politics in my office." Everyone within hearing distance would nod sympathetically. You could hear them in the cafeteria and in the coffee room saying, "I can't figure out what's going on—or why—but who cares?" It was chic to deprecate the office political system.

Most people quietly and firmly believed in the work ethic. If they worked hard, the effect of politics on them personally would be minimal to nonexistent. Enough people believed in the myth that hard work equals success to make that cliché a reality in some places. At least that's what people told each other.

Were they sincere? Focus groups conducted in 1984 in five major metropolitan areas (Chicago, New York, Dallas, Los Angeles, and Washington, D.C.) indicate that, while aware of politics, the average professional or manager believed she or he could blunt negative politics by working a problem to death. One woman in Washington, D.C., said,

"I knew my boss didn't really like me. I knew he would prefer a man in my spot. Still, until two years ago [1983] he didn't act that out. Now he is."

There were gentlemanly rules to the "game" of politics that reflected social values at the time. These were unwritten, but still powerful, limits to what could and couldn't be done. One of the most powerful rules was "Know thy place," or "Respect the hierarchy." It was almost universally taboo to leapfrog over your boss and plot with his/her boss—especially if you would benefit professionally from the discussion. People had a sense of place within the structure. It meant something that your boss was a box above you on the organizational chart. There was a determined effort to honor the hierarchy. Besides, you might be fired if he or she found out you'd pulled an end run to his/her boss. If you did breach office protocol, your boss's boss was often part of your denouement because he/she told your boss what you'd done. This response reflected the need of each higher level of management to set a good example in honoring the hierarchy.

A second example of the political rules of this era was "Preserve face for the members of our team." You never embarrassed a co-worker, however much he or she deserved it. You didn't even help when someone did it to him/herself. Sometimes you saved the culprit from himself. To do otherwise would do public violence to the "team" facade that every department sought to preserve. You were expected to cover for the less capable. It was suspect to appear too competitive. "What's she trying to prove?" "She's certainly not part of our team," they'd whisper. Preserving the teamwork facade mattered to the majority.

Since 1979 more talk has spewed forth about the virtues of teamwork than ever before. However, there was more genuine teamwork before 1979 than at present. Now the rule is "Give the team lip service but no emotional support."

A third political rule was "The weak and incompetent must be protected." The incompetent or criminally bewildered person, who littered the organizational chart, usually because top management was doing some pal or business connection a favor by hiring the person, was tolerated. Why not? It kept someone's minimally useful relative off the street and off welfare—an accepted, although non-tax-deductible form of philanthropy. Other workers tolerated the person with as much good grace as their individual temperaments allowed. People who publicly objected were thought of as loners, chronic complainers, people who didn't want to be part of the team. Peer outplacement would have seemed a terrible overreaction at the time.

A fourth rule was "The boat will come back. One missed promotion isn't the end of the world." A missed promotion or plum assignment, while disappointing, was not cause for extreme alarm. Other opportunities would arise. Organizations were expanding, creating upward thrust. Despite several business downturns, many people were still optimistic. If you weren't promoted this time, there was certain to be another chance. Women believed this far less often than men. There was also a residue of loyalty on both sides of the desk. Your boss seemed to care how well you did. He or she was looking out for you. Paternalism was submerged, but was a real cultural and political value.

A fifth rule was "Keep the company green." Age discrimination was tolerated. Until the early 1980s, people seemed less anxious to sue, especially those just over forty whose values did not include suing a long-term employer or boss. Some companies deflected potential age discrimination suits by using a "golden handshake." This was an individual payoff plan in which, when a person's years of service plus age totaled a certain number, say seventy-five, the person could take his or her retirement pay in cash and/or receive a year's salary including benefits in exchange for leaving the company permanently. If the

worker in question believed that he or she could get another job—or simply wanted out of the present job—it was
a good deal. There was an involuntary dimension, too.
Many people took such offers because they felt they'd be
pushed out under less favorable circumstances if they refused. Their foreboding was usually justified. In fact, in all
of the companies offering such deals, golden handshakes
were politically mandatory, according to messages passed
through the grapevine, as often as they were voluntary.

The golden handshake didn't always get the job done,
however. Universities, overstocked with tenured faculty,
watched companies thin their ranks of older, supposedly
less productive people, and tried to do the same. When they
made the same kind of buy-out offers, the results were
quite different. The computer science, math, and engineering faculties loved it. They left for industry, financially
enriched by the experience. However, faculty in depressed
and threatened departments, such as English and education, resisted enthusiastically, heating up the war. This resistance forced university CEOs to explore other ways to
get rid of people.

It became nearly impossible for younger faculty to get
tenure track positions, much less actually get tenure.
Imagine the effect this had on office politics! (This is still a
major problem.) Younger faculty found themselves in paroxysms of publishing and bootlicking—while feeling
deeply resentful and sometimes punishing students in the
process.

Rule six was "Hire women only when forced to."
Women were protected, at least nominally, by the affirma-
tive action programs in larger companies. Looking back,
the period from 1975 to 1979 looks like the golden age of
upward mobility for women. Today's increasing on-the-job
political action by women is motivated by the belief (and
the fact) that President Ronald Reagan gutted the affir-
mative action programs, thereby making it easier for large
companies to do as they please. Interestingly enough, not

much has really changed. Few *Fortune* 500 companies have restricted the hiring of women. As one CEO said, "We'll be here long after Reagan has gone. We have to be careful." Many medium- to small-sized companies continued to discriminate. They saw the gutted programs as excellent justification for discrimination and also as a guilt eraser. If the emphasis on bottom-line productivity continues, however, this may change. Companies may still resist women in general but welcome the overachievers.

The New Economics

Economics as well as values changed the political environment. Economic reality intruded on the American dream, the work ethic, and people's expectations. Remember the last big recession? That was the period from roughly mid-1979 through mid-1982. (Some economists argue that it was two different downturns, but for political purposes that's not important.) It wasn't the longest or deepest recession but it was very different from its predecessors. Previous recessions were shakeout periods for individuals and businesses. There were cutbacks and redirections of resources, but once recovery set in, it was business as usual. This recession, however, really was the coda to a particular way of doing business. It buried the "old" office politics. It was a psychological as well as a financial event, especially for the baby boomers. As one thirty-two-year-old said, "For the first time, I realized that I was involved in politics—not voluntarily, God knows, but there I was anyway—up to my eyebrows, just as the game turned mean." This attitude was reflected in people's on-the-job behavior.

Before 1979 most of the baby boomers, those people born between 1946 and 1959, believed that they would earn at least as much money as, if not more than, their parents had. They took the American dream for granted.

They expected to buy a house in an appropriate neighborhood (a bit better than they'd known as children), raise families, and enjoy reasonable job security. Even the most ambitious believed that job tenure was as much within their control as within the company's. After all, in stable businesses few people expected to be laid off. They would move from job to job, climbing the ladder as they went, finally coming to rest on a really good perch. They'd stay there until retirement—unless they were recruited to become CEO of a major firm.

The Bubble Bursts

That dream has ended. Between 1979 and the present, baby boomers were forced to face some terrible truths. These cropped up one by one in an inexorable, unending stream.

1. Single-family housing had become prohibitively expensive. About 50 percent of the baby boomers were priced out of the single-family housing market unless their families lent or gave them money for down payments and continued to subsidize the monthly payments. Even with financial help from their families, many of them still found single-family housing out of reach. This became *the* topic both of conversation and lamentation at cocktail parties. Condominium sales boomed among this age group, but condominiums were a poor substitute for the dream house. It's interesting to note that the young couples who buy rundown, center-city houses and regentrify them expect these neighborhoods to be just like the ones they can't afford in more established areas. They haven't changed the dream, just its location.

2. The competition got much fiercer. The competition for professional and managerial jobs was much tougher. Who hasn't heard about the surplus of physicians and lawyers? Age discrimination laws helped a group least in need —those over forty from lower birthrate years—and did nothing for the people under thirty whose job prospects were the worst they had been in the last twenty years. Management welcomed older workers because it wanted people with the "lived in" look. Proven people were less risky. (This is changing in the mid-eighties as these people become disproportionately expensive and refuse to retire.) Many companies dropped expensive, year-long training programs for new workers. It was cheaper to pay more for an older worker than to bring along a beginner. People with MBAs from the top ten graduate business school programs could no longer count on five to ten job choices upon graduation. There were still recruiters for the top few students in each program, but those at the bottom of the class had to scratch for good jobs.

The joke in Chicago is that some of the University of Chicago Business School graduates are driving taxis. You can immediately identify them as U of C grads because they use city maps, a thing unknown to the majority of cab drivers. Normal taxi drivers simply hurl themselves in the general direction you want to go and expect you to signal when ready to get out.

3. "Deflation" arrived with mixed results. The rate of economic growth slowed dramatically. Double digit inflation ceased. Some jobs disappeared entirely. Smokestack America began to wind down; it was clearly cheaper to import many products. United States Steel closed its Gary, Indiana, plant. An industrial or mechanical engineer, with a few years' experience and the desire to move up, inevitably had fewer choices. Many went back for MBAs just as a surplus of people with those degrees emerged. It didn't matter that engineering jobs were still there—it was the sense that many options had been eliminated. A career claustrophobia set in. This happened even though there was sustained growth in service businesses. Things looked normal—but they weren't.

4. People stayed on the job longer. Older workers weren't opting for early retirement as often as they had in the 1970s. That slowed promotions. The social security system was threatening to self-destruct, despite massive tax increases. Furthermore, those just beginning to collect social security benefits under the present program were taxed on these benefits! This provided, and continues to provide, tremendous incentive for people to stay at their jobs until they are literally carried out. Besides, many Americans in their fifties and sixties still believe retirement is a synonym for death. You can track the resistance to retirement by watching large companies instituting preretirement planning programs for employees. Employees attend, participate in the discussions, act interested, but stay on the job. One *Fortune* 500 company put seven hundred people through a week-long program with their spouses. Only sixty of the 700 retired at sixty-five.

5. Large numbers of companies jettisoned the annual across-the-board salary increase for nonunion employees. Instead of a yearly raise, however small, the time between pay increases had been deliberately lengthened. Even after the recession officially ended, companies didn't return to their former salary policies. While it had become clear that nonexempt people, particularly secretaries and word processing operators, were going to resist any change in compensation policies, professional and managerial people were, and are, expected to get with the program. So far the results are not as predicted. Those employees, regardless of level, who believe they're employable elsewhere leave. The barnacles who know they've got as good a deal as possible stay, without significantly increasing their work effort. You can easily predict the long-term effect on productivity and turnover.

6. Company loyalty bottomed out. Employer/employee bonds weakened absolutely and changed character. It became clear to large numbers of people that company loyalty bought you nothing. It was a gift—frequently ungratefully received if acknowledged at all by management. Better to be mentally an independent contractor. Work for the company and move when convenient or profitable.

Ask people between twenty-five and forty what job security is and many will respond without hesitation, "Job security means that I'll always be able to get a job." A sixty-year-old upon hearing that reply must feel like a visitor from Mars. Apparently the younger group retained nothing from their grandparents' accounts of the Great Depression.

7. Productivity replaced Management By Objectives as the corporate fad of the 1980s. Now during performance appraisals the smart people trotted out evidence not of what they'd tried but of what they'd accomplished. Most popular is how much money you saved the company, either by working harder or by getting your subordinates to work harder. Harder in this context always means more output, of the same or higher quality, for less money. The implications of this trend haven't even begun to be felt. In the 1970s "having potential" was important, now getting results is top priority. Rarely has the contrast between fat think and thin think been so stark.

Middle managers and professionals know that their careers are implicitly threatened by the productivity movement and its spawn, but often they don't understand why. The generalized response to the productivity movement has been one of greater competitiveness for promotions and political leverage. In some companies there's a frantic attempt by managers in staff areas to move to line areas, the assumption being that line management is "safer." The people whose job tenure is greatest are revenue producers. They are usually asked later than staff people are to take pay cuts in a downturn. They are also there to turn out the lights. Still, both staff and line people will eventually report to the same unemployment office—and the same line!

8. Terror replaced outright firing for getting rid of unwanted or obsolete middle managers and professional talent. For some reason, the legal uncertainty over the employment-at-will doctrines caused companies to move very cautiously when eliminating surplus people, except in divisional or company-wide layoffs. Employment at will (in some states it's known as "wrongful discharge") means that you have no legal right to your job, regardless of quality of performance or years of service, unless you're covered by a labor union or employment contract. At any time, you and the company can get rid of each other without explanation. Employers have been sued and plaintiffs have collected for what courts thought was too free a use of the Divine Right of Kings in employee-employer relations. This left many companies looking for alternative ways to thin the ranks. Terror and creating uncertainty suggested themselves. For the risk avoider it was and is a successful management strategy.

The emerging philosophy is to make the expendable people so uncomfortable that they'll be delighted to go. Give them an incentive to leave and it will be cheaper than either firing or outplacing them, and far less risky. Few judges—especially since most are political appointees anyway—are going to see a legal cause for action because the company's politics were creatively hardball. As long as the victim is under forty, white, and male, it's successful.

These tactics substantially change the internal political climate. Once it's known that management's displeasure will be felt through the informal (terror) system and not through the formal one (firing or outplacement), all bets are off. Anything an employee wants to do through the informal system is justified. It's axiomatic that if top management uses a particular tactic, that makes it allowable and just. Everyone feels free to follow suit. Top management faces its own terrors, as boards of directors become less manageable and more demanding. Of course, nobody has publicly announced this change in policy, but one merely has to watch the ratcheting up of the terror among peers and below the level of top management in order to see this policy's effects.

Why hasn't this program of terror, usually done to people in their late forties or fifties who are at the top of their salary grades, produced a response from the baby boom crowd? What happened to the thirst for social justice? Apparently it ran aground when the economy continued to stagger. As one thirty-five-year-old engineer said, "Of course I see what's going on. Yes, I know it's unfair. However, can you think of a single reason to interfere when Rob's [the victim] leaving creates an opening? Incidentally, it will be the first supervisory opening since 1981."

9. People have weaned themselves from the notion that job security as a company employee exists or is even worth pursuit. The rising numbers of successful small businesses reflect the realization that since job security with one company isn't really possible, it's better (and maybe more profitable) to create your own. That way, if the business fails, at least the founder knows he/she did it to him/herself. He or she wasn't someone else's victim. Expect this trend to continue and the number of new business failures to fall sharply. That's because the new businesses are mostly low-capital, labor-intensive service businesses. This trend has been helped by large numbers of people who actively seek out small businesses to patronize. Witness the rise of small consulting firms, small highly specialized retailers, "garage shop" service organizations. With the advent of reasonably priced computers and word processing systems, the need for expensive clerical and support staffs disappears.

10. Women under forty in two-income families have found that they have to work. More than 60 percent of women with children under the age of five work, and the percentage is still rising. They can't go home again even if they want to.

Scratch a liberated woman and you sometimes find a latent housewife. Baby boomers can't live as they feel entitled to without two incomes. What their parents managed on one paycheck, they now struggle to achieve with two.

That means that women who previously longed for and expected a "choice" really don't have one. At least it's not the choice they envisioned. They can only quit work by halving the family's standard of living. These baby boom women, finally convinced they're in for the long run, have come alive as motivated competitors. That heats things up. Women under thirty don't yet have the same commitment to work as married women in their thirties. They usually haven't developed the combination of economic need and ambition that their married counterparts have.

All of these changes, which baby boomers are currently facing, affect the political climate. They are subtle changes; you must look below the surface in order to see their effect.

Old Politics versus New Politics

Office politics isn't a recent phenomenon. Most of the really good theory was developed by Machiavelli hundreds of years ago. Although his interest was primarily the Italian city-state and not the office, his concepts are still applicable. There are, however, some new developments in political mores and folkways that make "office warfare" the right term for what's happening in the majority of workplaces today.

The new politics has heavy economic overtones. Imagine that you meet an old pal, Richard, at your professional society meeting. You and he have a desultory conversation and you mention you are interviewing for a job at the XYZ Corporation. Your pal says, "Good luck." You and he part amiably. Two weeks later the person you interviewed with at XYZ tells you that he's decided to hire someone else. A friend calls to tell you XYZ hired your erstwhile pal, Richard. Confronted, Richard says, "Hey, you mentioned the opening, why shouldn't I go for it? It pays thirty percent more than my present job."

People who believe they are deprived of what they "deserve" can justify more elastic ethics. These can be stretched to cover virtually any decision and action. For example, one woman in justifying her whisper campaign against a co-worker said, "Look, they [presumably her boss or top management collectively] are only going to promote one woman. Realistically, there is a quota. Either she moves up or I do. I decided that I was going to get the promotion no matter what it took. I can't afford ethical quibbles right now. I need the money." Although these tactics occurred in the 1970s, they were much less common than they are today, probably because of the sixties' peace and love hangover.

Politics is now out in the open. It's no longer necessary to speak in euphemisms. It's perfectly OK to talk openly about the political situation. Why pretend that hard work equals success? To suggest this immediately invites others to brand you as a political neophyte. While this new realism is an improvement over the silence of previous times, many people use it to free themselves of any pretense that their interests are identical with peers', bosses', or even with the company's. It's license to take whatever action they choose.

Since open politics plays a major part in management decision making, the tendency to devalue such old-fashioned virtues as sincerity, positive attitude, loyalty, and extra effort has increased. Instead of recognizing that these are also political virtues, there's been a wholesale change. People see political planning and the development of action strategies as a substitute for such attitudes and behavior. This weakens the ethics that the majority of office players subscribe to. Listen to the grapevine in your office. It carries more negative judgments than in the past. A dark cynicism coupled with impatience seems to dominate in many companies. There's a tendency to label anyone who has any of the old-fashioned virtues as naive or as a "wimp." For a manager trying to raise productivity it's a double problem. Productivity and negativism are not good bedfellows.

Middle managers are intently studying how top management acts out its values and are trying to figure out ways to follow suit. For instance, if top management shows extreme interest in financial return, every middle manager will, too—sometimes with disastrous results. The tendency is to fixate on the obvious at the expense of the long-term. If top management thinks terror works better than improving quality of work life to motivate the majority of workers, middle management collectively makes a fist. The lemmings-to-the-sea approach can be disastrous for both the internal politics and the long-term survival of the business. Even the business press has picked this up since 1980, as evidenced by the increasing coverage of the shortsightedness of managers who stress only this quarter's profits while touting strategic planning—something never done short-term.

Politics in the 1980s can be most accurately characterized as the politics of brinksmanship. More and more people are making extreme decisions about how they'll behave in the office. This is often quite shocking to people in their fifties and sixties. For instance, one spouse in a two-income family may deliver an "up or out" ultimatum to his or her boss, knowing that the mortgage is covered. Another may threaten to resign in the midst of an important project, knowing the boss will retaliate down the road but planning to be gone before that happens. Top management responds with quicker cuts of surplus workers, more switching around of people, and less personal concern. Top management's risk, of course, is that the company will lose critical talent, but since they are sitting on the largest talent bank ever, it seems a small, and wholly acceptable, risk.

Never discount the willingness of top management to be shortsighted and act spitefully. Strategic planning and reasoned, bottom-line decisions work better in theory than in the field. The *Wall Street Journal* bears this out in many of its feature stories. Some of the companies it reports on seem to have a death wish.

In the past, political power has been based on building stable personal relationships. People cooperated over a period of years and relationships developed that were so mutually beneficial it was advantageous to maintain them. These relationships allowed workers to overlook fairly obvious defects in their co-workers and bosses because of the warmth and habitual nature of such friendships. Not anymore. Relationships are now situation-specific on both sides. Why get involved long-term? Who knows how long you'll be in that job or even in that company? This means every relationship by definition is both transitory and superficial. How could it be otherwise when developing long-term relationships in a short-term environment practically guarantees stress and pain?

If people do form closer relationships in which they have a personal stake they will find these relationships threatened rather regularly by the company's groping to stay afloat. Hurting someone's reputation, when the relationship is purely surface, seems less of an ethical problem than destroying the reputation of a friend. Why get involved? Greater freedom of action is possible when you don't. This is the wrong way to analyze the politics of instability, even though it's by far the most common approach.

Outsiders replace insiders as the primary source of support for individuals. Recognizing that the company is permanently unstable, people form the strongest peer relationships outside of the company. The growth in trade and professional society meeting attendance and the mushrooming of special interest networks reflects much more than a heightened awareness of the power of networking. It reflects the growing identification of people with an industry, e.g., health care, or a particular skills group, e.g., communications, rather than with an individual company.

Test this by going to the monthly meeting of any trade

or professional group and listening to the small talk. You'll find people talking about their jobs and companies much more frankly than would have been customary ten years ago. There's less pretense. Companies call it a lack of loyalty. Employees call it "hedging your bets." As one thirty-two-year-old lawyer said, "My law firm's OK now but it will be three years before I know if I'll be made a partner. In the meantime I'm going to be very, very visible at the bar association meetings and active in the corporate law section."

No company or firm can promise not to go out of business or be acquired and gutted. It can't even promise its stockholders that it will be regularly profitable—much less make such promises to its employees! Therefore, anything goes. For example, many industrial firms have become aware of the need for escalating security precautions and are actively trying to persuade managers not to talk freely to outsiders. It's only partly successful. No trade secrets are shared, but employees see no harm in sharing what top management believes is sensitive information. Workers deprecate their exchanges as gossip. After all, they need each other. If someone needs a job quickly, who could help as readily as a competitor? This line of reasoning is especially prevalent among people whose companies would be unlikely to provide any kind of outplacement help—or even a few weeks' severance pay.

Workers under forty seem to have a heightened sense of time. They very specifically record, lament, and worry about the passage of time. They can't or won't wait to see "if things turn around." If a company gets into trouble, the uncertainty means that many talented people will bolt. For them, ambiguity means flight. These workers also arbitrarily set limits for how long they'll wait for promotion. A thirty-three-year-old manager in a Big Eight accounting firm said, "They've got six weeks to make me a partner." (That would be the time of the next announcement of who had been elected.) "I don't care if it's the middle of tax season. If it doesn't happen, I'm leaving. I've already got three jobs lined up. I just haven't let anyone make me a final offer yet." He hadn't shared his timetable with management and he was one of the firm's top tax people and a real client pleaser. Top management was thinking in terms of five-year plans, middle management was looking ahead to weeks and months. Many companies have been slow to respond to the end of the recession. The employees, thinking they have suffered sufficiently, are quick to move on once business improves.

It's inescapable, looking at this behavior, that politics in the 1980s is appallingly self-centered. The "me" generation has become middle management. It now has a very broad stage on which to act out its desires and display its values. Many of these people have no sense of teamwork at all. They talk about teams and play team sports but have never really transferred those values to the workplace. As one vice president said of his three subordinates, "Their idea of a team is that we are all in the same geographic area at the same time." These workers are entirely isolated within their own values, wants, needs, and plans, so teamwork really means nothing to them.

The rising number of entrepreneurs among this group bears witness to the fact that large numbers of the thirty-to forty-five-year-old crowd want to do it entirely their own way, in their own time frame, accepting whatever risks are involved. Having decided real job security doesn't exist, many abandon *Fortune* 500s for smaller, more responsive employers.

More than any other factor, including economics, the "me first and last" attitude accounts for many of the changes in politics. Lamenting this, while mildly cathartic, is not productive. It's more important to look specifically at, and analyze, individual changes. Knowing the mindset of your competitors is going to affect your goals and strategies. Unless you can uncover the motives behind your competitor's actions, you will be setting yourself up as an ideal victim of office warfare.

As you'll see in the next chapter, this is happening every day to people who should, and claim they do, know better.

◊ FINDING THE HIDDEN AGENDA

Focus groups often reveal startling attitudes among people whose unvarying Brooks Brothers mien misleads the casual observer. The people most security-oriented are those with nonworking or economically disadvantaged spouses (nurses, teachers, social workers), not people from working class backgrounds whose parents or grandparents suffered through the Depression.

A second group who are highly security-minded are the bootstrappers, mostly women, with a few men from technical backgrounds, who've moved from lower-level jobs into middle management. Since they know they lack educational credentials and were promoted on merit, they are never quite sure they could have done as well elsewhere. Would another company have recognized their talents? Their need for security within the company and the search for it is all-consuming. They are much touted by their companies because they were "promoted from within." These people wreak so much political havoc when threatened, companies are beginning to examine whether they are such a plus after all.

Chapter 2. Identifying Company War Zones

Why War Zones Occur

We've talked about the big picture. We've seen how and why the political environment heated up in the 1980s. Now it's time to get more specific and scrutinize the individual company, your company in particular. We're going to look for war zones. A war zone is any part of an organization, regardless of size, in which the political climate is such that all employees must prepare to act decisively to avoid victimization. We need to see what internal conditions can occur that complement and intensify what's going on outside the company to create war zones. The victims and victimizers may change places during a single siege. There's no consistency and no real predictability.

War zones develop, sometimes with startling rapidity, because management creates and/or tolerates conditions that breed them. Top management may not even be aware of what it's doing to create war zones, but you will, once you learn how to recognize and analyze these conditions. War zones aren't particularly difficult to identify. It's simply human nature to ignore unpleasant situations. You may, on an unconscious level, know that your job is about to become a nightmare, but do you really want to confront the details of the whole bloody scenario before lunch? You must, if you don't want to become a victim. Identifying the warfare potential of a situation, before it unfolds, gives you time to plan rather than be forced to react under less desirable circumstances.

Although there are many internal conditions that will set the stage for office warfare, there are ten that virtually guarantee war zones will be created. A company never needs reason or excuse to fall into destructive politics. It can happen for many reasons. However, the following ten conditions are most likely to create a state of seige. Where did this information come from? It's the result of observing victims in companies (some self-described and some identified by others) and meeting with them outside of the workplace. You are bound to recognize some of these conditions if you've been working five or ten years, although you may not have identified them as such at the time. Remember, at any time three or four of these conditions can coexist. They rarely occur one at a time.

CONDITION ONE: Financial Instability

Financial instability, if it can't be changed by individual actions and keeps people wondering if the company will survive, precedes the onset of political warfare. If people see a logical reason for financial instability, such as a sales decline, then it's just another business problem. It may be very serious. It may prove fatal in the long run, but it doesn't necessarily provoke political warfare. In order to heat up the internal politics noticeably, the financial instability must have no discernable cause and must be a long-term problem. Bankers and accountants come and go with beetled brows and worried expressions. They spend inordinate amounts of time in closed-door sessions with a dour top management. Despite all this attention, whatever is tried neither improves nor worsens the situation. People feel threatened but helpless. It must be clear that even a messiah would be mesmerized by the complexity of the problems. A state of predictable, monotonous financial instability seems entrenched, even never-ending. Watch companies in which one division regularly loses money even though its planning is good and its product is excellent. The people there are shell-shocked and comatose.

People who've never lived through the gradual weakening of a division or a once-successful product and watched it bleed have never known a peculiar, but very real, professional agony. If your Aunt June had cancer, even a very virulent form, you'd have the comfort of knowing she was getting state-of-the-art medical care. The Mayo Clinic, Northwestern, Johns Hopkins, nothing would be too good or too risky for Aunt June to try.

Imagine instead that Aunt June called in a series of witch doctors who waved printouts and mumbled incantations. No two "doctors" (consultants) could agree on the problem, much less the solution. You'd soon move from fear through anger to numbness. Numbness, of course, protects people from the stark terror of having to confront and cope with the fact that things are out of control.

When this form of financial instability exists, top management can't—for a collection of political, ego, and overall prestige reasons—pull the plug. A trickle-down panic effect starts when operating managers begin to realize that the status quo is management's permanent choice, not a temporary aberration. They hear the door closing on their careers. If they care about the company, and many still do, they are literally bathed in fury and intense frustration.

Why does this situation breed destructive politics? The major reason is that it says to workers, "This company is out of control. Top management is deliberately incompetent. We are careening down an unknown road at top speed and we don't know why or where we're going." That throws people back on their own resources. It loosens their ethical and emotional ties to others in the organization and even to the idea of a cohesive organization. It promotes aggressive and systematic disintegration. It does not breed teamwork. A thrall comes over the employees. They realize that they are experiencing the calm before a major storm. During that uneasy quiet, anyone who can improve him/

herself feels entirely justified in doing so. All bets are off. This may mean nothing more than trying to get an expensive lamp for one's office or ratcheting up the level of expense account cheating. It may also mean trying to derail someone else's career, sometimes merely to see if it can be done—a macabre practice session.

Sometimes the things people do to divert themselves from the perpetual fog are comic. In a drug company that was struggling through its third recall in eighteen months, someone organized a "horse race." Anonymously, pictures of the three top people in the embattled division appeared on the coffee room bulletin board. As rumors cropped up, one of the three pictures would move to the right. Then a new rumor would surface and a different person would move out front. The anonymous handicapper kept moving his horses until personnel issued a memo and removed the pictures.

The Outward Signs   Here are some sure signs of chronic financial instability. If your company meets more than five of these ten conditions, consider yourself in a war zone and prepare either to be a full-fledged combatant or to bail out. Since that usually can't be done instantly, you need as much advance warning as possible.

1. The company's profits have declined each quarter for more than two years, even though the amount of the decline is not great. The company has reserves but shows an increasingly smaller profit. The outside directors bluster and eye the CEO menacingly but do nothing. Periodically, something profitable is sold to improve the bottom line.

2. The grapevine has reported that the auditors weren't eager to sign the management letter. They insisted certain changes be made before doing so, even at the risk of the audit committee's wrath. Accounting firms don't casually refuse to sign off on an audit. An accountant's displeasure is important, even critical, and rarely political. The consequences for everyone in the company, however, are political. This news in the grapevine (you can bet it won't be published in the house organ) may be the rank and file's first exposure to the chronic nature of the company's problems. Until this happens, many employees will believe it's the boogie man or the competition that is causing the problems—anything but the management. Most employees prefer, look for, even hope for, an outside explanation.

3. The company has changed its accounting system twice in the past five years. Companies often change accounting procedures when they need to plump up earnings. There may be many other legitimate reasons for these changes, but anytime it happens, especially if statement number 1 is true, it's worth investigating. Solicit reasons from the grapevine. Have you taken an accountant to lunch lately?

4. The company has changed banks and the bank(s) they dropped didn't work very hard to keep the business. The grapevine does not report a reason for the change. Bankers live by their intuition as well as their financial workups. They'll fight for clients they want to keep. The lack of fight signals a withdrawal of confidence in the company's viability. The lending officer who let the account go may have upped his/her profit participation. Remember, bankers like safe risks, not "it could go either way and we can't predict" situations.

5. A pattern of new product failures has occurred, which has drained the company financially. There is no clear reason why any of the new products should have failed. Outsiders say the company has lost its touch. Insiders say each of the new products was underpromoted, undercapitalized, or both. A company unable to adequately finance new product development may cut corners elsewhere, thereby creating a money drain equivalent to the energy drain of a Black Hole.

"Throwing good money after bad" is a cliché but also an often-repeated truth. Witness the companies that introduce a new product nobody will buy and, not content with having the market validate this, introduce "improvements" six months later. No wonder so many marketing people are gypsies.

6. The company's stock price has declined over the past five years. It has had a few, very small, increases, usually when the market overheated, but has fallen back after each one. Nobody suggests the stock is underpriced. Since many people are unaware of what's going on, the news of the totality of the company's sickness travels slowly through the investor grapevine. Putting the whims and fads of Wall Street aside, stock prices can reflect a lack of analyst and institutional investor confidence in the long-term viability of the company. This is different from the vicissitudes Chrysler's stock underwent during the massive effort to save the company. Investors knew something was being done. In companies with chronic financial troubles, investors don't see any positive steps being taken.

7. The research and development budget has been gutted. The cash needed for innovation has been redirected to operating costs or paid out in dividends. This is especially significant in service businesses and high technology companies. A company that doesn't support research and orderly innovation will eventually die or be acquired at a "fire sale." The death throes will be painful and lengthy because the lack of will to keep up is identical to the lack of will to survive.

Consider the advertising agency or public relations firm that repeatedly does the minimum for its clients, keeping the business profitable at the expense of long-term viability. That happens more frequently than people in those industries like to admit. The employees may know what's going on but they often feel powerless to change things. Some of them probably aren't aware that this is even the problem. As one account executive in the branch office of a major advertising agency recalled, "No one seemed to realize that the client's dissatisfaction was submerged but always there. We thought it was normal, because there was no one specific time when we'd seriously failed to perform.

Client sales were good but never spectacular. My boss seemed to be in a trance. We kept recycling ideas and whole campaigns. I knew it was going to catch up with us, but since no one else cared, I just gave up. I decided to concentrate on what was happening in the office. Eventually we lost the account, but that was five years after I first realized we were drifting and using the client as a cash cow."

8. Comptrollers and treasurers change annually. Nobody lasts in the job more than twelve to eighteen months. The cynics form a quarter pool to guess the longevity of each new hire. Management, not just the troops, ante up. Killing the (financial) messenger is an extremely popular form of top management action. Sometimes the CEO acts as if he or she believed changing financial advisers would solve the problem. It never does—and it almost always causes middle management to start war games. The damage is caused because employees believe that each new financial wizard will help. Since the problems get more difficult and management is indecisive, no one seems able to make a difference. This can have a curious fallout. One chapter of a state CPA society actually put a notice in its monthly newsletter that said, "Seven of our members have been through the treasurer's job at the XYZ Company. If you're asked to interview for that job proceed with caution!" The company, deeply offended, threatened to sue. Its corporate counsel dissuaded management and advocated hiring a search firm to bring in someone from a remote part of the country.

9. The company's marketing department has been reorganized and staff reduced at least twice in the past three years. If it's a consumer products company, the advertising agency may have changed annually with a press flurry. Each time, the new agency showed more urgency to make back its initial investment. Most top management people, unless they have marketing backgrounds, don't really know what marketing does or what its capabilities and limitations are. Changing marketers gives them the same sense of dealing with the problem that changing comptrollers does, and it is just as useless. Advertising agencies expect to take the blame for top management's errors by being unjustly fired, and they are rarely disappointed. Change here rarely gets to the guts of the problem, particularly if it's largely due to management myopia or indecisiveness.

10. Top management meets more frequently and for longer periods of time with investment analysts. A consultant has been called by management to touch up the numbers for these presentations. Management gets coaching in projecting strength, warmth, and sincerity. (The cynics say if they were doing their jobs it wouldn't be necessary.) This can be carried to such extremes that analysts will say to each other, "I love the people, but don't buy their stock."

Financial analysts earn their keep by seeing through such presentations to the troubled guts of the company. However, it's not always clear whether top management knows that. Unless the press takes an interest, the analysts' opinions aren't widely known, and many people—but not the employees—will be unaware of their collective judgment. If you're too far from the financial area to observe what's going on, you should be able to garner this information from the office grapevine. It will appear as a rumor that the analysts don't think the company is very hot.

CONDITION TWO: Inexplicable Events

Arbitrary, irrational, and inexplicable occurrences, which large numbers of employees observe or hear of, should alert you that warfare conditions exist. The grapevine fairly vibrates with surprises. These occurrences can indirectly reflect financial problems. It isn't necessary for the company to suddenly run short of cash. Several key executives, last seen at the golf outing licking the CEO's

nine iron, suddenly disappear. There is no official (or unofficial) explanation. The grapevine is silent. The only reason the grapevine is quiet (and the condition is temporary)
is because the skullduggery happened away from the office, and absolute silence on departure was the price paid
by the dear departed for a good severance package. Although explicable financial problems may give birth to task
forces, reorganizations, and rah-rah speeches, as long as
management seems in control, these problems seldom
cause warfare. However, if management seems too dazed,
people will revert to the law of the jungle. Few people
reckon with the fury of the departed people's secretaries.
Sufficiently aroused, they can cause serious problems. At
the least, the grapevine will carry their versions of events
and their predictions about the next crisis.

Arbitrary behavior is a hallmark of a top management
under siege. The two kinds of arbitrary behavior likely to
produce a war zone are: firing people without apparent
reason, and major, abrupt changes in direction without
preparing the troops.

Firings always affect the political climate and heat up
the war; however, certain ways of firing people create immediate conflict. Firing people who should have been fired
years ago for taking unauthorized and premature retirement produces more political problems than firing people
unfairly. The employees reason that management, having
tolerated the nonproducers for years, must now be changing its values. Where will the change lead? What other
deadwood is likely to feel the cut? The employees assume
that something terrible is about to befall the company or
management would let its dogs lie. These born-again cynics are almost always right. Overriding all, however, is the
fear that top management's definition of "deadwood" may
have been revised.

It's no news that some employees retire on the payroll.
That's deadwood. However, it's not an absolute definition.
Suppose one day management redefined the term to mean

older and more expensive, even though competent, help. It may affect everyone in a particular department, because top management wants instant change. If everyone is fired or bought off, the new people will head in a brand-new direction. In financially troubled companies, an entirely new sales force may find a solution rather than merely identify a new set of problems. The support people who remain, however, are not enthralled with having all of their networks suddenly shredded. They may strategize ways to undermine the new messiahs. Since they're insiders and the new messiahs are outsiders, this can be done fairly easily.

Irrational behavior is different from, although just as dangerous as, arbitrary behavior. Irrational doesn't mean that the troops don't understand why something is being done. It means the troops believe management doesn't understand why they are doing it. It heats up the political environment. The best example of this in recent history is the selling off of a profitable division while continuing to fund a dying one. Another example would be the manufacturer who, while searching for a merger partner, decides to build a new factory. It has happened!

Finally, inexplicable behavior means that what has happened so defies logic that no one can reason out its cause. The best example of this is the hospital that added a wing just as two hospitals in the same town closed wards because of the citywide surplus of hospital beds. A year later the same hospital expanded a ward just as government-imposed cost controls began to be felt. This time, not only was the paid staff concerned, the attending physicians began to sweat. From sweat to seeking admitting privileges elsewhere is a baby step.

CONDITION THREE: Secrecy

Secrecy creates a red alert anywhere. The more secretive top management is, the more time the rest of the company spends trying to get the facts. Productivity drops off dramatically. If the company was doing as well as it should, top management would be trumpeting its leadership triumph to the internal press. That isn't happening. The editor of the house organ uses more linage for softball scores than on sales news. People can't rest until they know why. Their jobs are at stake. Secrecy never works because most organizations are run by men with secretaries. They know the truth and usually tell their buddies. Secrecy also produces a virulent "we versus they" mentality. Secrecy puts a premium on information-gathering skills at the price of getting on with business.

A drug company may decide its employees don't need to know that its most profitable product has hit a snag with the Food and Drug Administration. Even if the recall of that drug might sink the already troubled company, the news is kept under wraps. What happens, of course, is that employees sense that those above them are scrambling to cover themselves. Why? It can only be because the higher-ups recognize that a bigger problem than anyone has been willing to acknowledge so far exists and they are now looking for a scapegoat. A war zone now exists.

CONDITION FOUR: Reorganizations

Reorganizations produce war zones because they change all internal power structures. Management may be reorganizing solely for that reason. Every company's internal power structure is based on a combination of position power and personal influence. If data processing was previously headed by a vice president and is now under an operating manager, the area's influence is weakened. Reorganizations can put influential people back to zero—each person is left with position power only. Ruthlessly reorganizing undercuts alliances—which may have been part of top management's motive in the first place! The top people understand that breaking up influence groups may be the only way, albeit a somewhat drastic one, to break up entrenched power.

What they usually don't count on, however, is how the rank and file will react. The rank and file react by fighting back, and after the new organizational structure is drawn and rationalized, the politics will be extremely vicious. Because the old power relationships have been disturbed, people jockey for position. Power is literally free-floating until people grasp and secure it by building new influence groups and new relationships. This can even disrupt long-standing individual networking groups as people are shuffled to different areas.

Since many people don't understand that the reorganization must change power relationships, career damage may literally fall on them. They weren't looking for trouble, but it found them. Those people who naively assume "nothing much has changed" can be reorganized to powerlessness without even seeing what's happening. For example, Janet M., the head nurse in a hospital neonatal unit, saw the shuffling of people above her but had no idea they would not bear all the brunt of the shuffling. Imagine her surprise when she learned one day that she was now reporting two levels lower in the organization than she had previously. The farther down the organization reorganization extends, the more likely that war zones will be created.

CONDITION FIVE: Product/Service Declines

Nothing can heat up the political warfare as much as the gradual, long-term weakening of the company's main product or service. Suppose the company is famous for breakfast cereal. Consumer tastes have changed. The company responds by trying to get its rapidly shrinking number of customers to eat cereal more often. They don't. When this happens the internal politics will be a politics of scarcity. Instead of accolades and money to the innovators, the string-recyclers will rise.

The imminent death of an established brand might cause everyone to pull together, but the slow weakening of a once-powerful star product will have a divisive effect.

Had the company acted decisively and introduced a new product or even effectively improved or repositioned its old one, people would have held off cannibalizing each other. Without a positive, energetic response, the troops play a destructive waiting game. Where you will sit at the funeral becomes important.

In service businesses the crisis may come when the largest client is ready to bolt and no replacement is coming on board. People try to find out who's going to be scapegoated and slow down their work so everything can be documented and justified.

CONDITION SIX: Climate Changes

Changes in the political climate and the style of the organization can cause major warfare. When management begins to reward a different sort of employee, it signals a change in the climate. For example, if "hands-on" managers had been regularly moving up and now think-tank graduates are on the rise, check the organization's climate. The choices for former "ins" are clear—revamp your style and become more theoretical or leave. Those who resist create a war zone. They may not intend to, but it happens as they react to the loss of personal power. They feel threatened, and most important, threatened without a reasonable cause. They haven't changed at all! They're still doing the job. Why has management changed? If the economy should happen to be in a downturn when the climate shifts, the old guard will be reluctant to job hunt and may launch guerrilla tactics.

The climate change may occur not because the organization has financial or product/service problems, but because a manager feels he can use that to shake up complacent people. The change will accomplish that, but the cost is often very high. A service business has always rewarded and pampered its salespeople. They are at the top of the pecking order. One day management decides that the people who really make a difference are those who provide, rather than sell, the service. Top management shifts its attention. The salespeople, even if they earn the same amount of money, will react instinctively to the shift. They won't like being former stars.

CONDITION SEVEN: Unfairness—Real or Imagined

Real or imagined unfairness or organizational victimization can provoke retaliation against the company as a whole, individuals in top management or a group of managers, and even against specific, isolated individuals in any slot. It may be unfashionable to talk about fairness, but it's a powerful part of the value system. What makes it so important in office wars is that each person acts as judge, jury, and executioner. There is no separation between an objective evaluation and a purely subjective one. Those people who apply logic may be the first victims!

In a *Fortune* 1000 company, two divisional managers, Robert R. and Jack V., both over forty, were given exceedingly brutal performance appraisals after years of very positive ones. Their boss, in delivering these appraisals, called one incompetent and the other inconsistent—and that was the nicest thing either heard. The boss's superior had directed that these two men be forced out and replaced with cheaper help.

Robert was practically in tears from the combination of sudden brutality and shock. His secretary, an employee of twenty-five years' standing, had worked for him for the last ten years. She thought her boss was extremely competent and his boss aggressively out of line. Since she was due to retire within five years, she reasoned that she had little to lose. (This was a misassessment on her part, but since things worked out, she never had to face the possible consequences.) She decided to fight back.

Her power was in the informal system. As a secretary, she had no real position power that gave her access to top management, but she did have informal power. She talked with several secretaries who were old pals. One was the right hand of the corporate CEO. She gathered the facts and saw to it that the CEO's secretary delivered them. Robert's boss was in outplacement within three months. Robert still believes justice was done because top management saw the light. He didn't understand the delivery system. He didn't understand that the object wasn't justice at all. Jack stayed on the job but only because the boss was fired.

Top management fired Robert and Jack's boss for his inability to fire cleanly and politically. He tried, but the informal system zapped him. The fear of lawsuits stops few managers—or companies—from doing whatever they choose. It is far more likely that top management wisely decided that the perception of injustice might spread and that other employees might widen the war. What they actually did was satisfy the secretary and reward her for her informal power. Not one of the top people involved even knew her boss!

That a company would sanction such crudeness is not surprising, nor is it unusual. What is unusual, though, is how swiftly top management moved when it realized a victim had allies who would fight back intelligently through the informal system. Ordinarily nothing would have happened until management had fired several people and the political situation had further deteriorated. Managing up (the art of guiding your superior's decisions) is done every day, but it's most successful when done in a situation such as this. When people are standing on a clear principle, it's very difficult to argue against them. Public opinion and the political climate generally support and reward them.

Corporate unfairness can be identified by a group of employees as something done to them selectively. If assembly line workers are asked to take salary cuts, staff and management better be doing the same. It doesn't matter about relative salaries or what's happened in the past. Those who are taking cuts are only interested in what happens now. No amount of union soothing can control workers who see themselves as victims.

CONDITION EIGHT: Top Management Ego Overkill

Nothing is as scary or overcharges the political environment as quickly as watching top management begin to believe its own press. Let a senior vice president be interviewed on network television and suddenly he really *knows*. We don't know exactly what he knows—neither does he—but he's acting as if he had invented the microchip. It's the same when management begins to hyperventilate about an idea, productivity, for instance, which clearly says to the employees, "These people have lost their footing. They're out of touch with reality." It has the same effect as a ski gondola hanging by one wire. The passengers react with panic.

In a sense, the company is out of control. If top management can't discern fact from fiction, what hope is there for the troops? This can happen in a consulting firm when the principals decide they have found or invented the definitive solution to a particular business problem. A tidal wave of cold water wouldn't deflect them. They've gotten lots of media splash. The troops are sweating because they know the new theory is unworkable. Top management can't really deliver what they've promised. Nothing substantive is being done to correct the media impression. Ego overkill can happen when management tries to avoid facing a serious problem.

CONDITION NINE: Loss of Corporate Will or Direction

A company that loses its will to succeed provokes warfare. If the company has always been the leader in consumer food products and now thinks that acquiring divisions of other types of companies is better than innovating, you'll see a marked change in the climate and the politics. Whether or not this strategy provokes a full-scale war depends on how serious the rank and file judge things to be or are likely to get. If they see that top management is nearing retirement and the next level down is lean and hungry, they'll control their panic and get on with the job. However, combine a loss of management will with a leadership vacuum caused by no succession planning, and you have fertile ground for a free-for-all.

Top management isn't the only group that has occasional blackouts in its collective reality-testing mechanism. Let middle management believe there is no ready successor for a top spot and many will begin seeing themselves as candidates. Before anyone can point out that it's not even remotely likely that one of them will get the job, they'll be scratching and biting. It's preventable and it's all too common.

CONDITION TEN: Nepotism

The first generation founded the printing business, and husband and wife worked tirelessly to build a strong customer base. As the firm celebrated its twenty-fifth year, the husband died. The wife brought a son and daughter into the business. The daughter married a man most charitably called "limited"—as in "Harry's a good enough salesman, but limited."

The sales manager and salespeople tried to help the son-in-law, but after two years the office, by now comprising twenty people, fell to feuding.

Family-owned businesses that employ even one slightly incompetent relative invite warfare. While most employees will grudgingly tolerate outstandingly competent nepots, they will be ruthless toward the less than outstanding. This is a real time bomb because eventually talented outsiders will refuse to work for the company. (The less talented will flock there.) Employees begin to believe their chances of moving to better jobs elsewhere have been damaged, because outsiders know what's going on. It's true often enough to cause the internal politics to overheat.

Family businesses also tend to be eccentric. While certain kinds of unacceptable behavior are tolerated, other, completely reasonable behavior is rejected. By building a hothouse environment and embalming strange ideas, even the minimal ethics and protocol that restrain most workers some of the time are weakened. In this kind of environment, it's suddenly all right to sidestep a boss to speak to the owner. It's also all right to exchange highly personal gossip. The minute things become so intensely personal, the politics really heat up.

Doctors who use their wives as appointment and billing clerks learn this when a succession of nurses leave in a huff. Not one nurse will point out why the doctor's wife poisons the workplace. Her habit of asking the nurse to "help out" while she gets her hair done and treating the nurse as an equal seems appropriate to her. The fact that the nurse sees herself as a trained professional and far superior to the wife won't penetrate the wife's blow-dried hair. Since it's unlikely the doctor does exit interviews with his nurses, he'll probably never know.

TRIGGERS

In theory anyone can see the impact of the conditions we've described, but there's another important question to be explored. Why, when more than one of these conditions exist, will whole groups of people continue to march in relative lockstep and harmony, while in other equally grim situations, warfare will break out?

In addition to internal conditions, there must also be triggers to get the war started. Thirty, 50, or even 350 miserable people working together is not enough to trigger a war. One or more of them must deliberately precipitate an event that brings people into real conflict. Keep in mind that not everyone, however harassed, frightened, or enraged, will participate. Some people believe, alas falsely, that if they keep very quiet, others will tiptoe around their still-warm bodies. That's absolutely not true, but enough people think that's the case to allow conflicts to widen.

People move from passivity to passive resistance to action reluctantly. The percentage of workers who thrive on conflict is probably less than 10 percent. There are excellent reasons for this reluctance. Even people who love taking risks know they will have to expend an enormous amount of energy on any conflict. More important, however, they fear that they can't control or limit what they start. Who knows who might become involved? Even for natural office warriors, the motivation must be strong, laced with a healthy dose of self-interest. Here are the main triggers that ignite conflict.

1. Threats, particularly nonverbal and therefore nonnegotiable or unanswerable ones, are the most important triggers to overheating the political environment. While most of the people seem to be working together with little friction, should someone threaten or appear to threaten another person's job tenure, there will be a response. (Note: There is no difference in the response to a real threat and one that's wildly improbable, since both will trigger equally strong defensive action. Informal systems have difficulty separating the actual from the imagined.)

If a boss tells a competent subordinate that he or she just doesn't fit in, the veiled threat will trigger a response. The issue will be raised in the grapevine. It's the beginning of gathering sympathy, raising visibility, and putting the boss under scrutiny in order to deflect the threat. It will cause other workers to become anxious. Productivity will decline as all the players begin to analyze why one worker or group of workers is either under attack or threat of attack. If people believe the worker or group is performing well, the reaction will be especially strong. People won't do anything overt but they will react through the informal system. That reaction changes the power structure, because when threatened, people tend to align themselves in new ways.

The regular networking groups, which form the basis of the grapevine, are disrupted as people scramble for information from new sources and seek to recruit new allies.

Once this kind of behavior begins, it is difficult to control the outcome and difficult for people to restabilize old relationships.

2. Management will sometimes play one individual off against another or play one group against another. It's a deliberate attempt to heat up the environment by creating an artificial and wholly unnecessary competition. This happens more often in service businesses than in manufacturing, but it can occur anywhere. For example, management may decide that the way to solve a problem is to form two marketing "teams," each of which will present its ideas to the executive committee. A man who's been through this continues the story: "There were twenty people in the marketing department at the beginning of June. On June 15 we were put into two teams, one with nine people, one with ten. The boss was the twentieth person and was overall manager and referee. We met with the CEO, who said, 'I want each team to prepare a total marketing plan for resurrecting this product. The winners will be rewarded.'

"All of a sudden the department split like a walnut. People I'd worked with for five years would stop talking when I met them in the hall. The level of secrecy was unbelievable! It was like being back in my MBA program, but the stakes were so much higher. We worked in this atmosphere for three months.

"I especially remember the ways in which people's behavior changed over time. At first, all of us treated this as friendly competition. At lunch we'd joke about what we were doing. After the first month the whole game turned sinister. You dared not be seen with people from the other team. There was a war zone mentality. The cocaptains on my team actually called me at home one night on a conference call to make sure I was still 'solid.' "

To trigger warfare a situation doesn't have to be this organized. A manager can tell three supervisors that only one will be promoted, and that he/she will back the winner. The "contest" may be about anything. It's still a game and is still likely to create massive conflict. It also contributes to polarizing people's thinking on a fair/unfair continuum. That's rarely helpful to the overall politics of the organization.

3. The buildup of stress in a work group, particularly if the source of that stress seems to be atmospheric rather than one specific event, is like stockpiling gasoline in open containers. The least spark can trigger a disaster. Stress occurs in offices as the result of shared perceptions of what's happening. For instance, the long-term financial erosion of the firm will cause stress as people gradually become aware of both the enormity and seriousness of the erosion. Those who fear that their jobs will be on the line will begin to stockpile successes, check out what their co-workers are doing to be sure no one's moving ahead, and generally look for ways to exert more control over the environment.

Stress will be reflected in short tempers, greater stroking of job descriptions, and more time spent wooing the boss—even if that relationship was considered solid until now. To a neophyte this activity will look like four-flushing or brownnosing. Others, with more experience, will view this behavior as something to be emulated, not condemned.

Eventually the stress reaction will cause people to separate into two loosely defined camps, the "nothing to lose" group and the "something might be gained" group. This is a sure sign that people are thinking about doing something.

4. The desire for excitement on the part of a person who has already decided he or she has a plethora of options or even has a job offer in his/her pocket can trigger an extreme reaction. His/her actions will signal others within the work arena that this person no longer needs to care about what happens. A worker has given two months' notice. He is going about his job but his heart's not in it, because he's already changed jobs mentally. He remembers that John and Bill caused him trouble and bum-rapped him in the past. He can work them over now through the grapevine and does. Others join the fray and find new areas of potential conflict. The instigator eventually leaves but the war goes on.

5. A variety of political disasters may be triggered if a competitor introduces a new product that takes off and everyone in the weakened company knows it. First, key people may leave. Second, the people who stay may throw in the towel. Third, top management may panic. Sometimes these disasters happen almost simultaneously. There will be peace one day, the next day the morning newspaper carries news of a major new product, and that afternoon two key people depart. The troops will stagger.

6. The federal, state, or local government may decide to investigate some part of the company or something it has done. This can trigger a panic response that will be difficult to contain. Multiply the shock by ten if people below the level of top and upper-middle management will be questioned or involved in some way. This usually occurs in manufacturing, where government-mandated recalls, in particular, cause problems.

7. Productivity programs are always triggers. They can and will cause more warfare than almost anything else likely to be introduced into an office between now and the year 2000. It's been said before, but it's always worth repeating, that "productivity movements. in order to work, must eliminate middle management, as well as blue-collar, jobs." A second maxim is "Productivity programs are a socio-political, not a technical, innovation." The bottom line is that productivity movements threaten the job tenure of the least productive and often the least political workers. As long as productivity programs don't seem to be having any effect and no one is really taking them too seriously, the majority of workers are neutral. The minute it's perceived that management is doing more than going through the motions, a war zone is born.

8. The worst warfare is triggered by the One Final Injustice. This is an event that polarizes people so completely that they respond at a gut level—the very worst thing they could do to themselves and for the company. It may be a minor event that is blown out of proportion, but it will be seen as the last in a series of events. If five employees are fired and the grapevine says now there should be a respite, a sixth firing will be seen as the One Final Injustice. Never underestimate the emotional frenzy people can be whipped into by an issue that is seen only in terms of black and white. Most major injustices have blurry gray areas, so the response is tepid. When the troops see a clear demarcation between the good and the bad, people will overreact.

Where does that leave you? Can you see the war zones? Are you aware of triggers with itchy fingers attached? In the next chapter we look at the individual's role.

◊ GAUGING THE DURATION

How long does a political war last? They start instantly, and that focuses people's attention on the event. They don't end as decisively. A hot war may last weeks or months. Like trench warfare, attrition is as likely to determine the outcome as is planning, particularly if management chooses to ignore the whole thing. You can tell the war is winding down when the internal situation is no longer the only topic of conversation in the grapevine. You can sometimes hasten the cool-down period by introducing a variety of topics into the grapevine.

Chapter 3. At the Front:

Why Are They Shooting at Me?

So far we've examined the changes in social and work values and how these have affected office politics. We've tracked the ways in which companies drift into war zones or contrive to create them. We've also seen what triggers open combat. In this chapter we will examine the individual's role in being cast as a victim. We'll see how people contribute to their own victimization, how they independently victimize themselves, and what happens when others, such as bosses, peers, and subordinates, victimize them. First, some case histories.

One Monday in May, two years ago, a problem loan manager at a bank arrived at her office and found it denuded. The furniture was there but all her personal effects had been removed—including a picture of her child. When she sought an explanation from her boss, he got up and closed the door—never a good sign. Then he said, "Elsbeth, we're outplacing you. You're good at your job but you're not a team player. The men in the department don't want to work for you. They think you're weak. I'm inclined to agree. It's either lose you or lose them." Stunned, she picked up her purse and briefcase and retired to personnel to be greeted by an enthusiastic outplacement consultant. Her career at the company was over.

Unfortunately, this is not an isolated incident. It happens often to both men and women. Professional and managerial people are being shaken awake from career slumber to find that their political skills have eroded and their careers are teetering. They are, or are on the verge of becoming, victims. Why? What's happened?

The world changed and with it, the office climate. People who previously embraced the productivity movement as a logical, unalloyed good are rapidly becoming its victims. Those who maintained good working relationships with everybody at the office are finding out that, in the quest for job security and advancement, there are no good relationships. Anyone can and will turn ugly if the stakes are sufficiently high. This change didn't occur overnight. Most of the current victims received plenty of notice. They chose to ignore the data because it didn't seem important at the time, or even worse, they didn't want to hear or acknowledge what was going on.,

When Elsbeth looked back on her two years as department manager she remembered incidents, ignored at the time, but ominous in hindsight. When another manager proposed that one part of her job fit more logically into his area she'd relinquished it gladly. Why not? Less work for her, more for him. When the men she managed pointedly excluded her from their lunchtime camaraderie she'd reasoned that she was still the boss—it was their problem, not hers. When her boss bypassed her to give a subordinate direct instructions, she hadn't questioned him. She'd misread the subtle challenges, and once her boss, peers, and subordinates recognized her lack of fight, they closed in. Their behavior wasn't even personal. They disliked Elsbeth no more than they would have disliked any other weak player. It hardly mattered that she was female, although they may have thought it easier to deal with her than with a man.

Martin G. was an outstanding tax lawyer with a major law firm. He was an associate who could reasonably look forward to a partnership within three to five years. His track record was excellent, his social skills adequate, his personal habits inoffensive. Two other tax lawyers, at his level, also expected to become partners. In four years, there would be two openings, both created by retirements. One of the three associates wouldn't make it.

Martin merely worked hard while his two peers worked and schemed. They saw to it that Martin got just enough difficult cases, because he was "so good at that kind of case," that his losses soon outnumbered his wins. Guess who didn't make partner and never knew why? Peers can always subtly influence work assignments. Sometimes victimizing someone is as simple as not getting in the way of the victim's eagerness. When Martin saw a tricky, iffy case he charged into it. Why should his competitors point out the folly of too much charging?

When Marie C. took over as manager of data processing, everybody cheered. The previous manager had been weak—vacillating between yes and no in the same sentence. Then Marie began to give some highly accurate performance appraisals. It had never been done in the department, which consequently had a high tolerance for, and an attraction to, marginal workers. Suddenly, Marie's mail began to disappear or arrive late. She missed an important staff meeting because her notice of the meeting "went astray" in the interoffice mail. Her boss, a male, tried to help but couldn't really involve himself in a "cat fight." The operators didn't like her. When important work was delayed once too often, she was fired.

What happened to Elsbeth, Martin, and Marie can happen to you. It's not a sex-related phenomenon at all. Women tend to be victimized slightly more often than men but usually in a less spectacular fashion. You have outstanding potential as a victim unless you understand how the political process in offices has changed. To do that, you need to understand what is at stake.

Suddenly people are playing politics with an intensity, and sometimes a viciousness, that's new. There's been a revolution in office politics, especially since the economic shakeout of 1979–82. People who were formerly "laid back" about politics have scurried to get involved. Instead of positive participation, they're now talking about methods of attack. Why? Survival is at stake. Either you learn the new rules, examine your ethics and options, and get involved, or you risk fairly speedy victimization. Those who are planning to end or truncate your career may not see it in those terms. They can easily persuade themselves that you did it to yourself. And in many ways they'll be right. If you have done nothing to change your analysis and then your approach, in light of a changed work environment, you have victimized yourself. If this seems harsh, consider the three sad tales that opened this chapter.

What Is a Victim?

It's inevitable that most people will link the word *innocent* with the word *victim* because they want to believe that self-victimization is only done by sickies or people with compelling needs to self-destruct. The reality of office warfare is not like that at all. A victim is anyone who, when under attack, fails to take action, either defensive or offensive. It's the man whose strategy is to wait patiently for the attack to cease. It's the woman who doesn't correct a false rumor she knows is circulating. It's the man who won't devote any time to observing and analyzing his colleagues' political moves. It's the person whose only concern is getting the job done well—the social and political aspects of the job be damned!

There are two ways people contribute to their own victimization. One is through ignorance, usually by failing to identify problems, and the other is failing to correct problems that interfere with accurate information gathering and analysis of the data. Ignorance is probably the more common, and it means refusing to recognize and process data. Let's look at the problems that arise from choosing to practice ignorance.

1. Failure to participate because you don't understand that participation in the grapevine and internal politics is not a choice but a necessity. Your choice is not whether to participate but where in the organization and at what level you should participate. If you aren't plugged in, you'll have to ask people what's going on. That's bad because it brands you as a beginner, and the questions you ask will give clues as to your agenda, your values, and even your strategies, if you have any. For instance, if you're always asking people what they think the boss is thinking, it can't help but occur to whomever you've asked that one of two conditions exists: Either you are having problems getting along with the boss, or you want to influence him/her in some way—probably you want a promotion or raise. The grapevine will transmit and embellish your interest. It may even reach your boss, who is likely to view it negatively.

2. Failure to build and maintain working relationships with everybody regardless of rank, social skills, or your personal preferences. Work is not the place to build support relationships that are personal rather than political. You need responsive political allies, not "buddies." It's axiomatic that friends often adjust the news to protect your feelings just when you need the baldest statement of the facts. Political allies, anchored by the need for your total reciprocity, are kinder in the end when they bring you the grimmest version.

3. Lack of separation between the real you and the political you. Elsbeth couldn't separate her personal desire not to get involved from her political need to be involved and watchful. If you think like that, you hand your enemies a weapon. Ignoring the petty is self-destructive because it dismisses small, but vital, facts. You must see the professional you as totally your own creation and always under your control.

4. Failure to practice predictability and consistency in your reactions to people and events. True sincerity is vastly overrated. If you respond positively only to those things you sincerely believe in, rather than to those things that politically serve your purposes, you're going to have a problem. People won't trust you, because your behavior is unpredictable. They can never be sure what will trigger an unanticipated response, however sincere it may be. This is especially critical when dealing with subordinates. The best stance for any politician seeking information is inscrutable enthusiasm.

5. Not taking people's hidden agendas seriously. Underestimating the essential pettiness and mean-mindedness of business transactions is political suicide. If you assume that all people share your values, want you to move ahead, and want the company to do well, you're making yourself an easy mark. Wouldn't you be further ahead if you began every political analysis by asking yourself, "What's in it for him? What's his hidden agenda? What can I do for the other person that will make him/her want to do it my way?"

6. Not respecting the informal rules because they aren't written down. Marie's problems stemmed from her zealousness. If your company has gone easy on performance appraisals in the past, you'll invite retaliation if you independently decide to change the system. A boss who tells you to go ahead but doesn't support you is giving mixed messages. The informal system, through the grapevine, gives the real word on what's politically acceptable and what's taboo.

How Close Are You to Becoming a Victim?

Now that you know what a victim is, how can you tell if you're about to become one? Here are a series of questions for you to answer. We'll show you how to score your responses later.

1. Has your company shown significant sales growth since the end of the recession (roughly late 1982 to early 1983)?

2. Has top management shown enthusiasm for the productivity movement (or one particular productivity scheme)? Have they hired "experts" to advise them or to work directly on and with middle management?

3. Is the company profitable? If your answer is yes, is the annual growth rate as much as 10 percent, adjusted for inflation?

4. Are there rumblings from top management about reorganizing the company, your division, or your department?

5. Have any employees been laid off in your area? Were you affected? How was it done? That is, did management provide severance pay, outplacement assistance, several months' notice, etc.?

6. Have any employees left because they feared outplacement or felt the company politics were "getting out of hand"?

7. How long have you been in your current job? What would be your next logical career move within the company? Outside the company?

8. Are you managing a profit or a cost center?

9. Do you have more than enough, just enough, or less than enough work to keep you busy between forty and fifty hours a week, assuming you work more quickly than the average?

10. Can you identify any changes in the political process as you understand it since 1983? What has your response been, if any?

11. Has your relationship with your current boss changed in the past six months? If so, is the relationship closer, more distant, less or more formal?

12. What is the age range among your peers? (Count as peers not only direct competitors but anyone who could do your job with a little training.) Are all of you about the same age? Are any peers near retirement?

13. Would you describe your peers as very much like you, similar, or to some degree unlike you? If they are very different, how is it manifested?

14. How much news about other divisions within the organization do you get from your subordinates? Are they quick to report problems and personnel changes?

[handwritten: VERY LITTLE]

15. When was the last promotion in your department or division?

16. Has anything happened in the past six months that made you uneasy about your performance or job tenure?

[handwritten: NO, AND DON'T CARE]

17. Whose career would be helped by your departure?

18. Have you been psychologically comfortable in your job during the past three years?

[handwritten: ANYMORE]

[handwritten: DEFINITELY NOT]

Scoring Your Answers

Now let's look at your answers. Keep a running total of your points in order to tabulate your victim potential.

1. If the company's growth rate is under 10 percent, it's worth 5 points. If it's over 10 but under 20 percent, it's worth 0 points. If it's over 20 percent, subtract 10 points. If you and everyone else are so overworked that you long for more help, subtract 5 points.

[handwritten: 0]

The faster the company grows, the less destructive the internal politics will be. This is true because plotting takes time and effort. Also, lots of work to be done breeds a sense of urgency and a sense of accomplishment.

2. If top management has hired a productivity expert, regardless of reputation, add 15 points. If management has talked about hiring a productivity expert, add 10 points. If management has firmly rejected such help, subtract 5 points.

Productivity experts must eliminate people, usually "surplus" managers, in order to help the company "reduce costs and run lean." Remember, unless there's some impact on the bottom line, top management is going to smell the snake oil immediately. Furthermore, the experts are likely to identify some people as more effective than others, and this will affect the power structure.

[handwritten: N/A]

3. If the company is profitable, subtract 5 points. If it's very profitable, subtract 10 points. If it's losing money, add 5 points. If it's in Chapter Eleven, add 0 points. (Everyone's effort must be directed to saving the company, so there's no time to play political games.)

This question is different from number 1, which asked about growth rate, because growth and profitability aren't necessarily connected. When companies are profitable, people expect there will be spoils to divide. They will behave properly to insure that they get a share. This puts a clamp on the more destructive games. The more profitable the company, the more optimistic people are likely to be— and the less destructive.

4. If management is reorganizing, add 20 points. If they are talking about it, add 10 points. If you've survived a reorganization, subtract 20 points.

There's nothing like a reorganization to unleash viciousness. It often reflects a lack of management imagination. If they had been able to conceive a better way to get people moving, they'd have done it. Even top management people can lose out if the process gets out of hand. This makes them more vicious toward subordinates! For example, a music company reorganized several employees into outplacement. Two months later, still bankrupt of ideas, two more managers were let go. One, feeling himself badly treated, reported some of the company's financial dalliances, triggering an IRS audit.

5. If there have been no layoffs, subtract 10 points. If fewer than 10 percent of the employees have been laid off at any one time, add 5 points. If 10 to 20 percent, add 10 points. If more than 20 percent, add 20 points. If the process was orderly and humane, however large, it's worth 0 points. If it was haphazard, and left the laid-off people nursing their psychic wounds, add 10 points. If there's a government age-discrimination charge pending against the company, add 25 points. Remember that age discrimination has a chilling effect even on people on the comfortable side of forty.

A management that doesn't consider the emotional fall-out when planning layoffs invites the troops to retaliate individually in whatever ways they think are useful. The company is probably guilty of more than age discrimination. This is the law of the jungle.

6. If an outplacement firm has been retained, add 10 points. If exit interviews are the talk of the company because people are saying really negative things about the organization as they leave, add 5 points. If security-minded colleagues are concerned and the word processing machines are still warm when the supervisor arrives in the morning, add 15 points. (The troops have been working on their resumes.)

Here's the rationale: Fear will force some people out; the rest will turn mean-minded and territorial. By the way, are you plugged in to the word processing department? They are a very important source of news. They will expect you to ante up equally important information.

7. If you have been in your present job fewer than three years, add 5 points. If three to five years, add 10 points. If five to ten years, add 15 points. Over ten years at the same job, add 15 points plus 1 additional point for each year over ten. If your next career move is obvious, subtract 5 points. If it's a lateral move, or a move up in a different department, subtract 10 points. If there's no logical move, add 0 points. Add 0 points if you can see logical moves outside the company. Add 10 points if there are no logical moves. Add 15 points if you can't see any move. Add 20 points if you have not been thinking at all about your options.

The longer you've been in your job, the more likely you are to be bored and vulnerable. You're also very likely overpaid. You could be replaced by someone who would do the same job for less money—possibly as much as one-third less. This provides your manager and peers with a reason to take action. If there is an obvious internal move, you are at less risk than if your only move is lateral and therefore more difficult. If there's no obvious move, people will assume you're dead-ended and leave you alone. If you know you must move outside for a better job, but you don't know where to begin job hunting, it's less likely to produce aggressive behavior than when you don't believe you are marketable elsewhere at all. In that case you'll be tempted to try to hold on to what you have, regardless of the career consequences, a situation that makes you politically a wounded lion.

8. If you're managing a profit center, add 0 points. If you're managing a staff area, add 10 points. If your area is data processing, add 20 points.

The closer you are to the guts of the business the more likely you are to be visible to top management. You are probably seen as "one of the team." Data processing is most vulnerable right now because so many managers, sometimes with top management's blessing, want to buy personal microcomputers and eliminate central data processing, except for accounting and inventory control.

9. If you're working more than fifty hours per week, add 0 points. If it's fewer than fifty hours per week, add 5 points. If it's fewer than forty hours, add 10 points. If you're doing fewer than thirty hours of work a week, add 15 points.

If you're not busy, chances are those around you are also underemployed. People who aren't kept busy have time to plot. They recognize, at least unconsciously, that they are very vulnerable. Top management is highly suggestible. Why not eliminate a position and save money, simultaneously improving productivity? This agenda does not promote brotherly (or sisterly) love; most often it promotes bloodshed. You can practically see the "team" fall apart.

10. If you see climatic changes in the organization, add 10 points. If other people remark about such changes and you don't see them, add 15 points. If you've responded to the changes by changing your attitude, approach, or packaging, subtract 10 points. If you haven't responded, add 10 points.

We're obviously measuring political savvy with this question. If you're not aware of political change, you have a problem. You're starting well behind the other players. Merely to survive you're going to be responding to crises on the wing with no thought in advance.

11. If you and your boss have a very stable relationship, your performance appraisals are above average, and you haven't had a serious falling out in the last year, subtract 5 points. If your boss actively pushes your career, add 0 points. If your boss regards you as a threat, add 5 points. If your boss has hinted at your impending demise, add 10 points. If your last performance appraisal was not as good as the previous one, add 10 points. If the relationship is longer than three years' duration and has had highs and lows, add 0 points.

〈 5 〉

Few things are as important to pure survival as your relationship with your boss. However, what's most important is how your peers perceive that relationship. If they think it's solid, even though you know it's occasionally bumpy, they're less likely to attack. If they think you've got problems with the boss, they may decide to add to them via the grapevine. You may have heard it: "Bob's in big trouble —Fred's gunning for him."

12. If the age range of you and your peers is roughly five to seven years, add 20 points. If there are twenty or more years between the youngest and oldest, add 5 points.

+ 20

When all of you are close in age and are vying for a few openings, tempting opportunities for aggression present themselves. If there are a few people nearing retirement, everyone will gear down and wait it out. After all, the oldsters have to leave eventually. This attitude is often an illusion, but right now we're concerned about what makes people act, not the verifiable facts. If no one can foresee any possibility of opportunity by attrition for many years, the environment will heat up.

13. If you and your peers are look-and-think-alikes, add 10 points. If demographically you're different, add 5 points. If you and your peers have a bell curve distribution of characteristics such as age, education, and previous work experience, add 0 points.

The more you and your peers are alike, the greater the potential for skullduggery. Why? Because you are likely to be equally ambitious or at least act as if you are. Peer pressure is enormous. You may, because of a good values and style match, work together effectively, but you're also likely to be highly competitive. Some companies practically clone people in some departments, which increases each worker's potential as a victim.

14. If your subordinates rarely repeat gossip to you, add 15 points. If they give you news, but edit it, add 10 points. If they give you the unvarnished, and often unpalatable truth, subtract 10 points.

There is no greater threat to a person's career than the lack of timely, accurate information. Subordinates hear things that no manager would be privy to. Unless your subordinates always share the awful facts, your job tenure is in danger. A disaster may be lurking that you won't learn about until doomsday. For them to share fully with you, you must encourage, thirst for, and reward them for the bad news.

15. If someone like you was promoted in the last year, subtract 5 points. If nobody has been promoted since 1983, add 10 points. If the company is just now recalling laid-off managers, add 20 points.

What we're measuring here is movement. Is there any? If not, the political environment will ache for some assassinations. How else can openings occur? Besides, the people being called back, once the euphoria wears off, will be anxious to secure themselves. They are going to resist being victimized again. They are in politics to stay—and as aggressive players. Companies rarely acknowledge or deal with the laid-off worker's desire for revenge once recalled.

Companies assume people are grateful to be back, ignoring the fact that many workers, especially managers, spent the layoff in frustrating and fruitless job hunting. If they had been successful, they wouldn't have been available for recall! There is a short honeymoon immediately after recall, but then it takes a long time for restored workers to get over their resentment and back on the team emotionally.

16. Forget trying to separate paranoia from healthy skepticism. If anything has happened that makes you feel vulnerable, you are vulnerable. If you feel vulnerable, but don't know why, add 10 points. If you have objectively determined that you are vulnerable, add 5 points. If you can't figure out what the fuss is about, add 15 points. +5

Being vulnerable isn't necessarily the same problem as feeling vulnerable. However, the effect is the same because your enemies can smell (literally) your tentativeness. If you've made a mistake, you can correct it. But if the problem is not any one thing you can put your finger on, you are going to feel like a character in a Kafka novel and give off an aura of fear and loss of confidence.

17. If one person's career would be helped by your departure, score 5 points. If two would be, that's worth 10. If more, it's 5 points per person. +5

If more than one person would benefit by your departure, there's an incentive to hasten it. If everyone's career would be helped by your departure or anyone else's, add a 10-point bonus.

18. If you are steaming along, comfortable in your niche, add 20 points. If you've had periods of black dread in the past three years, add 10 points. If you can't remember the last time you truly relaxed on the job, subtract 5 points. ⟨5⟩

We're coming at the awareness issue from a different angle. The last three to five years were relaxing only if you were comatose. If you thought you were relaxing on the job, it means you missed a lot that may harm you now.

Now add up your points. The highest possible score is 250 or more. If you scored more than 150 points, you have outstanding victim potential. You are at the apex of the kind of personal, professional, and organizational forces that produce serious career and ego damage. (The latter can devastate your career by reducing your confidence level and hampering your job hunting.) A score between 100 and 150 means that some of the dangerous circumstances are there, but not all. If your score is in this range, refer back to the questions. How many points did you score on questions 11, 14, and 16? If you added more than 10 points for each of those three questions, you deserve a negative "bonus." Add enough points to put yourself in the high risk category (over 150 points). Why? Because, while the questions aren't really weighted, those three questions describe circumstances in which victimization can occur very quickly. If you're a high scorer there, you are proportionately more vulnerable.

If you scored fewer than 100 points, you may not be in immediate danger. However, you have only a snapshot of the political situation. It shows how things stand at one moment, and circumstances could be radically different tomorrow. Your company's political situation continually changes. For this reason, you need to reexamine your victimization potential regularly.

Knowing you are vulnerable should make you rethink your strategy. You aren't a victim yet, but you may be drifting in that direction. You can learn to assess risks and even predict the probable outcome. Certainly inaction is an option but a very high risk one. You need survival tools.

Self-Victimization—Doing Yourself In

We've touched on this in the first section; now we need to get much more specific. There are many things you may do—however unconsciously—that result in self-victimization. Here are some of the most common.

Inaccurate Listening

Inaccurate listening is such a common problem that companies actually pay for what are called "active listening" courses to teach their employees to listen and process what they hear more accurately. If you aren't getting all the information or not picking up on the nonverbal clues when you talk to people, you have a serious political handicap. How will you know if this is your problem? Answer the following questions.

Do you often ask people to repeat what they've said or have to return for a rerun of oral instructions? You may be a sloppy listener. Your attention is probably diverted near the middle of whatever is being said. You'll have to teach yourself to listen far more attentively. The best way to do this is to make notes as people talk to you. Not only will it provide you with a check on your memory, but it flatters people to think you're so interested in what they say. Once they realize you're making notes because you very much want to get every word, there will be no political fallout.

Do you edit or reject everything you hear that you disagree with? Do you think to yourself, "I'm sure he doesn't mean it" or "I'm sure it's not that bad"? Not only does he mean it, but it really is that bad! It may be worse than bad. This is a very dangerous habit. By rejecting unpalatable information on principle, you don't listen as closely as you should. It's hard to break the habit but you must try. Otherwise you're going to be in a perpetual state of shock and surprise as careers (maybe your own?) crash around you. The best method is to say to yourself, "I want to hear the negatives." This means you will consciously examine events and rumors to find the "hook." Never lightly dismiss a rumor, however ridiculous, until you've examined it. You have to suspend your natural disbelief about what you hear is happening or could happen, particularly if your company is changing.

Are you easily distracted? Does a change in the lighting, the temperature of the room, or someone else's fidgeting cause you to lose your train of thought? If so, you'll have to work at acquiring greater concentration and control. Otherwise you're likely to miss clues you need to accurately assess your present situation. If you have trouble blotting out distractions, try these techniques:

1. Take notes in meetings even if nothing is happening. Tell yourself you'll concentrate for two full minutes and then do it. Increase the time in thirty-second increments until you can follow a conversation for four full minutes without letting your mind wander. Practice intense concentration during every meeting.

2. Focus on the speaker and don't take your eyes from that person until he finishes what he's saying. Repeat what he's saying to yourself word for word.

3. After someone has made a statement, say, "Are you saying . . ." and rephrase what she said back to her. If the speaker says, "No, I didn't mean that," seek clarification. You may find that you habitually block certain messages.

Improper Analysis

There's no foolproof system for correctly analyzing a highly volatile office situation, especially when you're in the middle of a crisis. However, there are some guidelines that will help.

1. "A pessimist has no ugly surprises." The author's husband, Daniel J. Kennedy, Jr., said that a few years ago and it's never been more true. If you are not emotionally, as well as intellectually, prepared for the "worst case" scenario, you can't analyze the situation properly. You'll always be surprised. However you've analyzed it, if you expect people to act rationally, fairly, or ethically, you are going to be surprised. The bleakest possible view of human nature should be your starting point. You can always revise your expectations upward if it's necessary.

2. Even though conflict avoiders litter the landscape, it's a dangerous practice and a virulent form of self-victimization. These are people who'd much rather switch than fight. They are annoying and no good as allies but not nearly as dangerous as those mental pygmies who routinely put the most positive construction on every circumstance, even when confronted by disturbing or unpleasant facts. When surprised, these people may lash out unexpectedly, further agitating an already volatile situation. First an explanation: There are only two kinds of truth in the world —verifiable facts and everything else. If the company is not making money, if it's undergoing a reorganization, or if the product or service isn't selling, no public assurances management gives are worth anything. The job of top management is to keep the company afloat and profitable for as long as possible. Anything and anybody will be sacrificed to that end, if necessary. If you're thinking, "Everybody knows that," ask yourself why you hear people say, "They'll never lay off Gladys. She's been here thirty years." They can and they will. If Gladys doesn't know it, she's a fact avoider. The company isn't going to fold to save her from premature unemployment. It may give her plenty of company in the unemployment line.

3. Political laziness is self-victimization. Understand that regular office networking is a nonnegotiable political necessity. Going off by yourself allows people to view you not as more conscientious and harder working but as someone who is avoiding them. They will reciprocate!

Organizational Victimization

Companies can victimize people institutionally. The most common way is to set formal and informal policies to keep certain people from succeeding. The manager who's proven himself an excellent leader but lacks a college degree isn't promoted. At forty-two, it's absurd to suggest that he'd gain enormously by going back to school. What he'd learn is that he's being put through two years of night school as a matter of principle. His company's values are as wrongheaded as he'd always suspected. Although he may be an outstanding performer, if someone higher up wants only people with B.A.'s and B.S.'s, that guy will be a victim. If he's told why he won't be promoted—a fifty-fifty chance in most places—he may not understand that the company really means it. It does. The reason he's held back may not be logical, but if he advances, others might get the notion they can get ahead without a degree. They will— but at other places.

Companies can also recruit people for impossible jobs and set them up to fail. Every organization with more than one hundred people has at least one criminally bewildered manager it "can't fire." Of course it can! Top management simply doesn't want to do it. Instead, they work around him. He's allowed to recruit and chew up talent because management has decided that it's less costly to sanction a revolving door in that department than confront the problem. No matter how many people are maimed psychologically, nothing will be done. It's just another form of organizational victimization. This is the best reason why you should ask during a job interview about the fate of your predecessor. Don't ask that way, however. Ask if your predecessor was promoted.

Companies can change recruiting strategies so that present employees are forced out. If your company has been recruiting MBAs exclusively from Midwestern universities and then suddenly decides that only Dartmouth and Harvard MBAs will do, watch out. This is calculated to force out the current crop. How? There are differences between the mindsets of Harvard and Dartmouth graduates and those from the University of Illinois and the University of Indiana. They're not going to get along. You can't immediately call which side will win, but a lot of bruising will go on before an accommodation occurs.

Companies can recruit the security-minded and then force them out by making the job appear unstable. A second form of this ploy is to import a productivity program that rewards certain kinds of skills and punishes others.

Companies don't victimize people randomly. There is a reason, however ill conceived. If you're going to deal with the warfare you encounter in the office, you must adopt a new mindset. From now on, no matter what happens or what you observe, you're going to treat it as a deliberate act. No more accidents, mistakes, mishaps, or excuses that someone "doesn't realize what he or she is doing." Of course the person does! You'll never be a winner at office politics or office warfare until you decide, on both an intellectual and emotional level, to hold everyone you deal with responsible for whatever he or she says or does. The underbelly of this is that you can't get away with "accidents" either!

Victimization by Individuals

Bosses can victimize individual workers most effectively one of two ways. They can change performance standards and job descriptions so that the current occupant of a particular job won't be able to do the new job, or they can withhold information about the job so the person will fail.

More subtle, but equally effective, is to deliberately misstate the message. A boss can say, "I have no problem with this assignment," but really mean, "This thing isn't going to fly." This technique is an art, and unless you adopt the stance that it's impossible to overestimate the lengths someone will go to when he/she is bent on getting rid of you or messing up your career, you could miss the signals.

Peers most often victimize each other by one of two techniques. Isolation is most popular. Simply cut the person who is targeted for involuntary severance out of the grapevine. If that person accepts such treatment, he or she is letting everyone know he/she doesn't care—or worse—doesn't understand what's going on.

The second method is the setup. In this instance, people actively work to make sure the victim appears either incompetent or foolish. Either technique will work.

Subordinates should not be left out. They can easily damage a boss's career if they are hardworking and have good political skills. Top management listens very carefully to secretaries. If secretaries don't like someone—or say they don't—that's important. It's political suicide if you don't care what the secretaries think, and you let them know it.

◊ DEBRIEFING THE TROOPS

Nothing is more valuable to a manager in an unstable situation than subordinates who are good news gatherers. Teach your subordinates to get the facts. Tell them to be on the lookout for news such as:

1. Who is moving up or on? What area is being reorganized? What do their pals say caused the change? Change is the most important news item.

2. Who's discontented? Who is known as a heavy-duty griper? Your people need to be in touch with such people. They often speak for an inchoate constituency.

3. Who's being isolated by former pals? People get vibrations when someone is in trouble, and they reduce the level of association. Reward your reporters with praise, warmth, inscrutable enthusiasm, and an occasional bit of analysis.

Chapter 4. Survival Tools:

What the Politically Savvy Know

A Fairy Tale for Our Time

Have you ever noticed that the serious business press, e.g., *Forbes,* the *Wall Street Journal, Fortune, Business Week*, etc., devote comparatively little time to the part that office politics plays in corporate decision making or in people's careers? Lee Iacocca, chairman of Chrysler, did it in his autobiography, but that's not the same as a news story. Granted, that sort of thing would be difficult to report accurately. When did you last (or ever) read an interview with a CEO that reported, "My competitors," he cackled gleefully, "had good political skills but mine were far superior," or "I would never have made it to the top without my in-depth knowledge of company politics and my ability to construct alliances out of thin air, not to mention my ability to deflect predators!" You also won't see analysts refer to either a company's or an individual's decline as due to "internal politics." The reticence of both CEOs and the media must be a deliberate policy of ignoring all but the most obvious about office politics. The *Wall Street Journal* may mention "board infighting" or "dissension within the executive suite," but when it comes to political savvy, it never calls a spade a spade—a digging implement perhaps, but never a spade.

Considering the fallout from the 1979–82 economic crisis, one would think that plain speaking about job staying-power and public recognition of the need for finely honed political skills would be common. Not so! Most people still won't speak honestly about political options or explain how they acquired good political skills. Some even deny they have political skills at all. That's why some neophytes still believe political skills are God-given or genetically transmitted, not learned systematically. It also explains why it takes otherwise bright young workers several years to grasp the role of politics in their careers. Rather than perpetuate such absurdities, here are the facts. There are tools that you can and must acquire if you want to reach the first, minimal level of political sophistication. Until you get your present job, your office contacts, and your outside network firmly under control, you're really in no position to worry about the second level. (Besides, that's the subject of the next chapter.) After we've talked about the basic survivalist's kit we'll move on to the next chapter and equip you with more survival tools.

Vital Political Skills

There are six skills that are essential for first-level political sophistication. These are: (1) consistent, accurate information gathering and processing; (2) mobility, i.e., independence from a fixed on-the-job networking group; (3) financial security, e.g., at least 10 percent of your annual take-home pay in a money market or other cash savings; (4) self-training and observation skills so you can pick up new job skills simply from observing other people work; (5) consistent productivity at least 10 percent greater than that of your peers; and (6) a consistent image as a sophisticated, dependable professional at whatever job you are paid to do.

Each of these skills is important politically but psychological benefits may even outweigh the political ones.

These psychological benefits include a sense of control over your career, a heightened self-confidence, a financial cushion that allows you to take risks, an assurance that you can educate yourself and thus assert more control over your job, and a recognition of your greater value to the organization because you return more per dollar invested in salary than your co-workers do. Without these psychological benefits your ability to act decisively may be impaired. You could be panicked by a story in the grapevine or by someone's actions because fear will cause you to magnify the risks to you and your job tenure. Let's look at each skill in detail.

Information Gathering/Analysis

Skill and accuracy in gathering and evaluating the information that flows through the organization's informal system is the sine qua non of organizational life. Without it you can't possibly accurately assess what is going on— much less plan a strategy to protect or enhance your position. Unless you hear rumors in their inchoate stage (the first time through the grapevine and before anyone reacts), you'll have too little time to think through your options and develop a plan of action.

Your gut-level response, while almost always the most personally satisfying, is usually the least politically successful one. Most people's gut response is purely defensive. They don't think about offensive action. They get emotional. For example, if there is a rumor your department is to be reorganized, your gut response may be to look immediately for another job. A considered response might be to check the accuracy of the rumor with other sources in other parts of the company. Is that news circulating in any of the other divisions? Your co-workers may hear it, panic, and, if you keep cool, leave you in a better position—the only experienced person available to move up!

Simply put, if you're not plugged in to the internal information network, née "gossip," you will never be able to protect and defend yourself politically. This applies to personal as well as professional gossip.

Consider the sad tale of Joe R. A brilliant engineer with a large oil company, he lived by a rigid code of ethics. Not only did Joe's code forbid repeating gossip, it forbade even hearing it. That meant that Joe did not receive any news except what came in printed form, such as instructions, memos, or policy statements from his boss. He believed that if his boss told him something, it was official. Otherwise, he closed his ears. He never listened to the latest scoop about the departmental secretary's husband "coming out of the closet." He continued to tell San Francisco "fairy" jokes because he personally thought them funny. This distressed the secretary terribly and offended all of his co-workers.

His boss's personal problems included a child who was having problems with drugs. Joe, in casual conversation with anyone who would listen, explained that the reason he had never tried drugs in his youth was because he'd had strong parents and the right sort of upbringing. This caused his boss to seethe inwardly. However, such is the protocol of the workplace that it was impossible to confront Joe and say, "Listen to the gossip around here. You are killing yourself with a combination of self-righteousness and ignorance." When Joe finally involuntarily resigned because of personality problems, which even he recognized could cause his dismissal, the collective sigh of relief was audible.

If you continue drinking coffee at your desk and brown-bagging it at lunch because you "don't have time to waste on gossip" you are a tailor-made victim. It's just a matter of time until someone who could benefit from your invisibility or departure figures out how to arrange it. You will be the last to know that you've created an enemy, bungled something, or offended a higher-up. You'll be the victim of a major blowup that would have been prevented if you had only heard the rumblings early on.

There are other major benefits to participation, some of which are monetary. If your boss knows that you aren't independently plugged in to the informal information network, he or she can tell you anything and you'll have to accept it as fact. What alternative do you have? For example, if your boss tells you that everyone in the organization got a 5 percent raise and you were lucky to get 6, how will you know if that's fact or hyperbole? The grapevine knows.

To review briefly, the grapevine is the blood and guts of the organization's informal power system, sometimes called the infrastructure. Eighty percent of what goes through the grapevine is verifiably true. You can take it to the bank. It may not be letter perfect all the time, but the players, their strategies, and who's likely to benefit are accurate. There are many reasons for the grapevine's veracity, but the most important one is that people who work together form coffee and lunch friendships. They tend to tell each other the truth to protect and enhance these relationships, which are stable over long periods. A person could have had three spouses in fifteen years but still be having coffee daily with the same four people.

Without these relationships it would be each individual against the system. Unless you touch base regularly with about a third of the people in your primary work arena or get news of them indirectly on a biweekly basis, you are not plugged in to the grapevine. Your first task should be to get into the internal network. You can't move beyond the beginner stage in your political development until you do.

Here is a question to test how wired in you are right now. Has anything happened in the past thirty days that you first heard about officially either from a memo or from your boss face to face? If something has surprised you it's because there are gaps in your network. Remember, there is no such thing as an organizational secret. There is only information that you can't access today.

Company news that can affect your career tomorrow is in the grapevine today. This is especially true if the company has any of the difficulties described in chapter 2. Here are just some of the kinds of information you can cull from the grapevine. (1) It's superb at carrying news of top management's impending decisions, groundswells of discontent, and news of what large numbers of employees are thinking about. (2) It will also carry "pure gossip," e.g., affairs, family troubles, etc., but while you may have to listen to such news, it's usually not worth repeating. Ironically, once it's known that you won't repeat the pure stuff, you'll hear more of it, not less. While you may not repeat what you hear, the news will significantly alter your approach to a peer or cause you to package an idea differently for a boss. (3) It will carry outside opinion such as the effect on your company of competitors' strategies and opinions.

Do not trust a boss or colleague who dismisses the informal system as people buzzing over the nonessential. Anyone who believes that has already been victimized or, even worse, is trying to victimize you! In fact, tremendous amounts of top management time and energy go into figuring out what those below them in the hierarchy are thinking and talking about. The search for that kind of information can take such extreme forms as listening in toilet stalls or actually giving bonuses to secretaries who deliver fresh information culled daily from the grapevine. Beneath every legendary corporate leader is a carefully maintained network of people who feed him/her regular doses of unpalatable facts.

Why the tremendous interest in gossip? Powerful people understand that leading the parade doesn't necessarily mean getting out in front and blowing a whistle. Powerful people know that in order to lead they need to know what people are thinking. They need to understand the subterranean opposition. Then they can package their decisions to win support from the troops.

No real leaders want malicious compliance when important work is at hand. They want a real team and the extra effort it involves. The grapevine helps surface objections and allows top management to repackage unhappy news more agreeably. It also allows them to gauge changes in relative power positions before the troops react.

In order to obtain information, you need a plan for quickly monitoring the grapevine on a regular basis. Since more than 80 percent of what people talk about really is trivia, listening to it in detail can become tedious. Your job is to make sure you don't miss the 20 percent that's vital. Here are ways to identify what's important.

1. Any rumor of change, whether it's in management, a policy change, or a change in a product/service or whatever is the company's main business is important to hear. The first hint of change will be in the grapevine. The mere fact that top management is thinking about change is important because any change, however slight, will alter the power structure. Someone will lose power, someone will gain more. The score of those changes will affect your career decisions.

For example, if it's rumored that top management is in conflict about whether the company should expand, finding out who takes which side can be important. Even if you're layers below the top, you're still in the chain of command. If your boss's boss stands to lose this round, it won't help your boss's career—or yours. If you knew beforehand that those above you were engaged in a battle to the death, you could decide your personal strategy based on your assessment of political realities. It is impossible to develop an intelligent response while you're sitting in your boss's office being officially notified that your division is cutting back in order to free resources for something new. Worse,

you're sitting there being told you are part of those cuts—
effective immediately! If you had prior knowledge of those
cutbacks (via the grapevine) you would have had ample
time to formulate a plan and even a Plan B.

2. Listen for reactions to any company news that's been
reported in the media. Your co-workers believe what the
broadcast and print media say. A major story on the business page in the local newspaper or a TV feature that questions or criticizes the company's business strategy will have
an internal impact. Even if top management initially ignores the story, they may later panic and decide to respond,
especially if the media follow up the original story with
additional coverage. Once an issue is publicly raised, companies often display a panicked, knee-jerk response. Top
management responds as if public opinion, the board, and
stockholder opinion were all identical. The grapevine will
carry details about those responses and, more important,
what people inside the company thought of the coverage.
The media force as many decisions in businesses as they
report. If it's decided that management can't solve the
problem, they may look for an internal goat to scape. In
such situations there's always room for human sacrifice.
The stockholders like blood. It doesn't replace unpaid dividends, but most CEOs firmly believe it helps.

A large law firm read about itself in the business pages
of the local newspaper and the management committee
learned something. They had not been plugged in to the
internal network and hadn't realized that their employees
were talking about the very issues the news story had
raised. Instead of seeing themselves as remiss in internal
news gathering, they began to scrutinize each employee,
looking for anyone who might have leaked the story. Large-
scale defections ensued, further weakening the firm.

3. Any rumor that consultants have been asked to bid on
a project, particularly an organizational study, is important.
Do not dismiss the fact that consultants are being interviewed, even if your boss says it's no big deal. Bosses fre-

quently tickle the truth in such situations because they don't want subordinates to become concerned as any sensible people would if they realized such studies were beginning. After all, if management pays the consultant they are almost certain to take recommendations seriously. If the rumor mill says it's a technical study, e.g., a new accounting or computer system, it's less important than if the study has something to do with the guts of the business, i.e., a product or service, marketing, or, most important, how the company is structured. Consultants are often catalysts for change. They don't always think up the change—it may be one top management intended to make anyway. The consulting firm's input simply confirms the decision. Ask any professional consultant—after a few drinks.

Only the most naive individual would believe that consultants have a free hand to reorganize or facilitate selling a troubled division independent of top management direction and input. Many companies believe that it softens the impact of major change if people focus their displeasure on outsiders instead of the real culprits. This may work short-term, but in the long run this strategy is transparent. If top management has abdicated its leadership role, a far greater cause for concern at every level exists.

Consultants may be used to delay decisions—especially unpleasant but necessary ones. "We can't act until we get the study results," management will say, buying some thinking time to further agonize over the unpalatable alternatives they have identified. This is especially attractive when management faces a surly board of directors itching for decisive action. For some irrational reason boards are often mollified by the fact that a reputable firm of consultants is on the scene, the corporate equivalent of paramedics.

In such situations you must keep your perspective. The consultants' advice or plans may be ignored. They can also be paid for, publicly praised, circulated in written form, touted in the press, and never used. The grapevine will carry details of why this happened. There may be political problems in doing what the consultants advised. It may be bad advice. Management may be too eccentric or simply too hardheaded to take the recommended action.

It's not unusual for employees to side with consultants against top management. A bakery was told by a consulting firm that three elderly sisters it had employed for forty years were driving business away. Not only did two of these sisters have memory lapses between the customer, the cash register, and the placement of goods in the bag, but one literally snarled at customers if they couldn't decide what they wanted as quickly as she thought they should. The owners thought about it and decided the three women were more important than the customers. They paid the consultants' fee without complaint and did nothing.

4. Any personnel decisions that show management changing its long-standing hiring patterns are important. If a business isn't prospering or it should be doing much better than it is, the easiest, quickest way to change things is to begin hiring people with different backgrounds and philosophies. This is especially true in service businesses. The sticky part is that few companies are willing to get rid of everyone who's already been molded in the old way. Conflict is inevitable as the veterans circle the wagons to fight off the newcomers.

An advertising agency lost a major client. The owners, unable to diagnose exactly why the client had defected, turned inward. They didn't fire anyone, but those with a low tolerance for terror left quickly. The survivors soon came into conflict with the new hires—none of whom had any agency experience. As one survivor said, "All I can figure out is that the owners believed that by hiring people who have worked only on the client side, they were buying insight into the client's thought processes."

In a law firm that had previously treated all new legal hires as indistinguishable one from another, the decision to hire from different law schools or to hire people with three to five years' experience instead of new graduates would be very important. It would be a major change in the preferred hiring profile, one that signals a deliberate effort to rearrange the internal power relationships. People, accustomed to seeing fellow alumni, will now wonder what's up. Changing recruiting and hiring practices doesn't reflect on the quality of either individuals or institutions. It may be nothing more than an attempt to insure that the present employees don't get too "cozy," i.e., establish a lock on a particular kind of business. It's often done in service businesses in order to prevent any one group of employees from getting big enough to break off from the parent firm and become competitors. It doesn't usually work if there are other grievances, but still it's done.

5. Any rumor of an acquisition, merger, or takeover signals a change in direction. Companies don't do this just because they're cash rich or growth-minded. It reflects top management's strategy to build profitability in the business, unless it's a defensive move, of course. Then the grapevine should report who the possible predator or predators are. Grapevines are remarkably good at separating fact from speculation in these cases. Someone within the company, independent of top management, usually has heard names of either predators or victims through an outsider. He or she puts them through the grapevine and awaits a reaction. If top management blusters or overreacts, or if there's a very uneasy silence, that confirms the news!

Top management always assumes that only they can add two plus two and get four. This is never the case. Most businesses would have failed years ago if the employees were as mentally bulletproof as top management likes to think. The truth is, employees are much less isolated from the other rank and file than top management is. They can put the puzzle together over coffee. Each person contributes a fact or an observation, and they can usually figure out what other companies are involved.

6. Any rumor of changes in the executive suite is important. If someone who thinks marketing is the guts of the business is deposed in favor of someone who thinks marketing and selling are synonyms, the informal system will react. People's individual philosophies are acted out concretely in the workplace. How much do you really understand about your top management's values and business philosophy? If the answer is "Not much," what plans are you formulating to increase your knowledge? There may be very strong factions in conflict right now in the executive suite. If you knew what they were you'd be able to tell whose internal influence should rise and whose should fall. Without this key bit of information some of the things that go on will make no sense at all.

A man employed by a large earth-moving contractor never understood why the company bid on every job that involved the construction of softball fields. While he recognized that softball was enjoying a boom, it made no sense to him. Other jobs the company didn't bid on were equally, sometimes more, profitable. Had he done his homework he would have learned that the two men who controlled the firm were vitally interested in softball facilities. So interested, in fact, a year later they ended up building an eight-diamond facility. One of his peers was tapped to manage it—a major promotion. Our man was never considered.

Any discussion of business philosophy is bound to come packed in euphemism simply because it's difficult for most people to admit they are guided by something that sounds as esoteric as a philosophy. It's a difficult subject to discuss without sounding either pompous or abstract. However, the word *philosophy* is usually just a term for a combination of ideas and beliefs that function as a gyroscope, keeping the company on course. If a company philosophy exists in writing it should not be dismissed as hot air. The people who wrote it are offering valuable clues not just to business practices and goals but to the fantasies that sustain them. Read everything your top management has written or commissioned. Talk to people in the public relations department. They're paid to package and interpret top management philosophy.

Political Independence

By the time someone has three to five years' work experience, the importance of at least minimal involvement in the office grapevine is obvious. Despite the moaning about "wasting time" and "petty gossip," recognition of political realities has set in. What's not so obvious, however, is the insidious pressures that exist everywhere to affiliate and remain with one primary networking group.

Primary networking groups consist of from four to six people who regularly meet for coffee or lunch and engage in the kind of casual—sometimes intense—gossip that the grapevine then carries. These groups form up very early when someone joins a company and are his or her initiation into the informal system. While the fact that they exist is important, it's their stability that is a key political fact. It's obvious if you look closely that most people have coffee and/or lunch with the same people several times a week. This is a political liability. These people share the same values and outlook or they'd be giving each other acute indigestion. They will protect that relationship at all costs. That means that no one in the group will report something negative that's circulating about the rest of the group. Certainly the victim of negative gossip won't hear it from his/ her primary networking group.

Not being tied to one coffee group so that you can circulate freely throughout the company or division is a priceless political asset. To the amazement of your co-workers, you may actually be able to predict events. Your secret, of course, is that you've collected and sifted more facts and rumors than those who maintain only their exclusive primary relationships. No one networking group could possibly gather all the complete facts. They hear only fragments. Someone, preferably you, must collect all of the raw data floating around and make sense of it. Flitting from group to group like a bee cross-pollinating is the mechanism.

The down side is that it's very lonely at times because no comfortable group of cronies waits for you to share rumors and coffee. But you will have a priceless political advantage. Someone who's locked into a group for ten years will have a far less accurate view of the total organization than someone who regularly drinks around.

If you are tied to a regular group now (most people are if they've been on the job more than a few months), it's time to start loosening those ties. However, don't—repeat don't—suddenly drop the people you've been networking with. Your name will be mud in foot-high letters in the grapevine. There is nothing more verboten in offices than high-hatting one's old pals, however it's done. You'll be thought to have ulterior motives, which you do, but why display them so transparently? Over time, however, you can ease out and begin circulating, first to one group and then to another. You'll gradually be accepted as someone who has many contacts within the organization and many people to keep tabs on. Your strange behavior will soon be seen as normal.

Money and Risk Taking

Anyone who wants to survive and move up in organizations has to expect to take risks. This may be nothing more than reaching out to people whose acceptance you can't count on. It may mean planting a rumor (trial balloon) in the grapevine to see what shakes out. It may involve some of the techniques described in the chapter on political euthanasia. To be able to take any risk there is one bottom line and that's money. If you don't see the relationship, consider this: Money buys independence of action. The way you manage your personal funds is a key to success in the office. Nobody takes political risks at any level except out of desperation until he or she has some personal financial cushion. If you are vulnerable to financial ruin if you lose your job, you'll always play it very safe. Live at 110 percent of your take-home pay and you have few political options—however well you may have analyzed the situation. You must cling to your job at all costs because you're always on the financial brink. Furthermore, should you be out of work, even a few weeks, you'd be tempted to take any job—however politically impossible—just to survive.

And don't think companies don't use this knowledge to get employees who've got financial problems to toe the mark. Is there anyone more vulnerable to a boss's pressure than a man with a stay-at-home wife and two children under the age of five? If she's a retired flight attendant, double the vulnerability. She and he may believe she couldn't easily get a job that would cover child care expenses—much less the mortgage! (This isn't true, of course, but it's widely believed. Ditto for retired teachers, nurses, etc.) His boss can give him assignments that keep him in East Overshoe for weeks at a time and he's unlikely to protest very much or show a flash of independence.

Contrast that situation with someone whose spouse is working. Many corporations have found, to their collective amazement, that people in two-income families can be very independent! They won't tolerate any management funny business—if weeks in East Overshoe could be called funny—because the mortgage is covered. You can't give ultimatums, seek secret revenge, or reinforce your value to the company if the only thing you're really worried about is staying on the payroll. Therefore a quiz on your financial management is in order.

1. How long could you cover the basics plus 20 percent, i.e., housing, medical insurance, food, transportation, and fixed monthly expenses plus 20 percent of that total, from current cash or cash equivalent savings?

2. What kind of work have you already investigated that

you could readily obtain if you were out of work? For example, many people who already moonlight at various jobs could increase their hours. Others know of small businesses that might regularly need temporary help.

3. Does your total debt load (the sum of all credit purchases including mortgage and car loans) exceed 35 percent of your take-home pay?

4. If you have a spouse at home, how quickly could he or she be employed? In the sixties the rallying cry of college placement counselors to women was "Get a degree in teaching and you'll always have a job." Never have so many received such poor, or shortsighted, advice. However, there are still plenty of things people who haven't worked in years can do to make a living. Have you investigated any of them?

5. Do you have a plan for raising cash quickly, for example, by selling something that has ready cash value, such as coins, stamps, gold, preferred stocks or bonds?

Clearly this is not a comprehensive quiz—but this isn't a book on financial planning either. Here's how to score.

1. If you can finance your basic expenses plus 20 percent for a year, give yourself 25 points. If for six months, give yourself 15 points. If for three months or less, subtract 10 points. This is not just a financial question. People who don't have a cash cushion are vulnerable to panic. They'll leap at a job that's totally wrong. They may also underestimate just how much money they need to survive. That's what the 20 percent cushion is for.

2. If you are "keeping your hand in," making money part-time from a hobby, from temporary work, or just keeping your contacts warm in case you need them, give yourself 15 points. If you've given some thought to what kind of work you'd do, it's worth 10. If you've never considered any kind of temporary or part-time work, subtract 5.

3. If your total debt load is under 20 percent, give yourself 25 points. If it's under 25 percent, give yourself 15 points.

If it's under 30 percent, give yourself 0 points. If it's 35 percent, subtract 10 points. If above 40 percent, subtract 25 points. You owe your heavily mortgaged soul to the company store. They own you.

4. If you and your spouse have an action plan for his/her return to work that would likely result in employment in less than three months, give yourself 25 points. If in six months, give yourself 15 points. If your spouse would need to return to school in order to secure a job, subtract 10 points.

5. If you've got a list of what you could sell and to whom, give yourself 25 points. If you've got ready assets but wouldn't part with them under most circumstances, it's worth 10 points. If you have no cash equivalent assets, subtract 10 points. If you got 25 points on this question, it means you are thinking of contingencies. If you're in minus numbers, you haven't assessed the risks.

If you scored 75 or more, you're able to sustain some on-the-job risk. If you scored 50 to 75, you should be very careful. If you scored fewer than 50 points, you need financial counseling and career counseling. You are in no position to take any risks for advancement.

This quiz won't make financial analysts happy. They favor long quizzes that analyze every aspect of the way you handle money. All we wanted was for you to see that you can't be anything but a nervous bystander in the political wars unless you're confident your next meal and mortgage payment are covered. If they're not, and you still play games, you're suicidal and should have your internal furniture rearranged by a competent therapist.

You may not attribute your own caution and desire to be a political bystander to your financial, rather than psychological, makeup. Few people recognize or like the idea that they are handicapped in office politics. However, financial problems are giant handicaps to political action.

Self-Training

Everybody is familiar with organization training. It may be done by a boss who says, "Do it this way." It may be done in-house in formal courses or off-site. However, important as this kind of training is, there is another kind equally or even more important. That is self-training. Self-training is the ability to learn how to do something by watching how another worker approaches a problem. It may entail more than watching. It may involve asking someone, "Why are you doing that? Why did you decide to approach the problem that way?" Bottom line, it's the ability to pick up new skills on the job without someone specifically showing you how.

Much of self-training will be trial and error. If you were involved in customer service, you'd undoubtedly have been taught how to meet certain kinds of customer complaints or needs. As you met new situations, you'd apply what you learned. If something didn't work, you'd scramble for a different solution. Eventually you'd have developed some theories that would work in most situations. There might be an oddball who'd occasionally throw you for a loss, but not often. That process, developing and testing theories, refining them, and reapplying them, is self-learning. If you are to progress politically and be a winner in the office wars, you've got to sharpen your self-training skills. To do that you need to sharpen your observation skills, your analysis skills, and your interview skills. After all, the kind of questions you ask your co-workers makes the difference in the quality of information you receive.

Observation begins with testing how much you know right now. Suppose one of your co-workers has been very busy putting together a three-month survey of employee opinion. Your job is quite different from your co-worker's but you can still see the value in knowing how to approach opinion research. You might take a course or read a book if you wanted to know in detail how to approach this kind of research. However, if you watch your co-worker while he works on the project, you might pick up enough information to perform creditably if given a similar assignment. What you want to look for are specific procedures. Where did he start? What assumptions did he seem to make? You might lunch with him and ask how he did the assignment. Then, with that fact foundation, you should look for the overall patterns in what your co-worker did.

You don't have to watch him every minute; even occasionally seeing what he is doing can be important to your self-training. Most procedures have shortcuts, which, once learned, bridge many theoretical gaps. This won't work for highly technical projects, but it will be useful in at least alerting you to what you don't know! Sometimes that's the most important thing you can learn.

Analysis skills consist of correctly interpreting data. This is not such a big problem when we're talking about money, materials, or anything concrete. It's a big problem when we're talking about human behavior and the ways people approach each other. Analyzing why someone used a particular approach is as important as watching him use the approach, because until you understand the theory, you'll never be able to develop your own.

Interviewing skills are learned by trial and error. There are rules for asking questions but they are by no means universal. The way you ask a question is as important as what you ask. This is especially true when you're trying to teach yourself something like tact or how to put people at ease. It's important to phrase your questions to your co-workers as compliments. People will usually share something they believe you greatly admire.

The reason this is so important is that most companies won't send you to courses, to learn management for instance, until you've been promoted to manager. They also won't promote you unless you already seem to be good at managing the work of others. It's catch-22. Breaking out requires that you observe others, analyze what they do, and then confirm that is what they are doing. Then, when you behave in the same way as people who are doing the job successfully, management thinks you have potential.

Productivity

We've already talked about productivity as an issue for both companies and individuals. However, what we haven't looked at is the political power that accrues to those who are visibly more productive than their competition.

Productivity can be defined and measured. Generally the term means the relationship between effort, output, and quality. Politically it means producing more work of higher quality than you are paid for and packaging your efforts so your superiors are aware of them. It doesn't necessarily mean working harder. In the trade it's the bang-to-buck ratio.

Even if you provide a service, there are certain ways in which your boss and those above him/her will judge your productivity. It may not have a thing to do with the quality or quantity of your work. Job one is to find out what productivity means in your organization both overall and to your boss. For example, consulting firms put management relationship with clients and working long hours high on their lists of productivity measures. You may be sitting at your desk at 7:00 P.M. lining up a date for Saturday night or surveying local hot spots for prime time reservations, but you're still fulfilling your company's productivity expectations. It may involve how you motivate others. Getting more out of your subordinates may be the only way your own productivity is judged.

Being productive is important, but being seen and acknowledged as productive moves your career ahead. You may be the best analyst in the company but if no one knows, you're not going to get credit. Doing the work for its own sake is fine—but not political. That means you have to sell what you are doing.

How does your level of output compare with your

peers'? No one measures productivity absolutely. It's measured against what others produce. Just keeping even won't help you politically, because it means you don't understand the shift in workplace values that has taken place. It may also occur to management you do know but refuse to get with the program. If all the people in your department have secretly begun working longer hours, but you're still leaving at five, that's going to create political problems, however laudable your motives or however productive you are from nine to five. It's symbolic but vital. You may want to ask yourself if people are changing how they do things. Look at your competitors carefully. What are they doing differently?

What plans are you formulating to increase your own productivity? One of the blessings of the so-called productivity movement is that it's a cacophony of ideas and plans from the ridiculous to the deadly serious. You need to measure how you're doing now, and then plan for improvements. If it currently takes you two hours to sketch out a project, can you reduce that to an hour and a half? Then, can you show your boss that you've done so? You need to keep notes on how you are increasing your productivity.

Have you learned the language of productivity and do you use it? Do you say, "I've discovered I can save hours by doing this," or are you keeping that knowledge to yourself? You need to package your communication to your boss and peers in terms of productivity. Those who don't understand this are saying in effect that they are noncompetitors.

The Role of Positioning in Politics

Positioning is a marketing term that refers to the process of making an idea or product attractive to a particular audience; literally placing it in relationship to its audience. Most political positioning is done with serious, elected office seekers, but there's no reason that what's known about the process shouldn't be helpful to you.

In an office, how you position yourself is vital to how you're seen by peers, management at all levels, and your subordinates. For example, Jim M. appeared to be on the fast track at his hospital consulting firm. He'd started there two years before as assistant comptroller, been promoted within six months to comptroller, and now seemed to have a clear shot at financial vice president. Jim's career took a left turn when he let drop the fact that his idea of entertainment was picking up people in singles bars. He was single and his behavior was really no problem. The problem was his talking about it! Since then his career has been on hold. Unfair? You bet—and very typical. Since more people are knocked out of the running by nonwork issues than is supposed, it's important to look at how you've positioned yourself verbally and visually in the office.

Answer the following questions.

1. How much have you told anyone in your office about your personal life, family, hobbies, lifestyle in general?

Unhappily, people make judgments on details that, politically speaking, they shouldn't even be aware of. Joking about your idiot relatives may come back to haunt you. Your peers may decide you're similarly afflicted when you say or do something they consider strange. If you and your spouse are going through separation or divorce, don't discuss it. It can—and will—come back to haunt you. People should not be able to discuss your lifestyle unless you're acting it out in the office. If they think you're frivolous because you spend every weekend enjoying yourself at the city's finest French restaurants, it's because you're positioning yourself in that way. Everything you say and do is An Official Policy Statement from You, Inc., even if you don't think so.

2. How differently do you dress from those one or two levels above you in the structure?

If you're wearing a down-filled jacket over a business suit because it's warmer than wool, you don't understand what politics is about. Warmth isn't the issue. If you're dressing casually or comfortably while everyone else is dressing professionally, you're making a values statement that will affect your career. There are still women (and men) who think clothing has something to do with self-expression. It does, but the impact is negative, not positive. The business uniform, a conservative suit for men and women, is just that, a uniform. Introduce your own ideas at peril to your career!

Unfortunately, clothing is a political issue in the 1980s. John Molloy (*Dress for Success* and *Dress for Success for Women*) is being attacked not because he's wrong but because he's right! Before you decide to deviate from the old ways, ask yourself if it's conceivable that the CEO of IBM says to himself in the morning, "I'm so bored with conservative suits and ties. I think I'll wear my peach leisure suit today."

3. Are you radically out of sync socially with your co-workers? If they go off for a beer after work on Friday, do you join them or duck? If you're not there more than half the time, you're positioning yourself not as a loner, but as someone who doesn't like them! They don't care if your child's day-care center closes at the stroke of six. They don't care if that's your evening for handball. What they register is that you don't like them.

4. Do you spend most of your time sitting in your office at your desk? Do you move around the office and drop a friendly word here and there? People who build invisible shields that say "Don't disturb me unless it's life or death" are positioning themselves as untouchables. It's not good politically because people interpret this as withdrawal from the team.

5. Are you standing at your office door at five o'clock? Nothing could more clearly position you as antimanagement rather than top management material—unless your boss is in line ahead of you watching the sweep of the second hand. But still, what is his or her boss watching?

This list could go on forever but you get the point. It's fine to talk about positioning yourself on the fast track unless what you do repositions you as an also-ran. You need to turn on your mind's eye and carefully examine what your nonverbal signals are. Nothing can help you if there's a disparity. You must get everything in line with corporate values.

In order to position yourself as a serious professional you need to go over every detail of your image. You'll have to give up some of the ideas you have about individuality and self-expression. When you decide your career is more important than whether your present employer will let you work dressed as a peasant, you'll be on the road to greater success—some of it political.

◊ TRUMPING YOUR OWN ACES

The war over appearances versus reality will not be won in our lifetime. However, you might want to think about this. If you insist on positioning yourself as the office eccentric, you're really playing a game. Could you have decided that you're so much better than your competitors you can put an obstacle in your own path and still win the race? Do you remember the fable of the tortoise and the hare? Do you recall the outcome? It's never wise, politically speaking, to add to your own obstacles, simply because the office environment has so many unanticipated pitfalls that could sink your strategy. Straight ahead works best.

Chapter 5. Advancement Tools:

Politics and the Upward Climb

Eavesdrop on a conversation between a couple of self-proclaimed "hard chargers" in your company. You will be amazed at the techniques they still believe will move them ahead. You'll hear a rehash of ideas and strategies based on "everyone knows" and "everyone says." Generalized ignorance is being traded with the clear expectation of gaining knowledge.

Even allowing for a bell curve distribution of top management skill in talent identification, a real knowledge chasm lies between why people are promoted and why those not promoted believe the lucky ones moved ahead. Unless you can collect and analyze the facts about your organization's promotion policies, you haven't much chance of joining the inner circle. Unless you're just lucky, of course, but who wants to rely on that? Many people assume there are all-inclusive rules or a general theory of promotability that applies to all companies. Not so. Each company is a unique culture with rules of its own. There are, however, some facts that explain why top management tends to promote certain people and not others. You need to be aware of these.

Promotion Influences

An organization's size and its management philosophy play important roles in determining who moves up, but not the roles you might expect. Philosophy has more effect on marketing and management styles than it does on promotability, especially in large companies. In an arm wrestle between philosophy and size, philosophy will lose. Size is the major factor. Larger companies tend to be conservative, tightly structured, and addicted to routine. Think of IBM, General Electric, 3M Corporation. They may be innovative and excellently run, but they also profile other large companies. Regardless of size, no company is always pragmatic. Each has traditions management reveres even after they've been proven inappropriate. In small companies philosophy may dominate the decision-making process. Owner/founders often become fixated on their own early experiences and believe the same are critical to personal growth and business success. A boss may decide that no one will move up until he or she has paid his/her dues in sales or in the plant. As a result, the most brilliant financial person may not be moved up in the company until he's met this particular initiation rite.

Who moves up reflects what top management thinks the business needs as well as the talents an individual can offer. Management looks for a combination of what it thinks the job requires and how it can fill the gaps in management expertise or experience of those already on board. For example, if almost everyone in top management is homegrown, they may decide it's important to hire an outsider for a key slot. If no one near the top is a long-term employee, someone internal may be a front runner, even though more competent outsiders are available.

This thought process is the essence of team building and management succession planning. Both terms refer to the search for that elusive quality called "balance." It appears to be almost instinctive with CEOs. If top management believes faster growth will result from shoring up the business's financial management, the greatest marketing executive in the world can find his or her career on hold. If management believes that marketing is the key to growth, the premier cost cutter, strategic planner, or number cruncher will languish under an invisible lead ceiling.

There is strong evidence that balance is the key to any company's long-term survival and growth. Witness the fate of companies in which management invested too heavily in one area, marketing, for instance, focusing all its attention and resources there. When tough manufacturing problems occurred, the marketing people couldn't help.

However, the quest for balance has a down side. It increases employee mobility. If you're not hot in one company, you move to another where your skills are given top priority. As a result, companies have problems keeping the stars who are working in deemphasized areas.

Only when the business basics are covered will individual attributes be evaluated. Skills as an important part of how an individual is evaluated is a 1980s development. The whole idea of skills analysis became widely known and accepted only in the late 1970s, largely as the result of work done by Richard N. Bolles, author of the perennially popular *What Color Is Your Parachute?* Before then, companies spent more time evaluating work experience and education and trying to divine the correct fit with a particular job description. Skills analysis will always be done within a political context. "He may be good," the CEO says, "but is he wired in?" Does one of the aspirants have a mentor who's carefully pushing his/her interests? Does the person fit the corporate style?

In the 1970s it was widely thought that it was possible to rise simply because you were the "right sort." (Whether it was true or not then is open to question.) It was a generalization for those people who had some potential or skill that top management felt the business would need down the road. In the current economic climate it has become increasingly unprofitable, and in low-growth times very risky, to warehouse talent. Hence a change in the market-ability of potential. In the early seventies top management's idea of succession planning was to try to identify and lash to the organization people with very high leadership poten-tial. "Find a place for Jack," a senior vice president would say. "He's going to be a key man ten or fifteen years from now—after a little seasoning."

In the 1980s the same vice president is likely to say, "Let Jack go if he wants to. If we need him later we'll hire him back. He can develop at someone else's expense." Clearly talent has become a commodity to be purchased on an "as needed" basis. In spite of the fact that many com-panies have all but put this people-as-resource concept into the policy manual, you will still hear long-term employees touting their loyalty as something the company ought to reward. The truly masochistic continue to do this even after being told that the company is now more interested in increased work loads and better results.

The personality type most likely to be moved up is the one that matches or complements the most powerful peo-ple currently in top management. That's why any pop-psych test or magazine article purporting to describe a universal "success personality" is mental chewing gum. What is identified by an individual company as a success personality always depends on who's making the decision and in what context. How else can you account for the broad spectrum of top management personality types? Haven't you met really top-level executives who would have scored in the minus numbers on any personality quiz? It's adult-in-fantasyland stuff to believe there is one set of characteristics that guarantees promotability.

This is equally true if the job you want is two or three rungs below the executive suite. You may want to be a department manager. That job may be so remote from top management that you'd be unlikely to interact regularly with any one of them. Nevertheless, corporate values, as top management acts them out, have enough direct and indirect effect on the overall climate that whoever has the power to promote people will not be unfamiliar with them or ignore them. For example, a departmental manager, three levels below vice president, was judged by her former peers as aggressively underqualified for the promotion she'd gotten until they discovered that she'd spent three years on assignment in a South American country. Since everyone in the executive suite also had had overseas experience, international experience was a part of the company's promotability profile. This illustrates why there's so much close scrutiny of organizational culture right now. This insight can be used to predict who will be eligible to move up in a particular company.

Impressing your immediate boss may help you move up, but only about 50 percent of the time. It's by no means a guaranteed or even a highly reliable strategy. Some companies have a policy against letting managers groom subordinates as successors. They are afraid the company will become resistant to change and less resilient. One CEO explained, "It's too dangerous. You risk embalming incompetence, not to mention complacency." So your boss may not have the power to promote you.

There's the possibility he/she may not want to. If the company is top-heavy with risk avoiders, i.e., people who want a sure thing—and your boss is a card-carrying member of that pack—you'll threaten rather than impress him or her if you're visibly ambitious. The specter of a credible competitor is unlikely to make him or her want to promote you and may prompt thoughts of lopping you off your branch. The thought processes of risk avoiders are such that they not only don't want to help you become competitive today, but they consciously work to secure the future by surrounding themselves with willing "also-rans." Top management may appear acquiescent if the company is very profitable. If it's not, watch out!

There must be no perceived antagonism between you and your boss unless your boss is already in trouble. In that case you can be a bit more high profile and even let it be known you don't agree point-by-point with his/her position on an issue. Otherwise, you must appear to want to impress your boss. You have to support the boss and even allow some of your ideas to be stolen and the credit for them unfairly withheld. Don't worry. Stealing ideas and credit is not totally without risk. Witness the manager who claimed credit for a brilliant piece of analysis done by Andy, his subordinate. At a formal presentation to a packed top management audience including outside directors, the boss gave a seamless performance. Andy maintained a look of enthusiastic support. Then a director threw out a tough, technical question. The boss stumbled and hedged. He understood the results but nothing about the methods Andy had used to get them. Another tough question was tossed at him, so he turned and said, deprecatingly, "I'm going to let Andy answer that." Who was fooled?

Such incidents are just part of the workplace game. Going along gracefully is a test of whether or not you know the rules. To object shows that you don't understand or respect the hierarchy. The less you dwell on small injustices, the more quickly you'll move up. In fact, the sooner you banish the just/unjust pattern of analysis, the better off you'll be.

The person whose opinion really counts is your boss's boss. Raising your visibility with that person and his or her peers means something. She/he and colleagues control not only your boss's future but yours as well. If you don't include the boss's boss in your plans, you may waste time impressing a boss who has neither the power nor motive to push you ahead. The boss's boss sees you, not as your immediate boss's competitor, but in competition with your peers in the same age, education, and experience brackets, inside and outside the organization. But if your boss is in trouble, your boss's boss can compound your vulnerability to being fired by seeing you as competitive with your boss. Furthermore, if your boss is in trouble, he/she might fire you, figuring that a lack of a ready replacement might delay his/her exit. You want to be seen as complementary to your boss and the logical successor but not someone who is snorting and pawing the carpet to get his or her job. You want to position yourself as someone who could also be promoted to another slot. It's critical to be visible to your boss's peers. Being wooed into a better job by someone on the next level up is not a bad way to rise.

Using outside connections in another generation, your parents' for instance, is not as useful as it was in the past. If your name is Rockefeller, it might help, but it could raise questions as to why you need that kind of push. Could it be you're not as clever as someone who's made his/her own connections? Call it neo-cynicism; it exists everywhere. Even banks, long plagued with customers' needy, semi-competent relatives, are now looking very critically at people who are "must hires" because of personal connections. The recession has made them as welcome as herpes because they bring such a bundle of political luggage. When promotions were more plentiful, the competent people might overlook an occasional management weakness or indiscretion in promoting a welfare case. Now the good people, recognizing they are blocked, either leave or reduce their productivity. The latter, of course, is far more serious.

What Does Not Matter

The desire to get ahead, i.e., your personal ambition, isn't nearly as important to the company as it is to you. In fact, promotion is thrust upon about one-third as many people who are barely willing to accept it as on those who actively seek it. It's true. Not everybody's idea of heaven is moving into or up in management. This isn't surprising when you consider that people are coached from college days to tout their ambition. Can you imagine a mid-level candidate not mentioning a desire to move up in an interview? That's what they think management wants to hear. Usually women must actively campaign for consideration in order to overcome institutionalized prejudice.

Subordinates who think you're terrific and a great leader don't make much difference. However, subordinates who think you aren't a good leader could have impact through the grapevine. Top management is more sensitive to the negative news than to the positive. There are many documented cases of this attitude, especially in operations and sales, because being an outstanding practitioner doesn't necessarily make you a leader. Any hint that your area is loaded with reluctant followers can raise questions about your leadership ability. Even though Liz's boss thought she had managed the audit very well, he was disturbed when he found out that more than half the staff people assigned to her said, if given a choice, they would not want to work with her again. This turned up on her evaluation, and her boss began sending her to seminars on human relations.

Length of service matters in public sector jobs. It still may matter in some very large companies. Before cost containment, it mattered in hospitals. Today you can't count on sheer length of service to be of much help in advancing. People who've held the same job for three to five years are often viewed as "settled in," a real impediment to advancement.

What Does Matter

There are five things that can provide upward thrust to your career. These are heightened visibility, external mentors and contacts, job redesign, job proposals, and structural analysis. If these seem to lack sex appeal, understand this: They work in today's business climate. Except for a small number of highly visible, high technology companies, business is looking a bit gray these days. Recession and economic uncertainties have produced large patches of gloom. However, even though top management may alternately be pessimistic or optimistic, sometimes in the same quarter, you can still move up. You have to think far more creatively than ever before. In many companies you'll have to create a new position. Certainly, you will have to take on more work and responsibility.

Before you map out extensive plans, you can always ask your boss for a promotion if he/she has that power. However, two conditions may defeat your bid. (1) The boss may be surprised by your ambition. If so, you haven't laid the proper groundwork. You may have mentioned promotion to him/her, but you haven't done what's necessary to appear serious, such as raising your internal and external visibility or coming up with a specific slot you could fill. (2) There may truly be no openings. You are knocking on a locked door. This situation is common right now. You can wait it out or you can carefully consider the alternatives.

Raising Your Visibility

The recent economic gloom has caused some ambitious souls to lose track of a fundamental principle everyone was supposed to have learned in the 1970s. You can be doing the best work in the world, but if nobody knows it except your boss (and tell us why it's in his/her best interest to sing your praises), you might as well be working for another organization. You must methodically and regularly publicize your achievements. The office grapevine must be talking about you in positive or respectful ways, and you must have stature in your industry. (It isn't necessary to campaign for the presidency of your trade association but you can if you decide it's worth it.) You must be known to people in your industry. There is, as the Old Testament points out, no use in hiding your light under a basket. Visibility in a trade organization enhances both your internal and external promotability quotient.

Of course, everyone knows this and it seems condescending to repeat it but, alas, so few people actually do it! Most people have a basic conflict between the need to protect themselves from too much involvement and the need to advance. The conflict must be resolved first. If you're going to make an intelligent choice about when and how to seek advancement, you need to understand three things.

1. Only you can make yourself visible. You've got to tell people about your accomplishments in small, regular doses —time release publicity! You should create a sustained presence in your office, instead of trying to stun and amaze the troops once or twice a year. If you single-handedly save the company from Chapter Eleven, everyone will know it. However, the applause will be a momentary high. Next, you will be expected to leap tall buildings, at the very least, and your audience will look elsewhere for Superman or Wonder Woman when you don't deliver.

Instead, your strategy should be to update your networking pals weekly on how well things are going. Your goal is a steady, medium-wattage glow. This would seem a natural thing to do, but few people can even recall at the end of the week what they accomplished, much less remember to put it into the grapevine.

If you prefer waiting for the recognition you've earned rather than seeking it, return this book to your bookstore. You can't benefit from it. A certain amount of active courting of internal publicity is necessary. Recognition must be grasped, regrasped, and monitored. To show how obtuse people really are—it may just be lethargy—consider this incident. Maria, the human resources manager for a software house, persuaded an employee with a bankable legal cause of action not to sue. Because the grapevine carried a garbled account of what occurred, her co-workers, one and all, believed she'd caused, not solved, the problem. Maria never deigned to correct the misconception and so her high-mindedness turned a coup into her eventual downfall.

2. Comfort and promotability are always in conflict. The energy needed to become and remain visible is about double what you'd expect. You'll have to force yourself to network regularly with the congenitally unlovable. This may require you to enroll in a course in method acting, but no one must ever suspect how personally and professionally tiresome you find them—and you know how much energy that takes! There are other discomforts. Many people, particularly women, have real problems in letting people see their competence. They can't decide whether they'd rather be Gloria Steinem or Scarlett O'Hara. If you're convinced that self-publicity will position you as a castrating female and you'll lose all your sex appeal, put your career on hold and get therapy. Men who suffer from a similar mindset frequently seem self-righteous. "Why should I have to say anything? They should notice," is their attitude.

3. Visibility has risks. It can make you unpopular. People will see you as the one to beat, the person to envy. That may cost you some friendships and make you unhappy occasionally. It's uncomfortable to feel you're being watched even when you know it's what your career plans require. Read some of Franz Kafka's novels if you want to get in the right frame of mind. Seriously, discomfort comes with the territory. A word of warning: Don't ever deprecate your efforts or say, "Aw shucks, that was no big deal." You will infuriate your co-workers who've watched as you worked like a Minnesota mosquito, and you'll be branded (possibly publicly) as a hypocrite.

Assuming that you've swallowed hard and decided your advancement is worth the effort, here are some ways to maintain and increase internal visibility.

The Game Plan   Decide how often you want your name mentioned and how you want to position yourself. What do you want to emphasize—your competence, your follow-through, one special skill? A salesman who set his sights on becoming sales manager began to let the grapevine know how much he enjoyed soothing angry customers and, incidentally, how good he was at it. He'd tell the folks back at the shop about the tough ones he'd faced and placated. He was both smart and honest. His track record wasn't 100 percent so he never pretended it was. He didn't broadcast his failures but he let his co-workers know that he, too, had times when nothing worked. This helped him build rapport with them. Since he was a top producer, his methods were taken seriously. His methods and ideas motivated others in a low-key way. When the sales manager retired, it was hardly a surprise that our man got the job. He'd positioned himself as a problem solver with integrity and good leadership skills, top priorities for a sales manager.

An accounting manager, Joanie L., figured the competition for partnership in her firm would be uncommonly tough the year she would be considered. She knew that technical skills were important but pleasing clients and getting them to increase billings was far more important, especially since a large audit client had recently gone Chapter Thirteen. She also knew that industry scuttlebutt said women didn't become partners, because even if they were highly skilled technically, they couldn't bring in new business. She began to position herself as someone looking for new business. Her clients began to give her some tips on new business prospects. They also mentioned her efforts to the partners in her firm. In effect, they became a pressure group in her favor. The partners voted for her. Who could refuse someone, even a woman, whose priorities and results were so obviously in line with the firm's culture?

Once you know how you want to position yourself, don't

launch your campaign unless and until you're sure it's going to help you advance. A highly temperamental copy-writer in an advertising agency was sure she was in line for promotion to copy chief. She worked on the firm's most profitable accounts and her work won awards and kudos from clients. Client company sales curves were gorgeous. However, she'd positioned herself as highly creative but temperamental—hardly the attributes a nervous top man-agement would want in its ranks. In order to move up she had to overhaul her behavior and her image—repositioning herself on the side of leadership and sweet reason. It took six months to convince management she'd made a perma-nent change.

Allow at least that much time before you begin looking for the effects of your efforts. People change their ideas slowly. If you've been Frantic Freddy for three years, a sudden calming may be attributed to Valium rather than a change in outlook. After six months your co-workers will be accustomed to, and accepting of, the new you. Then you can gradually begin raising your visibility.

Actively seek out opportunities to meet people within the organization. Working on a charity fund-raising drive is a pain but it does allow you to be visible in positive ways. Agree to solicit pledges in the executive suite. You'll have a chance to chat with people who are not otherwise acces-sible. The company's internal newsletter always needs re-porters. Sign up. Then interview the people you want to be aware of you and your work. This is not just a junior-level strategy. Senior-level people can write articles that require input from others. Nobody refuses an interview when it's for the company paper.

Speak well of your boss even if you could be charged with criminal misrepresentation or a misdemeanor. You are an extension of, and a reflection of, that person. If he's such an incompetent why are you working for him? Any negatives about him/her, however well founded, reflect on you. They're also political dynamite. If your boss is founder-

ing, he/she still has some good qualities. Find them and
tout them. Besides, if your boss so much as hears a whisper
that you don't support him/her, your career in that department will be in jeopardy.

External Mentors and Contacts

The need for and the importance of external mentors
and contacts can't be overemphasized. Understand that
every mentor is a contact, but every contact is not a mentor.
A contact is anyone who can be useful to you and vice
versa. Mostly these are people you meet through trade and
professional society meetings. You might meet them at a
single-sex networking group. These contacts probably
won't help your upward climb as much as they will be a
source of job leads and information.

Mentors are teachers/enhancers. They are people who
do one of three things. (1) They show you how to behave
in a role you want to assume but have no experience with.
(2) They provide a sounding board for your ideas which co-
workers, who are very close to a particular problem, cannot
do. (3) They speak well of you to people within your organization who can help you.

The Role of Contacts in Mobility   Moving up usually involves using contacts creatively, especially if you don't have
an internal mentor. Here are some more sophisticated ways
they can help you and you can help them.

1. Feedback from a competitive viewpoint becomes increasingly important as you bump your head at the highest
levels of middle management. It's hard to know why the
word *competitor* is commonly used as a synonym for
enemy. Nothing could be further from the truth! Competitors need each other if only to have someone worth beating.
Peers who work for competitive companies can give you a
leg up in many ways. They will tell you the ugliest gossip
circulating in their firm about your company. This may

alert you to problems that your internal grapevine hasn't picked up. They show you by example the skills and qualities a competitive company thinks are necessary for someone doing your job in that firm.

They may inadvertently come up with a fresh approach to solving a problem. A small food processing company had a dying snack food on its hands until a salesman had lunch with a friend from another firm. His buddy commented, "You know what's wrong with that stuff? It tastes like almonds and it's not supposed to be almonds." The salesman talked to his company's R and D people, who thought about it and reflavored the product. Sales took off. An insider who suggested the flavoring was a problem might have been shoved aside, but a competitor's opinion was listened to.

2. Your outside contacts may let you know who in your company has approached the competitor for a job. If your boss is looking for a different job, it's unlikely he or she would let the word get out internally because of fear of reprisals from his or her boss. However, any sensible person would recognize that the most immediate market for his/her services would be a direct competitor and would approach them first. If you have the right contacts, you'll probably hear that your boss has approached them. This information could be useful to you. You might want your boss's job. Knowing in advance that the boss is trying to move would give you time to position yourself as the logical successor—and at a time when your peers are unaware of a possible change.

It might be a good strategy to try to figure out who would be most likely to replace your boss and begin building a relationship with that person. If it's to be an outsider, where would that person logically come from? How would a successor's skills or experience be different from the present boss's? Would a different sort of boss value your work and style more or less highly? Fact gathering is the key to preventing nasty surprises that leave you with inadequate time to mount a campaign or give a reasoned response.

You need to ask yourself what will happen if your boss doesn't get another job. Will disappointment in his/her apparent unmarketability change the nature of the department or your relationship to him/her? Competitors can give you an outsider's view of these issues and possibly help you change or rethink strategies.

3. Talking with a competitor allows you to test an idea without risk. If you think you have the best idea to improve your department that anyone has ever had, the best strategy is not to dump it on your boss or co-workers immediately. It's to your advantage to pretest it on someone who can give you perspective and feedback. This is especially true if the idea has political aspects, such as reorganizing the department or changing people's duties. A competitor could share how his/her company handled a similar situation. There's nothing unethical about talking to a competitor in these situations, because you're discussing structural problems, not products or services. In other words, how a company has approached an organizational problem isn't a competitive secret.

It may help to have someone who isn't an insider but knows something about your operation play the devil's advocate. A competitor brings a different perspective and frequently raises issues you'd never have considered. It's also easier on your ego to have your hottest ideas shredded by someone who isn't in your office every day.

4. The relationship can be noncompetitive. One of the blessings of these relationships is that you can't be bushwhacked by someone you've mistakenly trusted. You can be mutually supportive and use one another as a sounding board, but not worry that your associate is after your job. That is an important dimension to any professional relationship. With your co-workers, you must always carefully package what you say. That diminishes the degree of trust in the relationship. An outside competitor has no interest in your job per se and needs you as a sounding board and source of information, too. That cements the relationship.

Job Redesign

Job redesign is the most practical way to approach advancement and takes the least sustained effort. Once learned, the technique can be applied anywhere. The theory is this: Your job description doesn't really describe your job; it tells you more about the boundaries of your territory than what you're supposed to accomplish. For some reason, possibly because there's usually a committee that develops job descriptions and approves changes, people believe there's something mystical about the process. Instead of treating job descriptions as The Word From On High and therefore cast in stone, it is better to study them as maps to the territory.

Study the organization chart of your department and the job descriptions, your own and those of your co-workers. If you can identify tasks that are not being done effectively, it's possible you can redefine your responsibilities and create a higher-level job by including them. You can then go to your boss and propose the changes. If you've followed the format your company uses, it's just a matter of winning your boss's support. Even if a salary adjustment is required, it could be a line item "adjustment," not an out-of-season raise.

Packaging becomes an important part of any effort to get your job redesigned. If you think and write like a job standards committee member, it's much easier to win approval. Go in with a vague idea and you won't succeed. Your boss will be content with the status quo unless he or she sees why it's in his/her best interest to change. There must be a clear payoff, such as savings, greater productivity, or enhancement of the department's power or reputation.

Once you've decided to use job redesign as part of your advancement campaign, here's what you need to do.

1. Develop an overall strategy in writing, in as much detail as possible. Use it as a spur to keep building momentum. Develop a timetable and include what you plan to do each week. Week one would include gathering all the job descriptions for your department and getting guidelines from personnel about the ways job descriptions are developed and then studying them carefully. Week two would call for writing and refining a new job description. This could take several evenings. Don't be satisfied with something casually roughed out on scrap paper. Revise and refine it. Remember, a potentially hostile committee (you're invading their territory) will review whatever you submit. In week three you would talk to contacts in competitive companies and ask them to look over what you've written and give feedback. Week four may be the time to put into the grapevine that you think there's a need for a change and your reasons. You must precondition people to expect change. Week five or six may be the week you talk to your boss. You want to give the grapevine time to build. This timetable may seem unnecessarily stretched out, but you still have your present job to do and life after work.

Don't start a campaign like this unless you intend an all-out effort. You can't quit midstream, so you must be both intellectually and emotionally prepared for failure as well as success. No one can anticipate every contingency. You may not have accurately assessed some part of the climate. However, if you don't follow through, you'll be forever branded as indecisive. "Sharon doesn't know what she wants. She gets hot about an idea and then she cools off." Nobody's reputation needs that label.

Your boss may need several months to think about what you've proposed. You can't expect instant action from either the boss or those above him/her who may have to approve a change. However, if you continue your publicity through the grapevine about the need for the change, you're creating an awareness that something should be done. Don't pressure, just repeat. Repetition begets acceptance. All new ideas initially create problems for those in power. You want to make job redesign seem both logical and inevitable.

2. Time your campaign carefully. Don't begin just as the company announces it's not paying dividends on its stock this quarter or the *Wall Street Journal* pontificates about a general business downturn. You might get what you want, but the overall climate is against you. If your company is going through a reorganization, wait until you are sure all the major structural changes have been made. You can't expect your new plan to fit into a structure that's still murky. Try to assess when the company's or the economy's major convulsions are over, then begin your campaign. Part of this caution is for your protection. What if the job you create is a step up but, because of reorganization or economic dislocation, it's one that logically should be eliminated in the changing business climate? You'll have talked yourself into and out of a job in record time!

3. Strategy is everything. Are you sure the job you envision will put you where you want to be long-term? The time to decide if it's really what you want is now, not after you get people hotted up. For example, being made a supervisor in an endangered department has pluses but also some powerful negatives. On the one hand, moving into management means you are likely to get another management job more easily when you need one. Still, if a job is eliminated, it's more likely to be yours than one of the troops'.

Job redesign is the most logical approach, and you'll want to explore this option first. However, it's by no means your only option. If it turns out that altering a job is the corporate equivalent of rewriting the Ten Commandments, you aren't necessarily stymied. You can try the other techniques described in this chapter.

Everything you learn in your advancement campaign can be put to use at another time if you're not successful now. You are practicing a process that can be used repeatedly. When David W. proposed that his job in data processing be altered from analyst to coordinator (which would give him some supervisory responsibilities), his boss refused. David persisted as long as he could, then rewrote his resume to show he'd done everything necessary to qualify himself for the higher-level job. He talked with some contacts at other firms and got in at the higher level in a competitive firm—with a 22 percent increase in salary. Although he's only been at the new firm for six months, he has already collected job descriptions in preparation for another assault on the system.

Even if you don't get promoted in the first pass, you've put everyone on definitive notice that you are vitally interested in moving up. The importance of this can't be overemphasized. Most people talk about promotion only because they've been programmed to do so. It's obligatory. Often they don't mean it. But when you try a job redesign, you are saying in actions, as well as words, "I want to move up." It's a very positive statement and positions you as someone who's working toward promotion, not just talking about it.

Job Proposals

Sometimes your job can't be redesigned. It's hopeless because the department is too small, too territorial, a boss or co-worker would be too threatened, or the company's policies are truly cast in cement. Don't despair. Leaving is not your only option. When job redesign won't work, it's time for a job proposal.

Once of the best ways to move up is by doing something patently political—proposing a new job only you can fill. This isn't a new idea. Richard Bolles and other career planners have advocated this tactic for job hunters who are trying to get into a company that interests them. What is different is that it's even easier to do and more effective when done internally. You have tremendous advantages over the outside job hunter because you know the culture from the inside. You also know your boss and boss's boss and their phobias and preferences.

A job proposal is essentially an outline for an entirely new job. It may include some parts of your present job, but generally even those will be recombined or reworked. For example, if you've been working as an accounting supervisor but there's little chance of promotion to manager, you may be able to create a new job. This may be a halfway house between supervisor and manager or it may be a job that's parallel with a manager's job. Let's say you look around and see that, because of the size of your division, there's little coordination between projects. Things that could threaten sensitive client relationships fall through the cracks. Everyone is aware of it, but no one wants to take the time to figure out how to improve the system. You can research how a coordinator would benefit the company, what the person would do, how much he or she should be paid, and, finally, why you'd be the best person to do the job.

As long as you create a more responsible and, incidentally, better paying job than you have now, it will move your career ahead. Don't worry that you're out of the ordinary advancement track. If you design the job properly, the next step should bring you back into the hierarchy. To do this, you will need job descriptions of those above you so you'll know what skills the next level requires. You build those skills into the new job.

One reason this works fairly often is that a company's ability to create new jobs, while phasing out those that are obsolete, is limited by the fact that everyone, including personnel, is preoccupied with the day-to-day business. There's a time lag between when the need arises and when anyone has time to deal with it.

Will you get the job you've proposed? About 60 percent of the time you will, and uncontested. If the company insists on posting the new job and allows open season on applications, you may have a problem, especially if you have created a job so attractive several of your peers are interested. However, you'll still have the inside track. Since you researched and created the job, you ought to be able to talk more persuasively about it than someone who's only read the job-posting announcement. Also, since you've thought in great detail about the positioning of the job, you can answer all the hard questions. A competitor would have to guess. Don't underestimate how important your knowledge of what other companies have done will be in persuading people to adopt your idea. Companies have a herd instinct, especially in matters such as job descriptions and salaries.

Writing a Job Proposal   Your starting point is the question: What is not functioning well in this organization? Not just in your department or similar departments, but overall? The first step is to identify problem areas. Why is the mail room such a mess? Don't put the blame solely on the people. They're probably working about as hard as any other department. What's wrong structurally? Make a list of all of the jobs you see that aren't being done and consider which of them you might want to do. It doesn't matter if there is already someone who's doing part of the job, because an unmet need still exists. However, the best strategy is always to identify a task or set of tasks that has no home.

Back to the mail room. Suppose it's attached to an already harassed operations area. The person in charge has three higher priority areas to manage. Truth to tell, it might be something she'd like to get rid of. Your task is to find several similar areas with some geographical connection that aren't functioning properly and put them together into a job. It's nice if there is some relationship among them but it's not essential. The only reason geography is an issue is that if the areas are too widely dispersed it will be apparent to everyone that you'd spend more time on the road than doing the job.

Now to the research. How have other companies handled these areas? Is there anything to be learned in the library from trade journals or the business press? If so, include clippings and your conclusions along with the sources in your proposal. This has a reassuring effect on your audience.

Next, write a job description. Go over it carefully. If your company has a highly structured salary/job grading system, get a copy of the explanation. Try to position the job at least one level above your present position. Two levels higher would be better. This may be difficult if it's a small company with no grade structure. However, you can give the job the same title as someone now above you in your organization.

Finally, price the job. Try for between 20 and 25 percent more than you now earn. This will be easier than you think because presumably the job you are proposing will result in an overall net savings, which you've estimated at least roughly. The company will not be spending any more money and the productivity gains will be substantial. Three or four people may now be covering these tasks at considerably more expense. Your proposal will cut costs and vastly improve efficiency.

Here's an example. An engineering firm had always had trouble with basic administration because a large number of secretaries and word processing people were needed, but the turnover was high. One engineer, Duncan R., tired of his straight engineering job, developed a scheme that allowed coverage of both the telephones and the word processing equipment with 20 percent fewer people. This involved a pool approach and incorporated some part-timers and home-based workers at peak times. He wrote a job description for the person who would manage the new system, including the purchase of microcomputers, and a new job title, director of staff service. At first there was considerable hemming and hawing because no one could understand why an engineer could do it better than the present nonengineering managers. He cleverly pointed out the greater likelihood of cooperation engineer-to-engineer than engineer-to-nonengineer. It worked, as did his new organizational scheme. His boss's only comment was "Why didn't you propose this job sooner?"

The footnote to this is that the reason he was able to sell his proposal was that he showed management how it would make their lives easier and more productive. If the proposal had been for his benefit alone, it would have been rejected. If it had only benefited the secretaries and their bosses, it wouldn't have been approved. He positioned the job entirely on the basis of benefits to senior management and cost reductions.

Structural Analysis

New jobs often come into existence because top management decides that the company must be restructured. That is, a redesign of the organizational chart is necessary. Get a copy of your company's organizational chart. Just as you did with a job description or job proposal, approach the chart, not as holy writ, but as a document probably put together by a committee. The structure represents a compromise that, at the time it was revised, seemed workable. It may be very simple. It may show a president, vice presidents, managers, and supervisors. It may be very complicated with three kinds of vice presidents, multiple grades of managers, and several levels of supervisors. Where are you on the chart? Are there jobs around you that, if they reported through you, would streamline things for the next level up? You have to see yourself as a cultural anthropologist on an expedition if you are to do any imaginative thinking about the company's structure.

It may help you to know that some organizations have standing structure committees that meet periodically to look at the effectiveness of the current chart. You won't shock anybody with your interest in the organization's skeleton—except your competitors, of course, so don't say anything to them.

Plenty of information on organizational design is available in a good business library. This can give you the background to justify changes that would help.

Overall, you need to be creative at the promotion game. You are in your worst competitive position when you wait for an opening to appear. It may not be anything you could do or would want to do. By taking pot luck, you may get something that cannot help your career and may do it significant harm.

You are the only one with a real stake in creating an opening tailor-made for you. In the process you will also learn about the style and the politics in your company in ways you never would if you didn't try to redo jobs and create new ones. Policies you've questioned may seem more rational when you're working with the same tasks and relationships and can't put them together any better than the company has. It's a humbling experience but also an important one for your professional growth and development.

Do not worry about what your boss, peers, or subordinates will think about what you're doing. They are going to react, but not necessarily negatively unless you seem bent on blasting them out of the organization. You won't cause nearly the uproar you'd provoke if instead you tried to one-up people or used other aggressive tactics.

All of these techniques share a key political element. They support the axiom that you have to give to get. They are based on trading, not manipulating. They frequently mean you take on more work, sometimes without a pay increase. Each forces you to please people you might find unpleasant. However, nothing unethical has been suggested. You aren't playing grab and snatch. You are less likely to arouse a protest or create enemies with these methods.

◊ STEALING FROM PERSONNEL

The best place to learn all of these techniques is to hang around with the personnel specialists who use them. It's easier than you think. Attend some meetings of the local personnel group and you'll pick up a lot. You don't have to be in personnel to benefit from adopting the mindset.

Barter should be a way of life for you. You'll be changing jobs or positions many more times before you retire. The best place to learn is flea markets. You don't have to buy anything, just go and observe. The rules there apply in the office as well. Most important is to have some alternatives. Most good deals at flea markets are gotten by putting together several things for one price. Keep it in mind.

Chapter 6. Political Euthanasia:

Removing the Still-Warm Bodies

Joe S., a regular church supporter and physician manager, has no problem with his intensive campaign to get his departmental secretary to leave. They've been at war for six months, but slowly he's seen her morale weaken. Robin J. knows her boss's marriage is shaky because the boss's wife finds Minneapolis a real bore after San Francisco. Robin encourages her boss's wife's dissatisfaction. If the wife puts enough heat on Robin's boss, they'll move back to San Francisco, and Robin can happily fill her boss's still-warm chair.

It's hard for people with benevolent opinions of themselves, those who treasure and cuddle their ethics at least as often as they violate them, to talk about inflicting damage on a co-worker's career or forcing him/her out of a job. Interfere with someone else's right to earn a living? Unthinkable! Besides, management is supposed to be running the organization. If someone's not working out, management should perform any necessary surgery. This is the theory. In practice, managers at any level act only when a person is grossly and publicly incompetent in a way that threatens the manager's career, but don't even react to borderline incompetence cases or when the situation is purely political.

Haven't you ever wondered why people turn aggressive in the office, e.g., arrange for someone else's departure? Before you throw this book down in righteous wrath, claiming you're not "that sort of person," consider this: You've probably seen such things happen in your office or at least you've heard whispers. You really need to know how it happens, if only so you can recognize the signs that someone is trying to do it to you!

Involuntary job or career change is rarely initiated for a single reason. It requires more motivation to sever someone from the organization than a sudden fit of pique. Thinking "He/she is a turkey so I'm going to arrange it so he/she no longer works here" is not sufficient motivation. Particularly in the 1980s it takes extraordinary circumstances to get anyone but the politically criminal to act. Most people are too busy trying to stay on top of their own careers. In a company whose financial people appear to be suffering from seasickness the last week of each quarter, holding on, not aggression, is the only priority.

Political euthanasia takes superb planning, careful execution, persistence, and a high tolerance for risk. Even with all that, there are no guarantees! Targets can have incredible staying power—especially when they garner sympathy as helpless (but rarely innocent) victims. They seldom go quietly once they realize what's going on. This is true even if they would actually like to leave or know moving on would be a career boost.

Aggressors are assisted by victims. The most powerful weapon the true aggressor has is the knowledge that most people don't want to confront unpleasant truths. They are textbook conflict avoiders. By the time the victim recognizes that his fears are reality, he may be past helping. He can't even help himself. In the worst case, the victim believes it's simply a problem of not being well liked. He noses adverse information aside and turns off his early warning system. When that happens, he's doomed. By that time the problem is too real, and too public, to be ignored. People will have begun to take sides and it will be too late to change events.

Realism is the best armor in any uncertain situation, but most people, victim and victimizer alike, can't separate fact from wish. For example, how often has a new co-worker said to you, "I don't think Harry (the boss) understands me"? Your instinct would be to reassure him. You might have said, "You're right, George. He doesn't. I'd say you are probably on the way out." You didn't say that, right? More likely you said, "Don't pay any attention to Harry, that's just his way." Or "I'm sure he likes you, he just doesn't show it." Had the boss said blatantly that he truly loathed your co-worker, would you have told George? More important, would you have expected the boss to act out his feelings or would you have dismissed the boss's remark as so much idle talk?

Personal animosity is a kind of truth many people feel too threatening to acknowledge publicly. Two workers may get into a blood feud over a seemingly minor occurrence. One may take an aggressive dislike to another and act it out, leaving the victim wailing, "What did I do to her?" The assassin may have suffered an ego wound at the victim's hand. It's irrelevant whether or not the wound was intentional. The tendency to underestimate ego slights as catalysts in office warfare is a universal sign of political naiveté. It may also reflect the very human belief that what wounds me deeply wouldn't even nick someone else. Don't you believe it! Everyone is microscopically thin-skinned.

Thankfully, incidents that involve mindless aggressors with overblown egos are rare. (Overblown egos are commonplace. It's the combination that's rare.) What's more common is an aggressor using the political process for benevolent, even team-spirited, reasons. Aggression doesn't necessarily mean doing deliberate harm. People who try to eliminate someone from the workplace often do so with altruistic motives. They may think it's a major assist to management to help correct a bad hiring decision. The reasons for aggression must be highly visible and the need to get rid of the person compelling. The most common stimulus is lack of action by those in power, so an individual decides to act.

If you decide to push someone out of a job, you will need assistance from co-workers or at least their silent acquiescence. An aggressor's motives will be examined. Most people aren't willing to cooperate if you are the only beneficiary. The group as a whole must benefit. Other careers must be in danger, not just yours. Other people must be unhappy with the status quo. Otherwise, a group of people banded together to eliminate someone strongly resembles a lynch mob, a situation guaranteed to make most workers uncomfortable. Even if it's been said often that "everyone hates Jim," the distance between that statement and aggressive group action is roughly the length plus the width of the Grand Canyon. And isn't that fortunate? Anyone can vent his/her strongest feelings, try to arouse others, but not actually have to follow through.

Political euthanasia is not a casual undertaking. People become political activists and aggressors because they strongly believe someone is creating a roadblock that endangers the business's survival, their own survival, or makes work so unpleasant that they develop a "him or me" mindset. There need be no personal relationship or personal problem between aggressor and victim. It's actually easier to outplace someone you don't have a personal relationship with. That's another reason victims so often misjudge what's happening. Why would someone cause so much trouble when the two of them have always gotten along so well or, even more puzzling, barely know each other?

There are a few wise people in the workplace who recognize that individually initiated, involuntary outplacement may actually benefit the victim and his/her career. It's true! At least one-third of working Americans are badly misplaced in their jobs. Either they are using the wrong skills or they are in an environment that magnifies their weaknesses and diminishes their skills. They are often paralyzed by indecision and a sense of failure. Their egos are weakened inexorably day by day.

If someone gives them the boot, they may wake up, take charge of their careers, and find a better job in an environment in which they can be effective. Six months after the incident, they will realize it was a boost, although most such victims won't forgive the perpetrator for years, if ever. It's a lot like surgery; it's no fun even if the results are very positive.

The trouble here is, everyone is expecting that management will do something about the problem person. The problem an aggressor tries to solve is already well known to management. That's what lends legitimacy to the process and keeps management on the sidelines. Management may have grappled with the problem and failed to develop a plan of action. They may be too busy and distracted to act. There may be gray areas. The person's performance has bright spots as well as black ones. The most common reasons for management inaction are reluctance and underestimation of the short- and long-term effects of inaction.

The best example of this is the ineffective manager over forty whose people skills are highly developed. Everyone likes good old Joe. He's easy to get along with. He knows the organization. Of course, his department is a disaster. Turnover there is so high just coping with the paperwork is a real strain on the personnel department. Productivity is half that of the rest of the company. But he's always been there, a permanent, though undesirable, fixture.

Another common candidate for political euthanasia is the highly emotional employee. That was one of Joe S.'s secretary's problems. Level of responsibility doesn't matter in this case. The effect is the same. The people who have to work with an emotional disaster are perpetually exhausted and spend hours seeking ways to avoid working with him/her. This person makes their work more difficult and they resent it. When asked to make sacrifices and put up with the unpleasant behavior, they can become rebellious. Management's excuse is that the problem person may be emotional but he's so personally productive. What doesn't get said is that if he's reducing five other people's output, what's the gain because he's such a star?

Why would you want to become involved in political euthanasia? It's not the best path to a promotion—even though if Robin J.'s scenario goes as planned, it might work for her. It might adversely affect your reputation. You almost certainly will make an enemy or two. If you're reasonably happy with what you do, will eliminating someone really make a big difference? Here are some of the reasons you might consider taking an active role in helping someone out of the organization. These come from people who've done it, however reluctantly.

1. Productivity and morale are at stake. One of your subordinates is unhappy with the job and/or company and spreads that unhappiness to everyone within earshot. As a division or department manager in a troubled company, you're desperately trying to shore up that area and increase productivity and profitability. This person is lowering productivity and profitability. The prospective victim could depress Pollyanna. He or she is influencing your most stouthearted people by chanting the worst case scenario at every opportunity. This person has a genuine talent for packaging and selling bad news. Unless he or she goes, your efforts are useless. Your hardworking, talented people may get fed up and bolt. Or worse, they will stay but reduce their efforts.

Firing the troublemaker might involve overwhelming political and legal problems. If this is a person with twenty-five years of service with the company and consistently above-average performance appraisals, management could face a clear case of age discrimination. That's the sticking point.

2. Your competence is threatening to others. Someone above you—a boss or a boss's peer—is blocking your career because she has such tremendous ego problems that your success, or potential success, isn't just a challenge, it's a personal affront. She's in a totally defensive mode because she always has to explain why you suggested or accomplished something first. If you don't act, you could be unjustly fired for a trivial reason. Outperforming a superior may not look like a cause for firing but it happens everywhere.

It happens most often in companies experiencing rapid growth. As the company expands it brings in trained personnel. Until this point credentials haven't mattered. A department manager may be a former secretary who got the job because she was there and was willing. She's done a good job but has become paranoid because suddenly her new subordinates have had formal training or degrees. They are light-years ahead of her technically and full of enthusiasm. They are able to do the work better than she can. She knows that a comparable job at another company is unlikely, given her lack of formal education and training. Instead of rejoicing over the excellent troops she's acquired to supervise, she's afraid and predatory. A man can have this problem, too, especially in high technology, rapidly growing companies that may be exploding with new products and services. If he had realized that credentials often equate with mobility, he might have acquired them. He suppressed any such messages, so he may be vulnerable. Growth, which he helped create, becomes an enormous source of anxiety. If there is a genuine tragedy in office politics, these two cases are it.

3. A jealous co-worker has surfaced. Despite your best efforts, what you seem to know that he or she doesn't makes this person pea-green and petulant. He is fixated on how you do your job. He is perpetually circling your desk like an emaciated buzzard after a two-month fast and either copying or criticizing your work. Unless he is removed you'll spend more time deflecting him than doing your work. You've talked to this person and he says he can't understand your concern. Honest confrontation won't help you because the concept of honesty was entirely left out of his personality. This person doesn't want to learn or model, just attack. You feel the pressure and it's affecting your performance. If you complain to your boss, you'll be told to "work it out." The hidden problem is that if you don't find a solution, your performance will continue to suffer, raising the specter of being fired. "Working it out" will be possible only if you can get your co-worker to admit he/she is jealous and should change. That's highly unlikely.

4. Your boss has retired on the payroll. Not only can you do your boss's job, you are doing it—but not for his or her salary or title. Your boss is blissfully happy in his/her coma. You like the company and your boss's boss. Your boss's boss seems unlikely to get rid of a pet drone since the work is being done splendidly. Eliminating your boss would benefit the company. When your boss was hired, he was a top producer. Now, he doesn't do much, but he also doesn't offend anyone. It's too much trouble to fire him and too expensive to outplace him. It is estimated that the cost of getting rid of a $75,000-a-year manager is $100,000 to $125,000 in severance and outplacement fees. Nothing will change unless you act.

5. A co-worker is engaged in unethical, but not illegal, practices. The fact that the person is doing these things blatantly, and management isn't reacting, is causing galloping depression throughout the department. The collective energy level doesn't match the room temperature. People are practically engaged in a sit-down strike. The problem is being ignored upstairs because action now would raise embarrassing questions, such as "How long has this been going on?" or "Why has this been allowed to continue?" Those in charge are hoping in vain that the problem will quietly go away. The situation may not involve shockingly unethical behavior. It's just as demotivating to see repeated small-scale sins—someone promising customers things that can't possibly happen, for example. This practice thrives in sales organizations when the only scorecard is the bottom line. There's a time bomb here. Customers may tolerate the situation for months or years, then defect en masse.

6. Someone hired in a shark. You have a genuine predator in your midst who loves to create unhappiness and has a real talent for doing so. He or she picks on the weak or meek but has sufficient political skills to keep those above him happy. He may feel his career is prematurely halted or he doesn't care about going any further. So why not have some fun? There is one shark in about every twenty-five people. They often surface when there is not enough work to do or the work isn't very interesting. Such people get started by victimizing someone in a small way, such as damaging a reputation for no reason. They find they love to make trouble. It's exciting. Left to themselves they'll keep seeking bigger highs from more blatant acts, especially when they know management won't take action. Lest you think we've identified a new species of being, these people can always either justify or convincingly deny.

7. Human blockage has developed. Your department is on the verge of a megadisaster that you can't prevent unless a human roadblock is removed. Your boss is in an extreme caution mode and refuses either to authorize a firing or deal with it himself. The project on which this year's profits and bonuses depend is two months behind. The roadblock is the woman who is producing the research. She hasn't done it despite pleas and threats. Her excuses are solid platinum. Unless she's removed, there is no chance the project can be completed on time. Even then, it will mean eighty-hour work weeks all round.

8. Your old enemies have long memories. You inadvertently created an enemy who has moved up and can now cause you a lot of trouble—which he is prepared to do. The old wound was an ego wound but when you were peers it didn't seem that important. Now it does. You're not being paranoid if you believe your enemy's career has been helped enormously by a burning ambition to get even. And all because you said that East Overshoe State University and its graduates weren't quite competitive with Northwestern's. You knew EOSU was his alma mater, but a fact is a fact, isn't it? You thought you were dealing from a strong position of principle.

9. Someone wants revenge. You criticized or humiliated a person who turned out to be a top management adoptee or welfare case. You spoke disparagingly of someone's performance, then learned she's a biggie's paramour. (Listen to the grapevine!) This powerful person has your name on a very short list. Do you remember the story of the emperor's new clothes? It's unlikely the child who pointed out that the emperor was naked grew up to be prime minister.

10. A job hunter is having a last hurrah. A co-worker is job hunting, sure of his prospects because he has two firm offers, and is determined to have a little short-term fun by creating as much trouble as possible. It's revenge time. His motto is "Don't get mad, get even." The only curve here is that this person wants to do it while still on the scene in order to savor the results. Most people depart after first planting a few time bombs.

11. Career disappointment has soured your boss. He has been told unofficially that he's topped out. He's gone as far as he can go. After thirty years of service he's furious but feels unprepared and unmotivated to job hunt. He's fully vested in the pension plan, has two kids in college, and who's going to hire him at fifty-four? The company should have offered him a golden handshake and outplacement. They have been penny-wise and pound-foolish, because he's going to get even by slow torture. He's going to make as much trouble as he can but expect you to carry on as usual.

The list of provocative situations provides endless variations on these themes, but you get the idea. In every situation the would-be victim is causing a problem that those in power refuse to acknowledge or address. Decisive action is needed. However, there are risks. Before you contemplate any action, it's important to decide how much risk you are willing to assume. Some people talk a good fight but develop hives at the thought of action.

Risk Analysis

Risk is the possibility that something will or will not happen. In office warfare, calculating the risk is the first step in planning any kind of action. The risk you need to measure is what the failure of your plans could do to your career with the company. If you opt to move on, the problem takes care of itself, unless your victim should be reincarnated at your new company.

Generally speaking, your career is at risk in three ways. You need to be concerned about exposure, retaliation by the victim, and peer group retaliation. The latter may involve people acting individually or it may be a group agreeing to act together. Oddly enough, it's rare for management to get involved. They simply ignore the whole incident! It never happened. Retaliation happens in the informal system, and management doesn't officially recognize what's going on there. In fact, in all of our interviews we could find only one example of management involvement and that was because someone blundered so badly that the grapevine began to carry protests, followed by the filing of a formal grievance with personnel.

Exposure

Never is it more true that "I know and you know but we (officially) don't know" than in any kind of aggressive action. If you are open about what you're doing—particularly if you talk about it—you invite exposure, which is a political sin. If the grapevine buzzes with your actions, you can count on your victim picking up support, even if previously everyone had agreed vehemently that the person should be removed. To participate openly in aggressive action is the worst mistake anyone can make. Do not tell anyone what you think, what you plan to do, or what you expect to accomplish. Any exposure will hurt your cause because it focuses attention on the dark side of the informal system—something no one, at any level in the organization, wants to see. You cannot recruit allies. If someone decides to help you, it will have to be a "spontaneous" decision. If asked about your plans, stonewall. Clearly signal that you have none. Neither confirm nor deny when you are questioned.

Retaliation by the Victim

As you strategize, you need to consider the possibility that whoever you're working on may decide to fight back. In light of the person's observed behavior, how likely is that to happen? The most common retaliation is accusatory exposure. You will be publicly confronted (in front of two or three co-workers) and accused of being unfair and/or harassing him/her. Avoid this at all costs, unless the person has a reputation for feeling persecuted. If that's the case, his or her credibility may not be high enough to cause trouble.

Someone may accuse you of victimizing him or her even when it's not true. The grapevine will give you an accurate reading on whether or not the accusation is believed. If the grapevine doesn't pick up this person's statements, it means that no one believes that he/she is being victimized. If people believe something, they will repeat it.

A second kind of retaliation occurs when the victim tries to turn your tactics back on you. This can work if you're not carefully keeping up your productivity and contacts. If you're very productive and working from a solid base of internal and external contacts, reverse retaliation is not likely to have much impact. If you've let either your work or contacts slide, you will have a problem. The corollary is that you don't begin an eighty-hour-per-week project and try to sever someone from the corporate umbilical cord at the same time.

Peer Group Retaliation

Occasionally, after a plan is underway and progressing nicely, someone will spread the alarm to your peers. A co-worker will say, "Joe is really giving Peter a hard time. We should speak to him about it." This is hypocritical, of course. Everyone is aware that Peter is not performing and is a major roadblock in the department. Your co-worker is really saying, "If Joe succeeds in forcing Peter out, he'll be significantly more powerful than we are. We must insure that Joe doesn't get too far ahead of us." Women in management positions often feel they are singled out as victims in situations like this because men are usually involved. Instead of realizing there is relative power among peers, both male and female, women attribute the lack of support to male bonding. Male bonding can be overrated (and often is) as a motivation. What really concerns men is the competitive advantage anyone acquires by acting decisively.

So far we haven't talked about the reaction of your immediate boss. Unless he or she is the intended victim, your actions are unlikely to attract his/her attention. Chain-of-command protocol goes down the pyramid as well as up. Unless the boss's boss calls attention to what is going on, you may very well hear nothing from your boss. A word of caution. If your boss has a weak ego and is easily threatened, he/she may cause problems later. The boss will figure out that if you can do it to a co-worker, you might turn the same tactics on him/her. That kind of reasoning is valid. You could cause your boss problems. This is another reason to think and plan carefully before doing anything. Your career at the company could be prematurely shortened for no better reason than that you have demonstrated acute political skills.

Victim Cooperation

Why would anyone go along with his/her own victimization? Most people do and for some very predictable reasons. If the informal system is to work, everyone must cooperate. Cut someone out of the network and he/she has a problem. When people sense that they are not welcome, that they are thought of as outsiders, about 20 percent will prepare to leave. This is especially true if they highly value the social aspects of work, an outstanding weakness of workers between the ages of twenty-five and forty. A secretary whose co-workers pointedly exclude her from their gossip and camaraderie will enjoy her job far less—regardless of her relationship with her boss—than if she is accepted as part of the crowd. She may tough it out for a short time but within six to nine months she'll decide she doesn't need that kind of aggravation. After all, good secretaries are in demand. Why not go where she's accepted?

A middle manager who's excluded from the after-work drinking group—unless it's his/her choice not to participate—will feel the same way. It's not important that he/she could force his/her way into the group; the withdrawal of the group's acceptance is judgment and sentence.

The need for acceptance is even stronger in top management. The only difference is the form this need takes. For example, a financial vice president who is never invited to parties given by directors or other senior-level people will definitely notice the snub. At this level there are no purely social functions. His exclusion also threatens his on-the-job effectiveness.

Planning Your Strategies

Once you've determined that someone needs to leave, you should consider three things. (1) How long will it take to get rid of the person? (2) What is the best and least painful or disruptive method you can use? (3) What will you do if your plan doesn't work? Remember, as long as there is nothing in writing and you're working through the informal system, nothing official has occurred. It's not anonymity—that's unobtainable—but nonofficial status that you must preserve.

Strategy planning involves deciding on action steps and setting a timetable. If you decide your plan will be to get a co-worker to take a job elsewhere, thus freeing his/her position for you, you need to plan a complete job search campaign exactly like the one you'd plan for yourself. One halfhearted attempt to contact a few headhunters won't do your victim any more good than it would do you.

The Best Tools for Everyone

Involuntary Outplacement

There is no better method for getting rid of anyone at any level, with the least fuss and the greatest pleasure all around, than finding the person a new and better paying or more prestigious job. This can be done in a variety of ways, such as writing a very good resume for the person and sending it to a large number of companies and search firms. Even someone who's sure today that he or she doesn't want to move can often be seduced tomorrow by an offer of a better job. This strategy is relatively risk-free because search firms are accustomed to receiving resumes without cover letters. You may be surprised to learn that this is done regularly. Search firm recruiters say that they suspect at least 30 percent of the resumes they receive aren't written by the person whose career is reprised. The only risk you run is that search firms, inherently sloppy, may send the resume to your own organization. Even that isn't a real problem because the victim can quite believably deny any knowledge. He/she will be telling the truth and therefore will be quite convincing.

If your quarry is competent and would do well in another firm, a few calls from recruiters may be the spur he or she needs. Even if the person doesn't get a new job, he or she may decide that job hunting isn't an unmitigated pain after all and begin vigorously to pursue the search him/herself. If your boss, co-worker, or subordinate gets a new job, you can confess that you put his/her name "into the pipeline" and demand dinner at the city's most expensive French restaurant.

Feeding Hot Job Leads

A second relatively risk-free strategy is feeding your person the kind of job leads you know he/she will respond to. You can do this with anyone because, whatever the person's level, he or she wants to keep affirming his/her professional marketability. It's quite common for a subordinate to feed a boss job leads. "Hey, Sally, did you hear that Mark is leaving XYZ? They haven't hired anyone yet and Mark had a really terrific job." Sally, if given enough tips, may begin to generate her own. She's not going to think that the person bringing her such hot information is predatory, because she likes what she hears. If you work for an egomaniac, he or she may interview routinely for better jobs, pretending all the while it's not serious. Such people may get serious when confronted with some very tempting opportunities.

Where do you find leads to pass on? All that time you have spent at trade/professional society meetings and serving on community boards will now pay off. You will hear about opportunities, would-be opportunities, and even some pie-in-the-sky at the monthly meetings. If not, you haven't built the network you need. Each of the leads you pass on must be legitimate and must be current. Otherwise, this strategy is worthless. Everyone who's in your professional network should understand that you are vitally interested in hearing about openings at all levels and that you'll trade such information.

Publicity

Never underestimate the long-term payback of speaking well of people you work with. Even if the person you're trying to get rid of has predominantly negative qualities, stress the positive ones. Failure, like success, is 90 percent situational. Therefore, if you want to help someone out long-term, it's useful to publicize them outside your firm. Don't say anything you don't believe or can't verify. That won't help your cause and your credibility will be undermined if you interest a prospective employer who finds on further investigation that you have misrepresented the person.

Tactics for Helping Out a Boss

Intrigue

Intrigue, the process of spreading information and ideas behind the scenes, is one of the better methods for planting the idea in your boss's mind that he/she should be looking for another position. If your boss's boss hears that he/she is looking, you may have created a self-fulfilling prophecy. The higher one moves in the corporate hierarchy, the greater the emphasis placed on visible loyalty and discretion. It's hardly unknown for someone to call a subordinate in and say, "I understand you're looking around. That's fine with me as long as you're out of here thirty days from today." Stark, yes; uncommon, no.

A pharmaceutical house undergoing recalls faced a real problem. The sixty-year-old production vice president seemed unable to get quality control straightened out. His harassed subordinate, the manager of manufacturing, tried everything until he hit on something that worked. He began playing golf with a financial vice president in another division. That man carried some casual tales to the president. Two months later the production vice president was outplaced, at his own request. He could see the fence-mending and the superhuman effort needed to regain control of his area. He got a better job in a smaller, less competitive firm.

Isolation

The ultimate political weapon is always isolation from the informal system. It's also the most subtle. That is, if your boss isn't getting the grass roots news, she may blunder. She may offend someone important. She may embarrass herself by talking about issues the grapevine says have already been resolved. How can you tell if your boss is isolated? If she is sticking close to her office and asking you for news, that's an important sign. She's lost contact and needs help. Your boss may try to pressure you into becoming a news gatherer. That's fine, but you don't have to tell everything you know. You do, however, have to report accurately anything you choose to report.

Staff Rebellions

Staff rebellions occur usually when a boss is so ineffective the troops feel they can rebel with impunity. You may help the rebels by pointing out that the boss can't retaliate, if that's true—because he/she is weak or personnel is very strong—or by suggesting strategies. Direct involvement would not be wise, because you would immediately be positioned as the leader. That gives your boss a focus for his/ her otherwise inchoate wrath.

Negative Publicity

We've talked about the value of raising visibility with positive publicity. Negative publicity has the same value when trying to remove someone. A boss who never hears anything about himself in the grapevine has reason to suspect (even if he is not correct) that the word is negative. Otherwise, why wouldn't someone pass it on? Fortunately for you, few bosses investigate, because it's difficult to ask subordinates, "What do you hear about me?"

Negative publicity must be based on verifiable facts. Anyone who puts something as nebulous as "Nobody likes working for Mary Beth" into the grapevine doesn't understand how the news is tagged. A reason must be given so that it will be repeated to her boss along with the information. If it's said that Mary Beth caused a project to go under because she couldn't decide on an overall game plan, everyone but Mary Beth will hear about it.

Torture

Nothing is more frustrating to a boss than to have everyone in the department working as slowly as possible but simultaneously observing every company rule. He or she knows the game that is being played—they're getting even with him for something—but can't really fight it. (It happens in consulting firms when bosses keep people on the road too long. The frequent flyer programs peak in their desirability at about 100,000 miles a year. After that, the last thing you want to do is travel—even free.) People get behind their deadlines by weeks. The boss keeps urging them on. They work overtime but the overall productivity doesn't increase. He/she would like to fire everyone but it would be too difficult to explain to an already doubting superior why wholesale firings should be necessary.

As you consider your tactical options, here are some guidelines to keep in mind.

1. It's always risky to attempt political euthanasia with a boss because it makes his/her peers nervous. Assuming your motives are both company-minded and prompted by some degree of desperation, you must be willing to assume the risk.

2. Don't overestimate or underestimate your boss's power. Some bosses can fire people; others can't unless the person is definitely not doing the work. What's the real situation in your department? The secretaries should be able to supply you with details on what has happened in the past. Take time to get the facts.

3. Don't involve your boss's boss. Remember that any suggestion, however faint, that your boss is incompetent is a not very subtle attack on his/her boss. Your boss reflects his boss's judgment and tastes. Several corporations have nearly been driven out of business by the ties of one layer to another, so strong that the boss's boss would not fire his subordinate even when confronted with the fact that the subordinate was clearly incompetent. It was too threatening to the senior manager. This happens more often in manufacturing than in service organizations, because mentoring is more important and creates longer-lasting relationships than in higher-turnover service companies.

4. Confide in nobody, but especially not your peers. This includes people outside the company as well as those within it. Any hint of your desire or strategy will be swiftly carried by the grapevine. Keep your own counsel entirely.

5. A short time frame works better. A plan for a twelve-month campaign is probably too long. Your boss, even if very withdrawn from office politics, would invariably learn something was going on in that time span. Plan a six-month campaign instead.

6. It will require more time to work on your boss than on a peer or subordinate. Get everything set and use several tactics at the same time. You can, for instance, raise doubts and send out the boss's resume at the same time. You have to adjust your timetable to how hard you're willing to work.

7. Protect your own career. Don't arrange a disaster that will give the whole department a bad name. That will do nothing for you even if your boss does decide to leave. When a disaster occurs, top management will assume there is nobody within the area who can take charge. A new boss, brought in from the outside, will be extremely interested in the circumstances of his/her predecessor's departure.

Tactics for Peers

Everything we've said about bosses applies to peers, especially about negative publicity and isolation. There are also some tactics that are tailor-made for use against them.

The Veiled Cut

In many companies, teamwork and the ability to play on the team are touted with religious conviction. Suggest someone is not a team player and it's serious. More serious is a continuing process of raising questions with the boss about a fellow employee. You ask the boss if he thinks Sharon is really happy in the department and comment, "She never gets together with the rest of us for a drink after work." The next thrust may be to ask if the boss has noticed that "Sharon always seems to be more interested in the people on the floor below than she is in us." Sharon won't be fired because she doesn't appear to be a team player, but her position will be weakened. Combined with other negative publicity, it could force her to leave.

Creating Obstacles

Anyone can withhold cooperation at any time. You may decline to help a harassed co-worker for very valid reasons.

Usually it's not a very good idea, especially if you have harassed periods yourself. However, if you are trying to get rid of the person, withholding cooperation will give him/her a message. People are generally very sensitive to how willingly others cooperate with them.

The Setup

This is a high-risk but frequently effective strategy, especially if the victim is a stoic and therefore unlikely to protest. It would have been a great way to eliminate John Wayne. If, for example, you feed someone the wrong information and he/she subsequently blunders into a fight with the work processing supervisor or the manager of information systems, he or she may believe it was a self-induced failure. However, if this tactic backfires, you are through. Your peers will jump on you like lions at feeding time. You are a walking time bomb, as would anyone be who could execute this strategy.

Tactics for Subordinates

Subordinates ought to be the easiest people to get moving, but frequently they turn out to have enormous staying power. Witness the secretary who's known to be totally ineffective but still hangs on. There are certain tactics, however, almost guaranteed to produce voluntary withdrawal. Most of these aren't predatory as much as calculated bad management.

Raising Ambiguity

The one tactic almost guaranteed to move up someone's departure date is gradually raising the level of vagueness. For example, if a subordinate is revising a report and you tell him it is due Friday, that's clear. However, when he presents the report, you say, "Oh, I meant to tell you we don't need that until next Thursday." Do this regularly and add some totally noncommittal answers to questions. You will get a response. The more organized, mentally and professionally, the victim is, the more unable he will be to tolerate ambiguity. Don't use this tactic unless you have time to do more work yourself. The victim may literally walk out, references be damned, giving no notice at all. Don't do it if your company has any kind of feedback system in which employees evaluate managers.

Emotional Blackmail

Some people work for the fun of it. They need the paycheck, but what really turns them on is fun work and fun people to work with. Work per se doesn't entrance them. Take away the fun and they will definitely leave. This is especially true with younger workers. They aren't as committed to long-term advancement. They want excitement and look for it at work. The easiest way to kill the fun is to overreact to everything, both good and bad, major and trivial. Treat every problem as an ordeal, not as an exciting challenge. Be as depressed and depressing as possible, but only with the victim. Everyone else gets sunshine. And you thought only the military was interested in psychological warfare.

Repetition

While every job has elements of scut work, bunching the particularly demeaning tasks together and assigning them to one person will almost always get a response. No one can mistake the intent even if this is his first job. It's an act of aggression. Scut work may be neither difficult nor stress producing—unless you consider boredom as a kind of stress. Repetition is most useful when you want someone to rethink his/her career plans. Repetitive tasks that have no obvious usefulness lower self-esteem. They also make the workday seem interminable.

Change

Occasionally someone comes along who loves repetition. The opposite tactic will eliminate him/her. Rearranging the work every day will offend him or her and produce anxiety. There are many security-oriented people among subordinates. They like predictability and routine. A daily dose of change, particularly arbitrary and capricious change, will motivate them to look elsewhere.

Carping

A lack of appreciation, when uniformly applied, will produce sullenness. However, it produces flight if appreciation is consistently withheld from only one or two people. Managers have long realized that support people bloom when told how much their efforts are appreciated. Carping, on the other hand, causes wilting. The more petty the carp, the greater the effect. Some people are natural carpers so everyone ignores them, but when someone who has always been a good guy begins to carp, the big chill sets in.

Terror and the Veiled Threat

Subordinates are very responsive to the veiled threat, even if they don't seem to understand it at the time. For example, telling someone in a quiet tone, "I'm not sure things are going to work out around here," can be very effective. The recipient of this information will feel something ominous is at work but won't know specifically what. It is her breath? Is the company in trouble in some mysterious way?

Summary

Are we encouraging you to employ these tactics? Certainly not! It's up to you to decide when, or if, you'll ever do any of these things. However, not everyone is as high-minded as you are. Suppose some of your co-workers decide to work on you. Isn't it better to be aware and prepared, so you can intelligently decide whether to fight back or move on? It's possible to deflect most of these tactics if you choose to. However, it can't be done if you are encased in mental Saran Wrap.

◊ A WORD ABOUT POLITICAL CRIMINALS

Sometime in your career you're going to run in to a genuine political criminal. You'll recognize him or her, not because the person comes across as predatory, but because the person gets a real buzz from office politics as a game. A PC is someone who lives for the game, regardless of outcome. A PC thrills to negative gossip, loves the showdown, thirsts for action.

Why is that criminal? Anyone who is pushing and shoving just for fun is going to hurt people to no constructive purpose. It's one thing to hurt someone because it can't be avoided; it's an entirely different matter to hurt anyone for the fun of it.

Deflecting a political criminal involves intensive consensus building. To do that the troops have to be aroused because each person feels threatened. Isolating the PC works but requires far more sustained effort than using the same techniques with anyone else. These people are like ticks—very hard to get rid of!

Chapter 7. Defensive Tactics I: Protecting Your Turf and Credibility

The Dangers of Encroachment

Until they have been victimized, most people have no interest in defensive tactics. Even then, many people refuse to recognize behind-the-scenes skullduggery because acknowledgment would require a response. Here's a recent example. While Don W., an assistant comptroller in a *Fortune* 500 company, was diligently working at his job, somebody stole a piece of it—just like that, with no warning! (The affrontery and dreary regularity of this sort of thievery boggles the imagination.) Once he realized he'd been done in and done to, Don was outraged but helpless. It was too late to do anything really effective.

Let's look at what happened. Don was responsible for handling international cash management for a *Fortune* 500 company. He had a peer, Fred, whose job involved the day-to-day work on domestic cash management but not the overall policy decisions. One day Fred began a campaign to increase his responsibilities and get his job reclassified at a higher level. Don saw Fred working on his job description and heard one of the secretaries joking with him about his big ambitions. But Don ignored the incidents, telling himself he was much too busy. Meantime, Fred prepared a job description that gave him both policy and operational control of domestic cash management. To everyone's amazement (including, we suspect, his own), he went to their mutual boss and sold the whole package. The boss seemed pleased with Fred's initiative. He said he'd been thinking about changing the structure but hadn't taken the time to do so.

When Don confronted him, Fred said, "Hey, it was just a logical move. You've got plenty to do anyway. What are you worried about?" That was a sham. Both knew perfectly well that work load was beside the point. Both also knew the risks Don would run if he made a fuss now. Asking a boss to rescind a decision requires far more compelling reasons than shrieking "Stop, thief!" especially after the official announcement has been made. The new situation brought out a weakness in Don's relationship with his boss. Domestic cash management was one of the higher visibility areas in the department and Fred had effectively cut Don out of it. Will Don be able to retaliate? Probably not in the near future, because everyone will be watching for his reaction.

Martha R. had a similar experience, but was saved at the last minute. She was the manager of a large, profitable ethnic restaurant. Her relationship with the owners, while not familial, was warm and mutually supportive. One day the head chef decided that he should look over the waiter applicants before Martha hired them. That way, he explained, he would know if they were capable of delivering his exquisite morsels to the customers. Before Martha really understood what the chef was plotting, he'd convinced the owners. The chef knew that once he had control over hiring the waiters, it was merely a matter of time before he could demand final approval on all hires.

In three months the owners were wondering why they needed Martha. What did a manager do who didn't handle the hiring and firing of personnel? The owners were pleased that their chef was so efficient. The only thing that saved Martha was that the chef soon tired of the people problems inherent in a restaurant operation. He voluntarily gave back the 50 percent of her job he'd taken so easily.

Before you conclude that Don and Martha need mental protein supplements, or have been jogging too many miles a week, consider this: Each was already on the way to losing part of the job before either realized a power play was in the works. They made it easy for an aggressor because neither one had thought about the reality that a co-worker might act aggressively. They believed in "rules," though neither could verify who had written them or what or where they were. Their job descriptions gave them a false sense of security because they believed they were being paid to do the specific tasks that were itemized therein.

Don and Martha didn't realize that territory is a vital issue in office warfare. Every office scrimmage, however unimportant it may appear on the surface, involves realignments of territory. A job description offers little protection (if a written one exists), however carefully the personnel department may have tried to lock in the specifics. Actually, your job description isn't truly a description of the tasks to be done. It is merely a fence around your particular turf, designed to keep others from overlapping your responsibilities, and you, theirs. Your actual job may barely resemble the written description. Think of all the things you do that aren't in your description but have been assigned to you or that you independently decided needed to be done. However, where one job ends and the next one begins is usually rather accurately spelled out. You probably could not encroach on another department's territory or easily stray from your division. You might think about it, but realize your boss or some other manager could intervene.

What Is Your Turf or Territory?

Your turf is a combination of physical boundaries, psychological factors, and areas of influence that affects your status, your power, and ultimately your survival within the company. Turf includes the tasks, the people, and the results for which you are responsible, and it also takes in whom you interact with. Turf may be broadly defined in a job description as "areas of responsibility." For example, the director of personnel's turf should include all transactions that dictate how, when, and under what circumstances people are hired or fired by the organization. However, as every personnel director realizes, when a manager tries to slip someone into the organization without going through personnel, there must be a scrimmage so that personnel can beat back the challenge. It can't be ignored lest other managers begin to hire and fire at will. After all, if managers can do it, why have a personnel department at all? This is as close to warfare on principle as most organizations get. Some departments, such as personnel, data processing, or public relations, have these problems regularly. They tend to look warily at anyone who tries to "help" or "improve" their assigned responsibilities.

Turf may be rearranged by individual initiative. A secretary may be assigned exclusively to one person, but if she decides to help another executive who's in need, her team-spiritedness may protect her from her boss's wrath. At the same time, she increases her power and her turf. The person she helps will begin to rely on her assistance, and her territory will be enlarged as surely as if her job description had been rewritten. It's a pity so many secretaries (and other workers) resist opportunities to take on more work and increase their turf, because, especially in large companies, it affects who moves up. In the guise of helping or playing on the team, almost anyone can enlarge his/her job. Most people won't enlarge their turf simply because they don't understand what it is or its importance.

Company tradition may limit a territory but logic and decisive action can overcome it. The employee relations manager may have always overseen the food service operation, but when a new manager with a food service background comes into the operations department, tradition may not hold. It will take very compelling arguments to show why food service shouldn't be detached from personnel and attached to operations. Should the operations manager actually want food service in her territory, it won't take much to convince management that reassignment is the logical thing to do. Personnel's protest—"But we've always done that!"—won't impress top management. In fact, unless top management has a stake in the area under attack, this argument never carries any weight.

If the problem arises in a profit center (marketing or sales) rather than a cost center (personnel), the defense might be more spirited but it wouldn't necessarily be more successful. Almost as often as personnel, members of the sales department are regularly and effectively undermined and have pieces of their jobs snatched away, if they don't resist. The reasoning will be fundamentally the same: "Jack's had more experience with high tech start-up companies so he'll be calling on those accounts from now on." The method may be more subtle, but not necessarily. It may be justified on the grounds of logic, as in Don's case. There is no automatic job protection built in to the system. Most people assume there is, because logic dictates that people shouldn't be able to rearrange jobs at will. After all, organizations should be rationally organized!

At this point we need to say something about that tedious cliché "We're doing this because it's logical." Politically speaking, the argument that something is logical may strengthen a position, but it doesn't begin or end it. Logic can push an idea over the top but lack of logic doesn't necessarily kill it. It's just an all-purpose justification that is very easy to invoke. If, for example, a job logically fits in operations but a very powerful vice president in finance wants that area to report to her, that will be the reporting relationship. Clout, not logic, is the determining factor.

Owner Inattention

Territories can be redrawn by owner indifference or inattention. An administrative assistant who is supposed to order supplies but neglects to do it because he/she is too busy will discover that an alert busybody has begun to order items independently. If the troops are satisfied, ordering supplies has been effectively detached from one person's job and attached to someone else's. People will go to the person who assumed the task. Bosses rarely get involved unless the job isn't getting done or a political problem is created. A new tradition has been created! Didn't you ever wonder where traditions came from? Fiat, not planning, creates them.

The same is true in the executive suite. If the vice president of communications neglects media relations, other vice presidents will begin talking to the television stations and newspapers. They'll do whatever they think best. What's more, if the vice president of communications is really inattentive, he may not know what is going on until he reads the local newspaper or someone from the TV station calls to confirm what one of the company's officers has said.

So far this sounds very reasonable. If someone wants a task and the person to whom it's presently assigned doesn't want it, why shouldn't reassignment take place? It benefits the workers and the company as well, doesn't it? The answer is that turf has symbolic, as well as practical, importance. Those who watch while someone allows a part of his/her job to be detached don't see the logic or reasonableness; they see a lack of assertive, defensive action. Don's co-workers probably don't know all the details of the incident between Fred and Don. Although they know Don is angry, they won't automatically conclude Fred is an aggressor. Their conclusion will be that Don is a chump. Was he blind? Even if Don continues to perform outstandingly, his reputation, his influence, and ultimately, his effectiveness are likely to be questioned. The people who sympathize with him are themselves potential victims. If they were not, their judgment of Don would be more negative.

Why Protection Is Important

There is an unwritten rule of organizational life that says, "Protect your job or lose it." The rule means that if you are not constantly on guard against encroachments on your territory, you may discover one day that you have none. The danger probably wasn't as widespread or serious ten years ago—BPM (Before Productivity Movement)—but now it is. When people lose parts of their jobs through inattention or theft, they may find a watchful management ready to redistribute the remainder. After all, a boss can reason this way: If your job isn't important to you, you're probably not being that productive. He or she may assume he/she has somehow missed seeing whatever it is you are not doing well. Here's an opportunity to eliminate a job and boost the department's input-to-output ratio.

People are finding that when they appear to be unable to defend themselves, they invite derision, not commiseration. For women trying to move up, the situation is especially critical. A woman who appears unable or unwilling to defend her territory is definitively labeled negatively.

"Don't worry about Mary," her peers will say. "She'll go along with anything." More women suffered setbacks in the recent recession from territorial ignorance than were wounded by Ronald Reagan's anti-affirmative action policies. The conclusion drawn about both men and women is that they don't know the game.

There is also the suspicion that the ignorance is deliberate. Those who appear oblivious to encroachments are signaling that they are just doing a job. They don't care about power. Another unwritten rule of corporate life is that people who are unable to capitalize on, and expand, the power inherent in their jobs don't get more. You must prove that you can hold on to power as well as use it aggressively to move up. If you don't understand that power is the most highly sought-after prize in office politics and office warfare, you are written off as naive. Power is the path to success.

Furthermore, money follows power, not the other way around. When someone says, "I'm just here for the money," she/he is actually telling people that she/he doesn't understand the issues. This concept often is hard for younger people to grasp. They may understand that money is the scorecard in life. What's not so clear is that moving up—which is necessary in order to get more money—is a power problem.

Allowing your turf to be rearranged by others positions you not as a leader, but as a reactor. This is not the sort of person management strives to boost into the executive suite, where the power skirmishes are very spirited indeed. There are already enough people with a follower mindset who have slipped in there. Top management looks for the seizers, not the seizees. This may account for the fact that when a "nice" CEO (or one whom the employees appear to be genuinely fond of) is uncovered, the media go into paroxysms of ecstasy. It's a media event because great power and niceness are rarely compatible.

How People Fail to Protect Themselves

There are several ways people fail to defend themselves, even when they realize someone is attempting to detach part of their job or undermine an area of influence. (1) They wait until something concrete occurs, such as a memo or announcement, before taking action. (2) They lack the political skills needed to use the informal system effectively. (3) They have hypocritical attitudes about the job or power issues. They should be somewhere that excites greater commitment. (4) They don't think it will matter much, because they believe the formal structure protects them. Let's look at these fatal misconceptions.

Waiting for the Word

We've already bludgeoned risk avoiders quite thoroughly. Suffice it to say that waiting for official notice is the acid test of how far someone will go to avoid direct confrontation over turf. When Don got the signals that Fred might be working on a job redesign, he should have said something immediately. He should have put Fred on notice that he'd retaliate if Fred attempted anything funny. Instead, Don waited, as most workers do, until something concrete happened. He was betting that the boss wouldn't agree. When the memo arrived, it was, of course, too late.

Any protective effort must be a preemptive strike. The minute he realized what Fred was planning to do (and any secretary could have filled him in), Don should have gone to the boss with persuasive reasons why it was essential that he remain involved in domestic cash management in order to be effective on the international side. He should have emphasized the benefits to the boss. He could have effectively forestalled Fred's move. Vince Lombardi was as right about office politics as about football when he said, "The best defense is a good offense."

Political Skills

Political skills allow you to work easily with others. People who show that they think their co-workers are tedious, especially when they are, usually have difficulty building the rapport needed to rally public opinion when they're under attack. Here are some of the essential political skills for protecting your turf.

1. You must be able to arouse the sympathy/empathy of others. That means that if you're keeping a low profile or have opted out of the grapevine, you're probably invisible. You have to get back in right now! When you decide it's convenient to do so or when the work load lightens, it may be too late. In organizational life, familiarity breeds acceptance and interest, not contempt. If you are a cipher to your co-workers, why should they empathize with you? You don't exist for them except as a mobile warm body.

2. You must be able to show others why an attack on you or your turf is also an attack on them. This isn't as difficult as it might seem. You have to articulate to others why it's in their best interest to help you. If Jack is allowed to preempt everyone in the department by going to all the industry trade shows on departmental money, won't everyone else face creeping obsolescence? Is it equitable—especially when several of these meetings are in Palm Springs in January and the rest of you will be shivering in St. Paul? He had the office suntan last year!

3. You must be able to create and maintain alliances that are mutually beneficial. Putting extra effort into helping others creates an obligation to you on their part. They'll owe you and you can collect if you get in a jam. Although you may take on more work, the rewards will vastly outweigh the effort. If you now realize that nobody owes you any favors, it should set off a strong mental alarm. You have been too remote from the politics of your office and need to get busy.

Hypocrisy

There are a great many people who do their jobs effectively while maintaining they are totally indifferent to turf issues. In fact, they have very mixed, almost contradictory feelings about the job. They believe that high productivity and good politics are incompatible even in theory. They justify these attitudes by saying that they are paid only to get the work out, not to play political games. This stance, while superficially true, raises questions in the minds of their co-workers. If the job isn't worth defending, why is it worth doing? Indifference equals ineffectiveness with hypocritical overtones in most people's minds. When people are disappointed in how far or how fast they are moving, they sometimes adopt this attitude. If someone you know was passed over recently, don't be surprised if he or she starts talking about politics as a "waste of time" and responsible for all of the company's troubles—not to mention his or her personal ones.

If you let everyone know that you think the marketing plan is really not a barn burner but you're executing your share superbly anyhow, you're sending mixed messages. You've really put out a welcome mat for aggressors. If you say you think the whole thing isn't worth doing, you shouldn't be surprised if your co-workers expect you to react softly if they try to grab an interesting project. You have also cast yourself in the role of resident hypocrite. Why are you taking the organization's money if you think your job is second-rate? You should move to a job with more sex appeal. Staying in a job you believe is not worth doing can damage your career. People tend to stagnate in this situation—inviting obsolescence.

If you appear to be indifferent when attacked, you may suffer greater damage down the road. People will remember that you rolled over when challenged, and they will assume that's your style. You've set a precedent. Your boss may not give you a crack at the next big job. This reputation may follow you to another company. You might have changed your attitude and become more turf-minded, but colleagues from your past may show up and raise doubts. That could cause needless work as you scramble to shore up your image.

Misread Political Signals

Every worker occasionally misreads political signals. Don never thought Fred would act aggressively, although a number of far from subtle clues turned up. He didn't think Fred was serious. Don't judge Don too harshly. Bank presidents, managing partners of law firms, and CEOs of consulting firms are just as capable of misjudging the intentions of others. This failing has no hierarchical boundaries. That's why doing a worst case analysis on every piece of disturbing information you hear is so important. Always say, "If this is true, what is the worst thing that could happen?" Then say, "What should I be doing now?"

If you find yourself misreading events and other people's actions regularly, you need to find out why. Are you blocking the message? Are you worrying about trivia rather than facing the fact that someone is after your job? If either is the problem, you need to ask yourself if you're really committed to the job and to staying with the company. Maybe your subconscious is signaling you to move on. Misreading the signals is almost always a deliberate decision. If you've been working for a few years, you have seen enough office warfare to recognize the symptoms.

Developing Radical Pragmatism

Most people, however unconsciously, want life to be more like a romance novel where the ideals of fairness and hard work rewarded always triumph. The mere mention of defensive tactics, much less preemptive ones, brings on a migraine. Well, the greatest defensive tool any worker can develop is an attitude of radical pragmatism. The importance of taking in and processing distressing information can never be overestimated. (Not to mention the practical benefits of doing so.) If nothing else is persuasive, imagine how much less bitterness and self-recrimination the realist experiences.

We've talked about rewarding your subordinates according to the quality and quantity of bad news they produce. Had Don done that, the grapevine would have given him more early warnings that Fred was taking an abnormal interest in Don's job description, as well as his own. He would have had time to plan a well-thought-out response. As it was, Don really victimized himself by not using the grapevine effectively.

Think what Martha might have learned had she been networking regularly with the kitchen help. It is highly unlikely that the predatory chef had failed to make his views known. In fact, he had been busy laying the groundwork for Martha's demise by complaining about the incompetents she was hiring. He knew he needed specific examples as ammunition to impress the owners and he collected them. Without these examples, whining about Martha's work would not have convinced the otherwise-satisfied owners.

People who pay close attention to the grapevine are rarely ambushed. Early warnings are always there to guide the wary. In order to recognize the early warnings that precede victimization, you must become turf conscious. That means changing your mindset from "I'll deal with that when it happens" to "Is anything happening?" and "What could happen?"

Pacifism on Principle

This is different from hypocrisy. Some people believe they shouldn't have to fight over turf issues. It's a matter of principle with them. They won't get involved at all. They may actually recognize that they should do something, but they hide behind an abstraction. This happens most often to professionals, physicians, accountants, lawyers, teachers. Something in their professional training has made such nitty-gritty activities seem beneath them. They'd rather lose than go to the mat over turf.

Public school teachers may refuse to attend PTA meetings because they believe nothing gets done there. "They are such a bore," one teacher said, "and all for show. Does anyone believe serious educational issues are discussed at meetings with parents present? I'd rather skip the whole thing. If a parent wants my opinion, that's what Parents' Night is for." This teacher would protest vehemently should parents make important decisions at one of these PTA meetings. She would dislike any policy decisions that encroached on her turf. She would whine about not having a chance to "react." She already had that opportunity at an open meeting but chose to turn it down.

The Company Will Provide Protection

So much honest misunderstanding about what the formal structure can and can't do exists that it's hard to convince people of how helpless the formal system is to cope with turf problems. Here's why the formal system is slow to respond: The formal system exists in writing. It can only be changed in writing. Whatever informal arrangements are made by individuals to get the work out aren't reflected in written documents. Remember, turf is as much a psychological issue as it is a physical issue. That means that something very specific must be done to you before the company can officially get involved and rewrite your job description.

If a co-worker comes to your desk and takes your files and work papers, you'd protest. Then personnel or your boss might tell the offender to stop. They may even rewrite your job description to make it official that whatever was snatched is part of your turf. This is rarely the way turf is snatched, however. Tasks or responsibilities are assumed and then something official happens. Someone, usually the boss, sees that things are being done differently with better results and then job descriptions are rewritten.

You can't count on the company to protect you officially unless whoever is seizing your turf is doing it through the official channels. In that case personnel will help you, because writing job descriptions is their turf, and that's being attacked!

Here are some guidelines to help you protect your turf.

1. Bad news and uncomfortable news must be considered true until disproved, not the other way around. Remember Kennedy's Truth, "A pessimist has no ugly surprises." Every cynic knows this but most people still dismiss it. Hoping that bad rumors will go away is always counterproductive and cuts down your planning time. Good strategy is never developed during a crisis, especially when someone is waiting for an immediate response. Face the facts, test your strategies, and be ready to implement them. In business you can't believe that "no news is good news," because the opposite is true. If everyone avoids talking to you about your work, a nasty rumor or two is probably being suppressed. Your friendly peers don't want to upset you even though they would actually help by telling you the bad news.

2. Other people are as ambitious as you are and frequently more ruthless. Very ambitious people don't necessarily talk about their goals, believing that the less said, the better. Your co-workers who appear very cool should be watched carefully. The ones who talk a lot about hard charging are dissipating energy and are probably less threatening. They don't require much of your time and attention.

3. Mr. Dooley (a character created by humorist Peter Finley Dunne) said, "Trust everybody but cut the cards." This thought should be a rule for protecting your turf, too. Assume that part of the reason for your involvement with your co-workers is to keep them honest. Let them know, in a nice way, that if you hear about any impending tricks that would threaten your position, you will respond. You're not a lawyer; you don't assume innocence until guilt is proven. You don't need courtroom proof to act.

4. Bosses only monitor and ratify subordinates' work. They do not warn them of turf encroachments nor do they protect one employee from another. Many people don't understand this. They insist on believing that the boss must be interested in their turf. Actually, the boss has no need to get involved in intra-departmental turf squabbles. Only if an outsider is trying to detach a large piece of your boss's turf will he/she react.

Most managers expect you to look after yourself. If you expect your boss to reprimand a co-worker for an aggressive move toward you, you'll be sadly surprised when nothing happens. Your boss will be surprised that you assumed something would. He or she will tell you that you must solve your problem with your co-worker. There is probably no experienced manager who doesn't say at least once a week, "You and June (or Larry) work it out."

5. Genuine friendships in an office are unlikely, and even hazardous to your career. This doesn't mean that you should be misanthropic, just be watchful. Everyone's primary duty is to stay on the payroll. If a co-worker sees an opportunity to boost his/her career by an aggressive act toward you, he/she will take it. Friendship is fleeting. Each worker's first responsibility is to defend his job and enlarge it. For many people in the twenty-five to forty age bracket, building a career is the number one interest. They will behave more aggressively than the person who has a broad range of interests outside the office.

6. There is no such thing as "fair" in business. Any tactic you can get away with that is legal and reasonably ethical is all right and may even be grudgingly admired by those who aren't as successful. Another way to say this is that there is no corporate department of political intervention that provides amnesty and safe passage for the inept. Nobody will help you if someone cuts up your territory. Every-one is too busy defending his/her own.

7. Kidding yourself or trying to look at events optimisti-cally is frequently fatal to your career in a company. If you don't want to defend yourself, withdraw. However, if you feel your job is worth it, strike first. You can affect the outcome only when the issue is unresolved and still circu-lating in the informal system. Once a boss has made an official announcement, it's too late.

8. "Nice" is in the eye of the beholder. "Necessary" is in the mind of the beholder. Neither word has any meaning outside a situational context. It may be both nice and nec-essary to assume a part of someone's job rather than let some tasks go undone or continue to be done ineffectively.

9. At least 25 percent of your job is protecting your turf. You must have access to the grapevine and have good re-lationships with your boss and co-workers at all times. This is probably the most neglected area of job maintenance, because many people think their work consists of only the product or service they are paid to provide. Above the cler-ical level, job descriptions rarely list the responsibility for building and maintaining good working relationships with everyone. It may not be included in your job description, but is essential, and it is assumed you will do so.

Have you ever read a more unpleasant set of facts? Or ideas that you know are absolutely true but you'd rather not think about? Probably not. No wonder people let situa-tions slide rather than swallow such an awful dose of cor-porate castor oil. However, we're betting that you care about your turf and won't shove this list into your mental out-box.

Your best defense is letting your peers know that any assault on your turf will be ruthlessly resisted. In casual conversations, you can let others know that you are on guard and that they should be watching their territories rather than casting covetous glances at yours. Some will protest, "Jason is so prickly. He really worries about minor details." Watch anyone who says that sort of thing. He or she is a predator. The number of people who have no sense of turf is enormous, probably as many as 75 percent. Don't put yourself in this unfortunate majority.

Don't underestimate the relative importance of turf protection to productivity. When you project an air of being in control, they'll be less tempted to move against you. Since the new theories of productivity assume an improvement in quality, is it likely that the quality of your work will be high if you are unable to protect and control your turf?

Protecting Your Credibility

Do the people in your department believe that if you say something they can take it to the bank? Is your word your bond? Do they think you have your job under control, that you perform competently? No work-related asset compares with credibility as a motor to move you up. All CEOs have it or they can't do the job. Who wants to work for someone whose believability or job skills are in question? You may think there's nothing new to be learned about creating and protecting credibility—until you look at the subtler ways in which your believability can be undercut. Lest your paranoia be steadily rising, understand that sometimes your credibility is undercut innocently by someone who truly isn't aggressive, just careless or being used by others. This is often the case with rumors that are quite farfetched. But just in case a predator is out to undermine you, here are the principal methods that should be used.

1. Co-workers can undermine you. They can watch you being undermined through the grapevine as you, happily unconscious of what's going on, concentrate on dotting all the *i*'s. This may take the form of challenging your data or raising doubts about your performance. They may say you don't have firm control of your job, i.e., your skills aren't state-of-the-art. They may say what you think about office events is purely your personal suppositions. You've lost your grass roots network. If enough people express such doubts, you'll have a problem because your allies will want guarantees that you're a credible source and a strong supporter.

One key to credibility is never talking about what may happen unless you are dead certain it will happen. Instead, you perform first and then let the grapevine know. If you're getting the news regularly, maintaining accuracy shouldn't be terribly challenging, unless your sources have become sloppy because you're not rewarding them appropriately. This happens often when people don't do regular maintenance. They may be giving you shaky data because they want to influence you. If that's the problem, you'll have to recement each of those key relationships without delay.

Consider this example. After Jennifer W. was promoted to media relations manager, she discovered that two co-workers, Larry and Bob, had each been dead certain he was the clear choice for that job. After the usual sour grapes, "They had to promote a woman, etc.," had gone through the grapevine, Larry and Bob began to do something far more subtle and potentially more damaging. Neither attacked, they merely questioned. Larry would say, within hearing distance of a secretary or another staff person, "Do you really think Jennifer has the kind of contacts at the newspaper to place this important story in the business section?" Larry knew the story in question was a particularly difficult placement for anyone—especially since the director of public relations had been stonewalling the newspaper on other issues. Bob would speculate with the department secretary as to why Jennifer thought a particular strategy would work, leaving the secretary wondering why Jennifer thought so.

Bob would say, "I'm wondering if we're getting all the

television coverage we should. Of course, I'm sure Jennifer tries, but the grapevine says she's always been weak in that area."

By raising doubts rather than attacking, they appeared to be concerned rather than merely predatory. Jennifer nearly lost her credibility—and put her job under a cloud —before someone finally repeated some of Larry's and Bob's remarks to her. She confronted both of them and cleared the air. She asked what either would have done differently. If they had better ideas, surely, in the spirit of team play, they would want to share them with her—for the good of all. By muscling Larry and Bob a bit she regained her credibility with others who then recognized the game—but it was a photo finish!

2. Your peers may informally challenge your commitment to the job, the department, or the company. This is only an attack on your credibility if you work for a company where loyalty is an important cultural value. If there's so much as a hint in their internal or external networks that you're job hunting, your credibility will be undercut. It's OK if it's known that headhunters lust after you, as long as you appear to keep them at an arm's length. If you seem eager to talk with them, your whole image will be shot. After all, if you're as dedicated as your co-workers have been led to believe, why do you appear eager? That behavior has overtones of a lack of commitment, which anyone can pick up.

Marty L. was a top salesman for his paper company. He had the highest volume four or five months in any year. He was clearly the current sales manager's choice as a successor. However, the sales manager wasn't going to retire for two or three years. Joel, the second highest producer, decided he'd like to reopen the contest for succession. He called several search firm contacts, praising Marty and hinting he might want to make a change. The word got around the industry that Marty was looking. When the headhunters called, Marty didn't turn them off as quickly as his boss would have liked. (Joel had, of course, made sure the boss was aware of the situation.) Marty allowed himself to be seen lunching with a headhunter! He didn't move, but his boss reopened the contest for sales manager. Fortunately for Marty, in the course of Joel's plotting he came across some very attractive opportunities and left. Marty had time to mend his fences before the manager retired. This story had a lucky ending for Marty, but not because he helped his luck along. He acted neither wisely nor decisively. He could easily have quelled the false rumors that he was job hunting simply by refusing to talk with the headhunters or produce a resume.

3. Your personal and professional images may seem unstable or unsuitable. A man who's been a preppy type most of his life and then begins to dress like a free-lance television producer will confuse his co-workers. It makes them think he doesn't know who he is. If that's true, his co-workers will tend to treat him warily until he decides. Women do this if they change from John Molloy's *Dress for Success* look to the Paris-dictated bag lady look—in the same week!

This happens rather often to younger, less self-confident types. Think about the recent fad of "having your colors done." It involved being draped with cloth swatches in a wide range of colors while a color consultant selected the most flattering colors for you. It was actually a helpful process unless your best colors turned out to be purple and pink or mustard and brown. If you worked for a bank and bought new business suits in any of those colors, you immediately had a credibility problem. Imagine a man who was advised that pink flattered his skin turning up in a pink shirt at IBM! If you're to keep your credibility, the acceptable conservative business colors have to be worn even if your color consultant disapproves.

Image consultants sometimes had the same effect in undercutting credibility when they convinced a person to change his/her persona in ways that, while personally positive, were still hopelessly out of step with a particular corporate culture. For example, convincing the rising female CPA that a more feminine silk dress and jacket would be just as businesslike as a suit. Wrong! The business suit is the uniform for all financial people. Women lawyers were often given bad advice about power clothing. They also heard the siren song of the silk dress. More bad advice. Only in creative areas like advertising can people follow fashion with some safety as they make personal statements with their wardrobes.

For some people it's not the wrong colors but the wrong mindset. Remember the fad for assertiveness training? All of a sudden, someone who'd been very considerate of other people's feelings became, not assertive, but downright rude! He or she began saying hideously insulting things like "What I think I hear you saying is" or (to a boss) "The way that comes across to me is . . ." Actually assertiveness is often a synonym for rudeness. Anything like assertiveness, which is bound to make almost everyone you try it on want to avoid you in the future, should be avoided. Besides, any fad undercuts credibility because it doesn't usually become part of your personality, just a momentary aberration.

Even worse than going the wrong direction is changing back and forth. Most people don't realize that what they believe to be useful experimentation—the search for the One Right Look—strikes business colleagues as professional instability. Pick a style and stay with it long enough for people to feel comfortable. If you'd like a change, make it gradually. If you decide to move from gray flannel to tweeds, try a gray tweed before hitting the troops with a more radical change.

4. If you seem vague or indecisive, people will get the idea you're physically there but have placed a "Vacancy" sign on your brain. Tentativeness absolutely undercuts your credibility and, equally as important, your alliances. Who wants to depend on someone who can't make up his/her mind whether the discussion is worth pursuing, much less what action should be taken?

Generally, vagueness is a sign your brain is in overload. It may be the result of job-related stress or some personal crisis. When Elsa began to lose her concentration after learning her mother had a rare form of cancer, she began to alarm her co-workers with memory lapses. While her mother's condition was by no means hopeless, Elsa was very anxious. When her mother began to rally, Elsa noticed the changes in her co-workers' attitudes. She resented having to go back and shore up her entire network. Why couldn't they have been more understanding?

Be aware that your personal problems have to be packaged to co-workers with instructions. Don't say, "I'm so worried about Mother that I can hardly think." Say, "My mother is really sick right now and I need your help. I know I'm distracted at times. If I seem vague when you're talking to me, please ask me if I understood what you said." Once your co-workers know that they must talk to you a bit differently during this temporary crisis, they'll do it. Your credibility won't become an issue at all. You can't expect people to be understanding unless you tell them what your definition of understanding is. Show them how.

What Doesn't Undercut Credibility

Oddly enough, your credibility usually isn't undercut when you change your mind if a clear cause-and-effect relationship exists. If you took one position on Monday and on Friday you're taking the opposite stance, you'll have no problem if there have been intervening facts or events. You won't be expected to stick with a position on an issue after it has clearly become outmoded.

You might have been squarely in favor of the new sales training program but the following week you raised serious questions about it. Be sure to explain why. Tell your boss and co-workers you have talked to a couple of college pals who said their company had used the same program with mixed results. Be specific. Secrecy undercuts credibility because people don't know what produced the radical change in your ideas. Let them know.

Nonassertiveness doesn't necessarily undercut credibility, nor does timidity. A mousy secretary, an almost mute programmer, a very taciturn office manager, can still have tremendous credibility. It's not charisma that makes credibility, it's the idea that when this person says something, it can be relied on. People often mistake forcefulness for credibility. That's ridiculous. Does booming out a doubtful statement make it less doubtful? Or is it just a louder mistake? Does becoming furious really make you seem more credible because you're willing to take such a strong stand or is it just a memorable temper tantrum?

Maintaining Credibility

There is no profile of the credible person. Credibility is achieved through a steady process of creating and protecting it over a period of time. Here are some ways you can do it.

1. Confront the source of false or misleading rumors. There is no such thing as an anonymous rumor. If something is circulating it has a parent—or several parents. It's up to you to locate the originator of false rumors about you or anything you're involved with, and say, "Jim, I understand you've been saying it was my participation that sank that last big contract. That's simply not true, and let me tell you why." Jim is likely to protest that he hasn't said a thing. His tongue is clean. Your response should be "Good, then I won't be hearing that rumor in the grapevine anymore with your name on it."

If Jim says, "I said it and I'm glad," keep your cool. Don't make provocative statements, ask questions instead. Say, "Aren't you worried about the damage to your credibility when people realize they can't really rely on what you say?" That should give him something to ponder.

If you let a false rumor linger in the grapevine more than a few days, it will be believed. Your belated denial won't change anybody's mind. After all, if it were really untrue, why didn't you jump on it immediately? Do not dismiss anything false that's said about you as "petty gossip." Life is petty.

2. Choose a management style and stick with it. Even if you feel a new management technique was made for you, you don't suddenly stop doing everything and adopt it. You must maintain some consistency in your style. If not, co-workers won't know on any given day which of your many personas they must deal with. Business fads aren't particularly good vehicles for expressing individuality. Everyone else in the office might not have read the latest book and will therefore think you're having a temporary breakdown, not trying the latest technique.

You can always modify your management style in subtle ways. For example, if your boss likes a very authoritarian approach in people at your level, you'll have to be consistently more authoritarian. If your boss is a consensus builder, you'll want to try using those techniques at least occasionally. If you immediately become the most ardent consensus builder in North America, your co-workers will believe it was not a desire to please the boss but something you smoked. As long as you are reasonably consistent, it won't matter which style you choose.

3. Analyze events and office news very carefully and respond appropriately and quickly. Don't lightly dismiss anything that seems unusual or seems to do violence to the organizational culture. Even if the event or problem is "no big deal," it's important that no one misunderstands your position on an issue. If you don't follow through on the little details—whether you're building alliances, tracking the gossip, or making sure people know what you're doing —you will undercut your position. During major upheavals, such as reorganizations or restructurings, every minor detail is important. If you don't process all the information you receive correctly, you can't plan an appropriate response.

4. Work at your alliances. There is more to building alliances than being nice to people. You also need to find opportunities to trade favors and then solicit favors in return. You have to anticipate people's needs sometimes before they are aware they have them. This solicitousness is attractive to everyone watching because it seems you're really aware of the other person.

Maintaining your alliances is the hardest thing to do in office politics because it's so boring and endlessly repetitive. How many times can you be nice to the same people? Forever, if necessary. Keeping people's egos plumped up is like plumping pillows in hotel rooms. There's an endless supply in need. Nonetheless, tell yourself that it's character building—and a necessary part of keeping your reputation burnished.

Protecting your turf and maintaining credibility requires that you take a long-range view of yourself and your career. Do you think of your career as a patchwork quilt or a pattern of interconnecting pieces? It makes a difference. You should be building for long-range success in the political wars, not settling for a quick hit today and letting tomorrow look after itself.

Finally, you should be giving yourself special rewards and psychological strokes when you do your maintenance and when you protect your career. Only you, ultimately, can reward you. That means you privately have a glass of champagne and toast the vanquished and your skill in vanquishing that enemy. You take someone special to dinner in celebration of another office victory. You don't have to explain the occasion to your companion. You buy the expensive hardcover novel that is a good read with absolutely no redeeming social value and spend a weekend in bed with it. You go off on an unfashionable vacation and spend a week as the primal grub. You have to pamper yourself occasionally to keep up your will to protect turf and credibility. Otherwise you may be overcome with tedium.

◊ A WORD ON TEMPORARY LAPSES

From time to time you'll be detonated by someone who has consistently been very irritating. You let the pressure build and one day you blow over some issue that is minuscule. You may dismiss this lapse as attributable to your humanity. Your co-workers won't. They don't remember years and days of sunny equanimity. They remember the storms. Moral: Don't think you can have a lapse without putting your career at risk. The argument "I'm only human" excuses nothing.

Chapter 8. Defensive Tactics II:

Fighting Back

One day Lily J. looked up to find herself enveloped in an ominous silence. It wasn't that she'd been dropped by her coffee group, it's just that these meetings seemed less frequent. In fact, while snowed under with work during the past few weeks, she'd really not been aware that her coffee regulars had made themselves scarce. She called one of them, Jeanne, and asked her for coffee. Jeanne was busy. She called up Ray. Ditto. She called Rose Ellen and she said yes, but reluctantly. Now somewhat alarmed, Lily decided to see what Rose Ellen had to say.

Rose Ellen's contribution to the mystery was more by what she didn't say than what she did. Lily left that conversation with the distinct impression that something was in the grapevine she wasn't supposed to know about. Rose Ellen's contribution to the facts had been that "everyone says the company is terribly prejudiced against women and won't ever name one to be assistant comptroller."

Since Lily was on the short list for promotion to assistant comptroller, it was clear that she hadn't gotten the job. Her acute disappointment caused her to look for a political explanation rather than a skills failure. After all, she was one of the final two. The only thing she could think of was that Ralph, who was also up for the job, had sabotaged her. Had he said something about her that caused her boss to pick him over her?

Ralph had said things, but not directly to the boss. What he'd done was to raise questions about Lily's commitment to her career and to the company. He'd asked questions that planted doubts. Was Lily really interested in so much extra responsibility, newlywed that she was? Was Lily committed to staying with the company? "I heard she's had resumes out," Ralph said. "Did you hear that?" Obviously Lily, buried in work, missed any report of this.

Ralph did get the promotion and Lily eventually left for a higher-level job in another company. She still smarts from the lack of support displayed by co-workers, especially the women. In fact, she misread the situation entirely. Her ignorance of Ralph's aggression made her pals' tentative response inevitable. She didn't seem alarmed. They thought they were protecting her feelings by not giving her the word on Ralph. How were they supposed to know she hadn't heard the rumors? They didn't see it as a loyalty issue at all.

She shouldn't have expected spontaneous support. Support always comes from trading favors. She should also have expected Ralph to do whatever he thought necessary to get the job. Expecting neutrality, as Lily did, from one's competitors is naive. If two people are head-to-head for a promotion, each should expect the other will do whatever he or she can to win.

Had Lily confronted Ralph, accusing him of badmouthing her, he would have been the picture of righteousness. He hadn't said a single negative thing about her! When he was asked, he said positive things. He commented enthusiastically about her competence. What he'd done was merely to insinuate that something might happen in the future. That's the kind of thing you need to learn to deflect.

Defensiveness isn't really the posture you want to take. Too often it raises the idea that perhaps you have some reason to defend yourself. Remember that old adage "Where there's smoke, there's fire"? People really believe that—at least enough do to begin sniffing for the smoke.

In competitive situations it's important to expect and prepare for attacks so you can minimize any potential damage.

How Assassins Work

All assassins, however they cloak their motives, share certain characteristics. (1) They prefer anonymity. They do not, if effective, seek publicity or long for public credit. If their actions were officially known, the victim might be awash in sympathy. This is especially true when the victim is competent. (2) They hope the victim will panic and behave foolishly. Better still is a victim who never figures out the game. Generally that's too much to hope for. (3) They want to conclude whatever they're doing as quickly as possible. As we discussed in chapter 6, anyone who's trying to undercut anyone else must move quickly before the victim and his/her allies respond.

The one fault in the value scheme of otherwise savvy people that seems to throw them off is the belief no one would attack unless they were doing something wrong. The game of promotion chasing should be fair. This is often a fatal assumption because it allows anyone who doesn't share those values a free hand. You end up rejecting intellectually what your gut is telling you. You always need to be on the lookout for competitors who want the job or promotion as much as you do. Underestimating people can insure failure, not to mention causing you great pain.

To prevent career damage you have to be able to recognize the earliest hints that someone is bent on causing you trouble. Only at that point can you squelch such attacks without bringing the whole sordid incident into the open. Publicity isn't usually any more helpful to the victim than the victimizer unless he or she is very popular. For men, especially, publicity seems a weakness.

Early Warning Signals

Even the most careful predator leaves a trail—as you would if you chose to employ any of the tactics in chapter 6. There is no such thing as true anonymity. Here are some ways to identify that you're about to become a victim or at least that's someone's intent. Initially, you don't need to know who's behind it to plan an effective response.

1. The quality and quantity of the information you collect from your network changes. All of your internal contacts seem to be waiting to hear what you say before getting on with the conversation. For instance, when you say, "What's going on?" the person says very quickly, "Nothing that I know of." (Pause) "Why, have you heard anything?" That person knows something. If you were alert to the signs, you'd try to squeeze the information out of him/her. You could do this in several ways, but the best way would be to trade him/her a piece of information for what you want to know. Even though Lily was busy, she should have realized early on that a long-standing habit (coffee every morning) was being broken. She'd have been wise to pin down each of her women friends until one broke. She should also have approached any men she'd helped in the past. Who could gauge their loyalty to Ralph until it was put to the test? You can't be powerful and wear velvet gloves all of the time. It's your career at stake.

A second way to get the information is to go outside the company. What have your peers in other companies heard? All you need is a clue. Is it likely Ralph never mentioned to anyone how hot he was for the assistant comptroller's job? Someone in the local CPA society knew. That person might have mentioned it to Lily. To him/her the information has no political luggage and can be passed on freely.

2. Your boss asks you questions about trivial issues or asks for your opinions on settled matters. You're asked about your continuing education plans. You're asked about something that happened on your last job, three years ago. A question out of the blue means someone is working against you. There's a hidden agenda. It's time to answer a question with a question. Say, "What brought that to mind just now? Has something come up?" Your boss may be trying to verify what she/he has heard. If so, it's important to find out what has been said and deal with it immediately. We'll identify and deal with the perpetrator later.

3. People are looking at you more closely when you meet or pass them in the halls. You feel this heightened scrutiny but may dismiss it as superficial—your new suit perhaps. It's not what you're wearing, unless you think there's a perfume or aftershave called Pending Political Disaster #5. You are definitely not imagining it. Most people will ignore this very clear signal that something is afoot. If this is happening, find the weakest person who's engaged in the practice and confront. Say, "What's going on, George? What don't I know that I should?" Nothing works in these situations like direct confrontation. George may spill his guts. He will run back to his source and confirm that now you know! This will have a dampening effect on your enemy's spirits, which is to the good.

4. People stop chatting when you join the group. There is no surer sign that someone is about to cause you real problems. No one wants to be the bearer of large-scale bad news. If people don't talk when you're around, you can be sure they were, and soon will continue, talking about you. Again find the weakest link in that group and press. Say, "Why did everyone stop talking when I came up? What's going on?" The more the person denies any such thing happened, the more certain you can be that someone is causing you a problem.

Who's the Culprit?

All this may be worth knowing, but the keystone is the name of the person who's planned and is now orchestrating the attack. How do you find that out? If you ask someone if Harry's behind the rumors, you may confuse the person. He or she has probably never thought about the original source of the rumor, and only knows who gave him/her the news. You need a much surer technique for getting at the source, especially if you don't pick up anything until it's been repeated by several groups. The real key to identifying the person is not why he or she is doing you dirt, but *how*. What is the method?

If you were a mystery writer, you would understand the adage "If you know how, you know who." If someone is after you, you are luckier than the victim in a mystery because you're going to survive. You're also going to need the same techniques a detective uses to bring the baddie in. Namely, you're going to have to get information on the perpetrator's modus operandi. People have characteristic ways of speaking and doing things. Their psychological makeup makes them choose particular weapons. They have particular skills. Someone who's a crack shot with a rifle is unlikely to choose a bow and arrow for the crime. It's less familiar and he's less skilled with it. People less sure of their people skills use different methods from master negotiators' or manipulators'.

Certain positions on the organizational ladder limit or enhance the tools an aggressor has available. Senior management can't use gossip as easily as the secretaries can. If you see what part of your image or reputation the victimizer has tried to attack, you can eliminate all the people who would never think of that tactic or who would be unable to use it. If you were tagged with a major project failure, who would be able to use that technique? A direct competitor or your boss is possible. A secretary is less likely because someone in that position would be unable to transfer blame as easily.

If someone is sabotaging your work, it's got to be someone with enough technical skill to understand exactly what you do and how it should be done. That suggests a peer. For example, someone whose mind glazes over at the thought of line item budgets is not likely to try to undercut you on that ground. Someone in accounting, on the other hand, has both knowledge and access.

Once you know who has opportunity, go to trusted sources not with a question, "Who's doing this to me?" but with a supposition. You say, "I think I know who's been telling everyone I dropped the ball on that commercial account. Harry's the only one who would have a motive." If your source disagrees, it probably isn't Harry. Insist that it must be, and you're likely to get some clues to the person's real identity. Don't directly accuse and don't seem particularly perturbed. It must appear your only motive is to set the record straight.

If someone agrees to give you the name in confidence, take it. You will have to find other ways to support this allegation or to clear the accused's name. That's not difficult, because rumors rarely circulate in the grapevine just once. If one person confides in another, the recipient of the confidence usually confides the same story to his/her own trusted source—especially if it's hot news. That means two people know. The word will gradually sift to other remote parts of the organization, but you'll be able to pick it up and trace it back through contacts.

Deductive reasoning comes into play here. Just for fun here are some office warfare mysteries for you to solve to help sharpen your skills. Who done it?

The Case of the Premature Departure

Three men—Dan, Jack and Roger—are assigned to analyze the financial data preparatory to the purchase of a small, troubled company. They are to work with Jane, the company's comptroller, in doing the workup. Roger, after examining the numbers carefully, begins to suspect that the company's finances are in far worse shape than his company had been told. Jane gives him all of the confidential information he asks for. Dan and Jack, sure they have the whole picture, are ready to wrap up the report when Roger presents his analysis. Both are surprised that they could have missed the critical angle. Jack is angry that Roger surprised them while he and Dan were working on an entirely different, and what he believed to be a clearly superior, approach. He blusters a bit about teamwork. Dan is' equally displeased but says nothing. Roger emerges triumphant and the boss is pleased. Two weeks later he learns from a contact that the grapevine reported he didn't play on the team. A second report comes through that he's trying to move ahead of the pack. Who started the rumors?

Note that Roger did nothing he was not assigned to do. He simply thought about the data differently. What angered his teammates was the way credit was distributed in the end. Dan is the source of the rumors. Here's why: He said nothing at the shoot-out because he believed nothing could be gained there. Jack spoke up and that was his attempt to go on the record condemning Roger's behavior. He's unlikely to use the grapevine after a public announcement. Principle: Those who don't speak up in a meeting use the grapevine more frequently as a tool.

The Case of the Purloined Memo

Amelia K. has spent weeks pulling together a massive research report for her boss, the operations vice president, which concluded that data processing was overstaffed by at least 10 percent. She is awaiting notice of the meeting date, which the CEO will set, when the vice president will present the data. The word is out in the grapevine that data processing will go under the knife. The word processing supervisor spilled the beans. Amelia and her boss are still waiting for their memo when the VP gets a call from an irate CEO. Where is he and where is the report? The troops are assembled and waiting! He rushes off to present the data. It's approved, but only after much tougher questioning than would have been generated by a less flustered presenter. Who purloined the memo?

The culprit had to have three things: knowledge of what Amelia and her boss were waiting for, access to an electronic memo machine, and the codes necessary to intercept the CEO's memo and take two names off the distribution list. The grapevine can easily identify the very short list of those who had access. The place to start is among the word processing supervisor's cronies.

The Case of the Altered Report

Max has been working for the company for twenty-five years. Each morning top management prays that he will retire next year when he becomes sixty-two. They are thinking up a buy-out plan to insure that he will. Max's secretary, Julie, is in her late fifties. She can retire on a full pension at sixty and she has no desire to break in a new boss. The CEO's secretary, Elaine, is a friend. One day Elaine mentions that Max's days are numbered. Max's secretary becomes agitated. She hates change and massive ones seem to be coming. Elaine discusses this with the CEO. He explains that it's company policy that when an executive leaves, his secretary is "thrown back into the pool" to be available for any other senior executive. Elaine types up the report that specifies when Max is to leave and what he'll receive if he goes quietly. It's entirely accurate, just as the CEO dictated it. When the report is distributed, several numbers have been changed. The CEO is furious because Max has declared the offer unacceptable. He'll be staying until sixty-five, at least! Who altered the report?

Blood is thicker than water. Elaine returned to alter the report (easy on a data processing terminal) to protect her friend. The CEO naturally assumed that Max had. Why Elaine? She had motive, the means, and the opportunity, plus the protection of knowing her boss would suspect her last. Principle: Those with access to tools are likely to use them. A senior executive would be unlikely to type his/her own material. Most men over forty, outside the communications and data processing businesses, can't type anyhow, which accounts for the large number of computer phobics in that group.

By now you should be thinking like Sam Spade. Always examine how something was done and then look for the one person who might have the greatest facility at doing it. Forget motives, murky at best, and concentrate on opportunity.

Do you confront the culprits? This is a situation-by-situation call. That means that you'll need to consider two things: What do you want to accomplish? Is confrontation the best method to achieve that? You may find quiet deflection more useful.

Deflection Tactics with Bosses

There are five excellent reasons a boss becomes a predator instead of firing you. (We'll allow that you may not find them particularly excellent.) You're performing well, so he or she is not helped there. Generally, the situation that causes the problem is chronic. What brings it to a head is a single event.

1. You are a threat to your boss. You haven't worked at this but it's a fact. Everyone knows that your boss is not competent. He got his present position in the much-missed sixties. The company is tolerating him but recent economic problems have made him feel less secure. People come to you for help and information, bypassing him. You have done nothing to encourage them but neither have you been able to discourage this behavior entirely. Someone must get the work out. It's in the grapevine that a shakeup is coming. Your boss wouldn't benefit from this. It would be an ideal time for the company to shunt him aside or even use outplacement. If you are there as not only the logical successor but an effective one, it would make top management's decision much easier.

Knowing this, your boss's tactics are likely to include a move to isolate you, undercut you with his/her peers, or find major errors in your work. The last isn't very likely, since clearly your competence and political skills created the problem to begin with. Your best strategy in this situation is to keep touching base with your boss and keep him/her tied in. That means you've got to check back even on the trivial decision. Say, "Dick, you know that big contract is almost ready to go. Want to see it before we send it out?" This is no time for an outbreak of prickly pride. Your strategy is to make sure that your boss has no surprises and that he's also incapable of surprising you.

Confrontation won't help. What can you two discuss that won't take more starch out of his ego? Bosses in such situations have one overriding sensitivity. They are paranoid about insubordination because it comes so close to public acknowledgment of impotence. To be seen as respectful, supportive, and cautious is your best posture. The harder it is for him to find fault, the more likely you'll eventually get the kingdom.

2. Your boss is jealous. If you work for someone who's inadequately educated, not plugged in as well as you are within the company, or lives an involuntarily frugal life, you could have a problem. Getting rid of you, or at least damaging your reputation, would restore his/her self-esteem. Managers who consider themselves professionals often discount such baseness. "We're so busy with the work here, who has time for that?" These are the same people who'll gather around a subordinate's Porsche in the parking lot and stroke the fenders while declaring they can't understand where he got it!

Your best strategy is always explanation. Did someone

die and leave you money? A jackpot at the roulette table perhaps? Conspicuous consumption in front of a boss is always a bad idea because money is the scorecard. Besides, it's your old school pals whose noses you'd like to rub in your success, not your boss.

3. Your boss has someone he/she would prefer in the job. It's not personal. It doesn't mean you're not a team player or that you're not good at what you do. Your boss has decided the chemistry with the other person is better. This is most likely to happen if a new boss has come in and you're a holdover from the previous regime. It's not pure prejudice, because it happens to men as often as to women and minorities.

Since there's no defensible reason to fire you, the only way your boss can handle the problem is to victimize you with the hope you'll leave or you'll become demoralized and your performance will decline. If your performance suffers seriously, you can be fired for nonperformance. Personnel won't investigate why your performance suddenly took a nosedive. Before you confront or respond you might want to consider whether leaving has career-enhancing possibilities and might not be a good idea. At least consider a transfer within the company.

If a boss really decides you should be replaced, it might be better to go along. However, if you want to stay, you'll have to confront him or her. Ask, "Are you unhappy with what I've been doing?" Put your boss on the spot to point out specific areas in which your performance needs to improve. Politely but relentlessly demand more details on exactly how he/she would like the work delivered. This is a situation in which confrontation protects. This is a far better strategy than accusing the boss of brazen favoritism in his office at 9:00 A.M. It's far better than quietly seething until you blow up over a minor detail. The larger the organization the more effective the strategy. Personnel departments can be so tiresome about "firing for cause." They can make managers squirm and be called to answer pointed questions before their bosses. They also demand mega detail and paperwork.

Can you win your boss over? Can you show you are firmly on his or her side? Probably not, but you can play a delaying action until it's convenient for you to move. Your boss may become discouraged and decide to get along with you and give up the project of replacing you. However, it will always be uncomfortable for both of you. If you think you can outlast this boss, and you really like the company, a transfer is preferable. Going to work for a competitor until your boss sinks would be next best. Sitting quietly and trying to wait it out is the last choice you should consider. You could be working productively and zestfully somewhere else.

4. Your boss is a perfectionist and you're not perfect. You don't make any more mistakes than anyone else, just too many for him/her. You can reduce the number of errors, but that generally doesn't help because perfectionists judge more by whether or not you are emotionally committed to the holy grail of perfection than by the win/loss score. You can generally deflect damage to your career by forcing your boss to specify what his/her ideas of perfection are and in which areas it's most important. Even a perfectionist must compromise occasionally. However, a perfectionist is less likely to cause major damage, because people, knowing his/her nature, reduce his credibility by 10 percent up front. The grapevine can help. Don't complain about the nitpicking. Question. "Why do you suppose Dave is so anal retentive? Do you suppose Dave is that careful because he's worried about his boss? Was he burned in the past?" Gently cover all of Dave's peculiarities.

5. You've acquired too much political power. You know too many people and too many of them owe you. Unless your boss undercuts you, your informal power will continue to grow. You'll be in a stronger position than your boss, and the boss wants to be the most powerful person in the department. Unfortunately for you, he/she doesn't want power enough to work for it. The result is that you have the power, he/she the position. This is a standoff that eventually must provoke him/her to action. It must because, long-term, position power isn't enough.

Eventually you and the boss will be forced to mortal combat because you can't peacefully coexist at cross-purposes. Your best strategy is to underplay everything you do. Don't be seen gossiping in the halls. Don't be seen hunched over the telephone cupping your hand over the receiver. Eat an occasional lunch in the cafeteria alone rather than as is normal, surrounded by your network. This is only a delaying action, but it can buy you some time to think about your options. It's always possible your boss won't have sufficient power to keep his/her position.

With Peers

Your peers are far more likely to try to cause you trouble than a boss because that's their only weapon. How else can they help you out of the organization? A boss could, if sufficiently creative, simply fire you even in organizations where that's generally a taboo. Even in not-for-profits, firings occur occasionally. Still, you can commonly expect trouble from peers rather than the boss. Here are some of the common tactics that should keep you looking at your peers appraisingly.

1. You have a direct competitor who's not confident he's going to win a promotion on merit. His strategy is to win by cutting you off at the knees. Two women, Joan E. and Triva M., office managers for different departments in a *Fortune* 500 company, got into a spitting contest over scheduling. Both were in line for promotion to assistant director of administration for the division. Joan, unsure of her ability to persuade the divisional vice president of her clear superiority, began to spread rumors to Triva's subordinates. She did this by getting her secretary to pass on tidbits to her network. Triva, realizing that top management might eventually hear something that wouldn't strengthen her chances for the promotion, retaliated. The result was that management ducked the situation and hired an outsider.

Triva's best strategy would have been to confront Joan. She could have asked what was going on. What did Joan hope to accomplish with this whisper campaign? Confronting would have made it very difficult for Joan to continue, because the grapevine would pick this up. As it was, the informal system lit up, reflecting badly on both. Moral: Don't fight fire with fire in the informal system. Confront the person privately. Dragging the culprit into the light of day focuses attention in harmful, not helpful, ways on both of you. Retaliation isn't usually the best strategy, because it widens the war.

2. You've aroused a peer's jealousy. She thinks your career-boosting tactics are questionable. You've merchandised your results while she's waiting for recognition. You've gotten the kind of recognition she's been dreaming about. People are not at all put off by your self-promotion as she is. In fact, you've got some admirers, some of them in top management.

This happens most often in service areas where results are hard to measure precisely. For example, Tom and Rob, customer service representatives for a hospital supply firm, did about the same work. Tom, however, let his cronies know about the interesting problems he'd solved. What caused Rob to do a slow burn was his feeling that Tom was violating some sort of customer confidentiality. He really wasn't but it rankled with Rob. Rob began to bad-mouth Tom and magnify his occasional errors. He even went to their boss with tales. While not critical to Tom's career, the pressure was uncomfortable. Tom had a choice: Feed the grapevine less information or bear the discomfort. No one can give an absolute solution to this one, because the key element is your tolerance for discomfort. Some people desperately need to be liked. Work is unsatisfying if this condition isn't met. For them, comfort far outweighs the value of publicity. If that's your position, your peers have an important, and timeless, weapon in dealing with you.

3. Your peer wants to even an old score. In the dimly recalled past, you and George worked together at another company. You were a smart mouth and used to tease him about his lack of tact. He's a smoothy now but your past behavior still rankles, and it shows in his attitude. The only thing to do is to confront George and clear the air. Say, "I used to tease you about your bluntness and apparently you're still angry with me about that, aren't you?" If he denies it, he'll have lost because he's saying there is no problem. He'll have to change his behavior. If he says, "Yes, I'm still angry," you two will have to seek an accommodation. Once you've talked with him he can't continue to punish you for something that happened years ago. This will work in any situation in which the past casts a shadow over the present.

With Subordinates

Being knifed by a subordinate is the unkindest cut imaginable, also very common in an era of climate surveys, employee evaluations of managers, and other instruments designed to torture managers into shape. Subordinates are almost always better plugged in to the grapevine than the people they report to. Remember our interest in getting our subordinates to work as information gatherers? They usually don't use what they know against a boss but, sufficiently provoked, they can. Here's what usually does provoke them sufficiently.

1. You were promoted out of the ranks, and the people who now report to you are former peers. Time is a major factor in your survival. Your first six months as a supervisor of former peers is going to be hellish. It can't be any other way. You're learning a new role. They're trying to adjust to the role of also-rans. They are testing to see if you understand your new role or if you are still just one of the folks.

If you put positive things about them into the grapevine, it may help the adjustment period. If you let them know that, much as you like them, work takes top priority, you're giving clear messages they will have to deal with. You're in charge now and you will set the ground rules.

The weapon they have is the difficulty you may have in shifting roles. If you show the slightest hesitation to take command, the slightest role ambivalence, you can count on their using it against you. You're on trial with them more than they are with you.

In the olden days, camaraderie caused you to confide several useful bits of information that would be acutely embarrassing if put into the grapevine now. Remember referring to your boss in less than flattering terms, as Old Shifty? He might not mind, but that's doubtful. If you said things that would embarrass you now, you should not go to your former peers and swear them to secrecy. If anything comes up through the grapevine, ignore it. Without some visible embarrassment on your part it's assumed they are indulging in sour grapes. In the future make no statements you wouldn't be happy to see written on your office wall. Moral: Don't expect cheers when you depart for management. The losers may decide to cut you up—or down to size. Give up the dream of popularity and get on with the work.

2. You have been unfair. You are only human, which is really no defense. You have favored one person over another. Of your two subordinates, Peggy is clearly your favorite. She's an excellent worker, easy to deal with, and she can practically anticipate what you want and how you want it delivered. Your other subordinate, Peter, while not bad, isn't nearly as good. You are always bending over backward to be fair to Peter, which rightfully irritates him. He feels as if he's the stepchild in a dark fairy tale. He also can't imagine why Peggy gets all the roses and begins to toy with the idea, which he shares with the grapevine, that you and Peggy know each other in a biblical sense. It isn't true.

Peter is just good enough at his job to make him difficult to fire. He also has some friends in high places who would frown on his being sacrificed. To mention why he was being let go, especially to mention Peter's rumor-mongering, would not hurt Peter. You and Peggy would become the objects of penetrating, unwanted scrutiny and speculation.

Confront Peter. Ask him what would make him happier with his job and more productive. If he suggests firing Peggy, you'll at least have a reading on his level of vehemence. Ask what getting rid of Peggy would do for his career. Ask why he thinks you and Peggy are involved. Let him sputter and deny it. Then say, "I'm glad we cleared the air. I guess I won't hear that in the grapevine with your name on it after this." If you don't let Peter see the risks in his behavior, he'll continue it. People will believe him. After all, he's close to the scene. Besides, they want to believe it. An office soap opera breaks up the boredom. Moral: Don't confirm, deny, or defend your liking of one employee over another. Contain the damage by putting people on notice that to challenge you will bring reprisals. You aren't going to be statesmanlike until you run for public office. In the meantime, it's office politics as usual!

3. As a new manager you have challenged or violated the organizational culture by bringing new job criteria and a tougher approach to the department. People who thought they had it made are worried they may be on the street. The grapevine has carried a date for the bloodbath and your boss is listening to the rumors.

Of course there were deadwood when you took over. You brought a different set of priorities and values to the job, which was reflected in how you evaluated what had been going on. Unfortunately, the deadwood weren't literally dead and they are working like termites to undermine your position. They've raised doubts about your competence, your politics, your values, everything but your eye color. They are keeping the grapevine alive with your exploits. The fact that you didn't clean your plate at lunch is passed on in hushed tones. Yesterday you left the spinach.

Do you confront? No. You have nothing to gain and everything to lose if you do. These people have a grievance. So far, they still have their jobs. You haven't made a single aggressive move that will cause their networking groups to wonder if these people are, just possibly, payroll freeloaders. If you get into the grapevine, you'll lose. You are too new, you are still an unknown quantity. If you get involved without allies and without the knowledge of the informal power structure that only six or eight months on the job can provide, you will have real problems. Preserve your silence. Discipline people when they don't perform. Let them position themselves as complainers without interfering.

◊ A FINAL WORD ABOUT CONFRONTATION

There are times when your best defense is silence. If nothing you say will help your cause, say nothing. This has two benefits. It keeps you from positioning yourself prematurely in an unsupportable position. It doesn't tip off your detractors as to the strategy you'll pursue. Both are important.

This is also the hardest thing to do, particularly when people ask direct questions. Remember, you're an office politician, not a candidate for election to public office. You can and should stonewall. You can push a two-pointed question aside quite nicely by saying, "What made you think of that?" or "What an odd question!"

You'll probably have to face the fallout of reacting prematurely a couple of times before you can stonewall effectively. You can shorten the learning curve by watching the way some skilled national politicians turn aside the questions they don't want to answer with a pleasant word and a smile. Only losers get angry. Seethe privately.

Chapter 9. The Politics of Nonprofit Organizations

Kathy M. went to work as administrative manager for a six-hundred-bed medical center. She agreed to take a 10 percent pay cut to get the job. After ten years with a *Fortune* 500 she longed for the simpler ways of a nonprofit. She envisioned less jockeying for position, less protocol, a more nurturing environment, and fewer overblown egos. Within six months she was interviewing with large corporations again, bitter about her experiences in the hospital. She'd found the politics were, if anything, more virulent; her co-workers were highly turf-minded; and she'd run afoul of entrenched power and the overwhelming pull of tradition every time she tried to make the smallest change. She left having delivered the single most scathing exit interview to the personnel director he had ever received. What happened?

Kathy had naively assumed, as most people do who've never worked for a nonprofit, that people who are engaged in a noble mission treat each other more kindly than those who merely pursue profits. Nothing could be further from the truth. Nonprofits are organized to circumvent paying taxes and take advantage of the IRS as much as possible. Otherwise, they do everything a business does and frequently more ruthlessly. In fact, the politics of a nonprofit is about 10 percent more vicious than any in business because, with implied job security, firing doesn't give management a safety valve for getting rid of nonperformers. They have to be tortured out. Unless you understand the peculiar nature of nonprofit organizations, you can be as disillusioned as Kathy should you go to work for one.

Nonprofits, especially hospitals, universities, social service agencies, trade associations and professional societies, and all branches of government, share certain characteristics that absolutely affect every aspect of the informal system and condition the politics. Unless you identify the values in those systems, you have no way of making an intelligent choice about whether you'd fit in and do well.

The Layer of Euphemism

Surrounding and connecting all communications within a nonprofit is a layer of euphemism. Because of the need always to appear to serve the larger public interest, ordinary messages must be packaged nobly. Hospitals write mission statements describing whom they intend to serve. Social service agencies talk about serving clients. Trade associations talk about advancing the goals of the industry. Professional societies want to show that they are highly credible and that only those who belong to the association truly meet the highest professional standards. Universities talk about an educational mission. The government talks about its service to the larger body politic. That's no problem, because IBM, RCA, and most other corporations talk about serving people as individuals or serving their customers and industry. The difference is not what is said but what can't be said publicly. The nonprofits can't officially talk about such things as making money or direct competition with the aim of putting a competitor (another frowned-on word) out of business, even in internal publications. This is partly a result of the relationship employees have with their institutions. While IBM employees are also sometimes stockholders and customers, their enthusiasm for the company follows a bell curve. Employees of nonprofits are independently employees and consumers/critics of the service. It isn't their hospital or agency. They don't own it. It isn't their mission. This affects the individual's relationship with the job. University professors have no trouble leading protest marches against the administration. Staff members of associations don't find it difficult to intrigue with members against the executive director. That doesn't happen in most companies.

There are major language differences. Imagine you are at a meeting of AT&T employees. The boss is up in front of the room saying things like "Our new microcomputer is the best in the world. When we get finished with IBM they'll be back in the business of making typewriters—and they'll all be manuals." The employees laugh and cheer and feel that indeed they are on the winning team.

Across the hall IBM is having its own pep rally. One of the marketing people is talking to her troops and, after a few telephone jokes, she says, "They think they've got a microcomputer, but ours is the standard of the world. When we get through with them they'll be back in the business of making equipment for the deaf!" All the IBM people cheer and, newly inspired, go forth to blanket the country with IBM microcomputers.

Now let's switch the scene. It's the same sort of employee pep rally but it's being held at Blessed Sufferer Hospital. The marketing director has brought his people together, and they're talking about the census (the number of beds filled at any one time) at the hospital. The hospital's chief competitor is City Community General. It's unthinkable that the Blessed Sufferer pep rally would include talking openly about arrangements for the early demise of City Community General. But that's what BS's marketing plan is all about, of course. There aren't enough sick people who can pay to be hospitalized to go around. One of the two will be out of business in the next two or three years. Each is plotting to make sure it will be the institution that will survive.

The folks at CCG aren't taking any of this lying down.

They're using marketing as a weapon. They're wooing physicians. They're engaged in every sophisticated—and some sophomoric—marketing practice they know about. The only difference between them and IBM is that they can't talk about it openly. A veneer of high-minded benevolence must blanket everything.

Associations have the same problems. They dare not point out publicly that they have more prestigious members than another association purporting to serve the same industry. Instead, they put a spotlight on the most important members with the hope others in the industry will conclude they're the better group.

The principal difference between corporations and nonprofits is that the latter must package every message in terms of its benefit to others. The hospital doesn't say it's working on cost efficiency in order to increase its reserve fund or to buy an expensive new high-technology medical gadget, which it thinks will give it a competitive advantage. It says the new cost containment program will serve the public good. People hired into that environment from business frequently kill themselves politically before they realize the heavy cloaking of euphemism necessary and the tremendous differences in language.

The Importance of Seniority

One of the things Kathy learned early on at the hospital was that seniority mattered far more than competence. This was shocking because she, like many people who've never thought about the issue deeply, had assumed that seniority had something to do with labor unions. It may. Unions are known to value seniority, too, but seniority exists and thrives far from the union environment.

Kathy had seen incompetents enshrined in several of the corporations she had worked for, but never to the extent she saw it done at the hospital. (This is not peculiar to hospitals. It's standard practice in every nonprofit.) She couldn't understand why the support staff seemed almost immune to accountability and dismissal for insubordination and nonperformance, not to mention the fact that they were filling jobs no longer wanted or needed.

Kathy tried to fire her secretary, or at least have her transferred to another department, upsetting the woman terribly and incurring the wrath of the personnel department. It was a totally unnecessary and damaging battle. Kathy lost. Had she done her homework, she would have learned that when people go to work for nonprofits they make a deal, just as she had. They agree to work for less money than they might get at General Motors in exchange for job security. Firing causes unrest because it's visible proof that job security isn't as absolute as the employees want it to be.

Job security, a primary psychological need of almost everyone who chooses nonprofits, means that even if your performance is barely average or even slightly below average, as long as you don't embezzle or get into a fight with top management, nobody is going to bother you. If you become seriously unproductive, your boss and other managers may try to torture you out of the organization or at least out of that department. This can be resisted if you listen to the grapevine. Your cronies will tell you what successful resistance has been staged in the past.

This seniority rule applies most particularly to support people. Secretaries, maintenance workers, clerks—all kinds of support people—have locks on their jobs. If an executive secretary loses a boss, whoever replaces her boss is expected to use her as his or her secretary. If the new boss refuses—political dynamite as Kathy found out—the secretary will have tremendous support from personnel and the troops to keep her job. She will be given the next executive-level secretarial position that opens up and her salary won't be reduced. Until a position becomes available she may warm a bench in personnel or count paper clips but she'll be on the payroll. Her new boss may have little say in the matter. Not being able to choose her own secretary rankled with Kathy more than anything. It seemed so illogical! However, it is part of the nonprofit culture.

Seniority is considered in promotions. A certain number of promotions must go to long-term employees regardless of job performance or managerial fitness if the rest are to believe seniority means something. In industry someone who's been in the same job for ten years would expect some behind-the-palm sniggering. He or she would be labeled dead-ended. In a university that person is seen as normal and "committed to the institution." These institutions discourage the fast track mentality and resist personnel changes along with most other change.

Fairness and Justice

Fairness is an important part of the nonprofit culture. Whatever action management ultimately takes, it will be weighed, patted here and there, sometimes bent out of shape, all with the single goal of making the decision seem "fair." Fair in nonprofits means that the decision was arrived at democratically or with the appearance of democracy. Should someone have to be fired, after months of turmoil and deliberation, management will work assiduously through the informal system to show the victim was given every consideration. Department heads will urge even hardened incompetents to resign. It's a way of making the departure acceptable to the troops.

Attitude Is Measurable and It Matters

Kathy talked in meetings just as she had talked in meetings at her corporate jobs. She talked about the bottom line. She talked about reducing personnel costs and trimming fat. She made everyone terribly nervous. They shared her goals completely, but to talk so boldly caused talk and worry for fear she really wasn't "one of them." Who knew what someone with such a different perspective and different values might do? Maybe she didn't understand the hospital. Clearly she didn't or she would have sensed that the newcomer's attitude was judged and if not found "supportive"—an ambiguous term for showing you agreed that management's goals and methods were the right ones—you did not advance and were unable to get the cooperation needed to do the job. To move slowly, making sure consensus had a chance to build, was the style that worked.

Kathy was clearly impatient with the issues that came before the administration committee. Why should the alcoholic janitor be kept on? He had already had two accidents that resulted in workman's compensation claims. He was sixty, why not offer him a deal to retire? The rest of the committee were silent when they heard Kathy's proposal. Although she thought her presentation was technically faultless, since it showed a sensible way to clear up a problem to the institution's benefit, it was not well received. The first question sank her. Another department administrator said, "But how would Jack feel about that? He might lose face and he's been such a loyal employee. Everyone likes him a lot. He plays Santa at the employees' children's Christmas party." It was decided to put Jack's problem off until another meeting. Kathy couldn't believe it. In any corporation she'd ever worked for his popularity wouldn't have mattered. Rent-A-Santa would have provided a replacement for the party.

In nonprofits the individual actually matters no more, and no less, than he or she does in a corporation. What does matter is adopting a public posture that says you care about the individual. The appearance that the institution isn't cold and heartless like a business but warm and nurturing like a family is important. In universities the students' interests are routinely sacrificed to the needs of an entrenched individual. A professor whose prime was in the fifties, if he had one at all, will be teaching economics. The university can't make him update because he's protected by academic freedom and tenure. He can be obsolete if he wants to be, and he has the freedom to pass on irrelevant, outdated information. If pressed, the administration would say that the professor had rights, too. Unarguable but it still begs the question.

This need to display the right attitude can't be ignored. Other skills do not overcome attitude deficiencies. Had Kathy included something in her proposal to get rid of Jack to the effect that Jack would probably enjoy spending more time with his grandchildren or playing golf, the committee could have gone along, assured that the cultural mandate to consider the individual had been fulfilled.

Credentials: The Absolute Arbiter

As anyone who's ever been in a hospital for a few days learns, all physicians aren't created equal. There are as many chronically bewildered, even incompetent ones as there are impaired professionals anyplace. It just looks like more because more people are terrified by the thought that even one underqualified M.D. is practicing anywhere. In business the incompetents bear the mark of Cain. In the nonprofit, incompetence is rarely addressed openly.

In a business someone whose incompetence endangers the survival of the business would be outplaced or fired outright. Although we're in an age of huge malpractice settlements, a doctor's mistakes would not necessarily lead to a loss of admitting privileges or, if on staff, to instant dismissal. Why doesn't it happen in hospitals? First, because in most cases doctors are not hospital employees but independent contractors, and second, because doctors will generally protect a less than sterling colleague.

In universities the level of impairment some tenured faculty are able to achieve and sustain is legendary. As long as they don't involve the university in a lawsuit—sometimes even if they do—they are safe. It's called academic freedom. The result is that the argument that someone is incompetent is no argument for taking action at all! Top management in a nonprofit has clear guidelines. As long as the doctor is licensed or the Ph.D. hasn't caused the university to be sued, nothing can or will be done. In the institution's opinion nothing even needs to be done.

Imagine you are a nurse in a hospital whose whole job seems to consist of nothing more than keeping a notoriously incompetent doctor from hurting himself and, incidentally, patients. His patients think he's marvelous. They think he's the original healer. You on the other hand can document—and have—incidents that have the risk management people breaking out in hives. What will happen?

Is he still licensed? Has anyone died? Is his malpractice insurance still in force? Yes. Then nothing will happen. If you complain that you're working to help patients get well, not prevent them from being made sicker, you may be asked to leave. Remember, a nurse is on the professional staff, not the support staff! Only the latter have locks on their jobs. In a hospital the doctor is always publicly right.

Have you ever wondered what role graduate students play in universities? They do the scut work. They grade the professor's papers—some of the more competent professors may give a cursory glance to see what the grad student is doing—and generally keep the professor from having too much contact with disgruntled students. Of course, there are outstanding teachers who grade their own papers and spend lots of time with students, but they are a minority.

Now, having thought about this, ask yourself what this does to the political climate. It makes a profound difference, because acted out in the university culture every day is one theme: Competence means nothing as long as you have the right credentials.

The Thrall of the Pecking Order

As any nurse will tell you, one incompetent, impaired physician will have more clout than ten competent hardworking nurses. One professor whose notes are so old they've had to be plasticized so they don't crumble on the podium is worth ten hardworking, caring graduate students with new and marvelous ideas on academia's scale of measurement. The most basic need of a nonprofit is to keep the pecking order intact. It's both the source of most political problems and the ultimate prize.

A few years ago a group of attending physicians got together to moan and groan over the latest mandates from the hospital's CEO. The CEO was forty, energetic, well liked by the board, and putting the hospital well into the black. He'd even started a program to teach doctors how to market their own practices, which was helping all who'd gotten involved. One of the M.D.'s, the medical director, said, "I don't know how we're ever going to keep George [the CEO] under control. He just doesn't have the right attitude. We can't get him out because he's got too much board [of trustees] support. He's turned the place around. Still, you know he's only an MBA."

A nonphysician at the meeting said, "I'll bet if you took George aside and said, 'George, you and I [the medical director] are equals in running this place. Let's call a truce and we'll play on the same team,' you'd have no trouble with him." A puzzled look came over the medical director's face and he said, "But George isn't equal. He's not a physician!"

The pecking order isn't just immutable, it's beloved and protected by those near the top. The full professor, although generally paid far less than someone with similar experience and training in business, doesn't mind. He has made a clean trade of prestige for money. In the university he's near the top of the pecking order. People have to respect his position even if they think he's not competent. The obedience to pecking order demands that once you've paid homage to those above you, those below you must do the same for you. There's never any pretense that this shouldn't be the order of things. In business his education wouldn't buy him that kind of prestige. He'd have to earn it with results.

In government agencies and associations this adherence to the pecking order sometimes becomes too obvious in implementation. The executive director of the association or agency head has a younger subordinate at his or her ear at all times. Like Svengali, the subordinate is pulling the strings. Still, no one who understands the system would dream of approaching the subordinate without the permission of the director. The director's high status must be honored regardless of his/her performance.

How Things Get Done

This recital would indicate that incompetence is running rampant and you should eschew education, hospitals, or other nonprofits. Wrong. Things are getting done as usual by hardworking subordinates who eventually hope to join that hierarchy. They're using fairly open, culturally approved manipulation. Manipulation is seen as teammindedness. People are often in jobs for very long periods, so that they may be falling toward obsolescence, if not already over the edge. Covering up and cleaning up for such people means that when you lose your effectiveness, someone who's sensitive to your need to feel in command will help you out.

In hospitals nurses don't contradict doctors. Often they don't do what the doctor orders, but they don't balk or refuse. If ordered to prescribe a medication that has been superseded by an updated version, the nurse says, "Of course we'll dispense Drug A for the patient immediately, but did you know Drs. Smith and Jones always use Drug B for that kind of problem?" Even if the doctor isn't all there, a red light comes on and he says, "Well, why don't we try Drug B this time?" The reason doctors generally get along with and trust nurses is not because of the similarity of training but because nurses tend to put the patient first and, often unwillingly, manage the doctor for the greater good.

Graduate students and secretaries in universities serve the same function. The graduate student will do some "research" that updates the professor and then sees that the information gets into the professor's notes. He sees that the brighter students are encouraged and the less bright ones are tutored.

The Political Fallout

The tragedy in the politics of hospitals, universities, and social service agencies is this: An overwhelming number of doctors, professors, nurses, social workers, executive directors, and administrators are dedicated, hardworking, and probably care more about helping people than is good for them. (These are the people most subject to job burnout.) They are up against a political system that preserves individual freedom of action often at the expense of the greater, organizational good. It makes risk avoiders of the competent and gives free rein to the incompetent, because the cost of blowing the whistle is the rupture of the political culture. Even if he or she feels no fallout would be likely, there is a reluctance to cause so many other people the pain and sharp pangs of insecurity.

A baby was admitted to the pediatric ward of a prestigious suburban hospital. The child's mother, appalled at the general conditions in the ward, including a free mixing between burn patients and children with highly contagious diseases, complained through channels. Nothing was done. She talked to head nurses, supervisors, even her child's pediatricians. She explained that if the place wasn't cleaned up she was going to the local network television investigative unit. It's not difficult to get media support and coverage in such cases if you know what the media want in stories. Besides, hospitals will sometimes do things when the public relations department explains the consequences of television coverage.

The child's pediatricians, both very good physicians, became terribly alarmed. They begged the child's mother not to involve them. They worried that the department chairman, who had the political skills of a radish, might retaliate against them since he could do nothing to the woman. In the end the mother acquiesced and didn't cause the stir she might have. In her conversation with the chairman of pediatric medicine, it became very clear that the pediatricians were right. He was unable to manage and unable to improve the situation. Revenge he understood. Why didn't the doctors fight? Because making changes in a hospital was nearly impossible until the recent and ongoing upheaval brought on by government-mandated cost controls. Doctors learned not to fight the system openly because it only aggravated them and the administration without changing anything.

The same is true in universities. If the administrative side goes into a nosedive, almost nothing can or will be done until a new president comes in. At that time the professional staff, especially department heads, will be expected to get on the new president's team or leave. The greater bureaucracy will remain unchanged.

Everything that is true of these institutions is even truer of all branches of government. Incompetence is entrenched. People are competent at risk to their own emotional health and job tenure. Consider the consternation with which civil servants greet new political appointees after every election. They know that many of the newcomers are not even minimally competent, need to make changes for instant media "scores," and have minimal interest in long-term consequences. The long-term government worker is often cast in a totally resistant mold. He or she must preserve sanity in the face of a value system that values competence last.

Why Do People Do It?

Why would any competent person go to work for a nonprofit, much less the government? Three reasons come out when you talk with them. (1) They sincerely want to help other people or work for a cause. (2) They believe, against all evidence to the contrary, that they will have job tenure or greater job security. (3) There is no other place to pursue that particular career choice. Nobody can be an air traffic controller for a private company. The diplomatic corps is entirely under the control of the federal government. Sick people are cared for in hospitals, most of them nonprofits, and students are educated in universities, overwhelmingly organized as nonprofits. It's as simple as that.

Your Choices

If you want to work for a nonprofit, this discussion shouldn't make a difference in your choice. It should make a difference in your language, your style, your attempts to work within that culture. It means you will go to work for the government, the hospital, the university, with a clear understanding of what's doable and what's not. You don't come blundering in, thinking the rules are going to change because you find them irrational. The need to put job security first must be respected, even if it seems both pointless and unlikely to be realized. These are some of the issues you need to keep in mind.

1. Secretaries have entrenched power and are to be cultivated even more than in business. Some of the secretaries
arrived before you came and will probably outlast you. Winning them to your side is necessary for mere survival, not
to mention any hope for advancement. Because secretaries
have a lock on a particular job, the secretary may train the
new bosses who rotate into that slot. The secretary to the
chairman of Obstetrics and Gynecology may have been
through three chairmen in her twenty-five-year career.
She understands how to make the system work. If the
chairman needs something, she brokers that need. As a
result, after a new chairman has been in office a few
months you'll often hear him say, "Don't let's get into that.
Someone tried it a few years ago. Besides, Hazel [the sec-
retary] gets upset if the subject is even mentioned!" Who's
really running the show? As long as she doesn't insist on
being called chairwoman she has a free hand. The new
chairman doesn't really know what his role is anyway. The
extent of his management training may be a two-day sem-
inar. She teaches him what to do, whom to do it with, what
to say. Entrenched power, in this instance, prevents any
kind of precipitous change, sometimes any change at all.
It's an interesting footnote that as more professional
women move into management, powerful secretaries in institutions give them far more trouble than men. Women
managers are a threat to women secretaries because
women have trouble manipulating women. You'll hear secretaries talking among themselves about never working for
a woman.

2. If you're working in a university or a hospital, you must
treat those at the top of the pecking order as if you sincerely
believed they were your professional betters. This is especially important when it's not true and you know it's not
true. To try to inject reality at this point would rupture the
structure. It wouldn't really change the pecking order, and
it threatens everyone else who's trying to rise. If doctors
aren't at the apex of power in the hospital and able to do as

they please, why are the interns and residents working so hard? If professors can't goldbrick, what's the point of the graduate student working for her less-than-minimum-wage stipend? Both groups believe they are "paying their dues." Challenge that and the people who are hurt are those who haven't made it yet. They'll fight back.

3. More is done through the informal system. If you're not good at political brokering through the system, you'll have problems. You can't demand or even ask forcefully. You have to barter and stroke and generally work through the system, satisfying myriad constituencies along the way. If you want a major change in a university, that change may be hostage to someone else's insecurities. You may have to promise no change in one department to be able to lop off an unproductive program in another. You may have to let one college have a highly visible visiting professor, in order to get rid of several untenured, but nonethless entrenched, nonperformers. All this would be settled over coffee or jogging or tennis or on the racketball court (women aren't as visible in management on the nonprofit side) before any memo is issued. What is different here from similar situations in business is that no memo announcing a meeting to consider a problem would be issued until after a solution had been brokered. The meeting would be held to ratify brokered decisions, not called to discuss the problem.

4. You can't harp on productivity at the expense of the individual. Consideration for the individual must be given lip service. You may net out the same way. The incompetent doctor may be forced to retire or become a "consultant," but his feelings have got to be considered. Try for public exposure of his incompetence and you'll be the loser. Remember, you are living in the land where security reigns supreme. These people don't want flash and drama. They don't particularly want truth. They want peace, quiet, and, above all, safety.

Productivity is not a safe issue. One of the greatest shocks a hospital administrator could have would be moving from a nonprofit hospital to one of the for-profit hospital chains. It would challenge all of his/her assumptions about getting things done. Doctors don't have as much control in for-profit hospitals, because there are demanding owners who have a very different view of productivity. They have a different view of service. There aren't many for-profit hospitals but the number is growing.

5. You would learn to torture the people whom you wanted to leave. You would always stage the battle on security issues. That is, if you kept threatening an entrenched employee (subtly, of course) with a transfer to a different, less desirable department or a change in hours, in order to make him/her live by the rules (such as arriving punctually), the person might eventually seek employment across town. However, you'd work hard to get your target to come to that decision.

6. You would have to memorize the mission statement or statement of purpose of the organization and then package the simplest change or acquisition within that. This is tedious, although necessary and effective. If you worked for a hospital run by a religious order dedicated to the poor, you might find it difficult to get a heart transplant unit going unless a few poor people might benefit, other than merely being donors. A high technology unit would have to be justified by showing that it could be expensed in such a way as to benefit some poor people. Even if poor people had long since decided to seek medical care elsewhere, you'd have to mention them in any serious proposal. You might rail at the hypocrisy of this, especially with the cost of heart transplants in the $200,000 range, but you would have to do it anyway.

7. You would learn to preserve appearances at all costs. Even if the few nuns of the founding order still living near the hospital or agency were entirely senile and had nothing to do with the day-to-day running of the institution, they'd have to be trotted out on public occasions. They couldn't be ignored. The public must see the institution as existing for the greater glory of whoever started it—and God. If this seems cynical, consider the number of universities begun by religious orders whose ranks of religious are so thin they couldn't fill the five top posts. Ignore their need to feel they still have control and influence at your own peril. There is a fine line between hypocrisy and honoring tradition, and that line is fuzzy.

8. You would learn to make individual members of your constituency look good, submerging your ego in the process. Particularly in associations there is a love/hate relationship between paid staff and the membership's elected representatives. The staff is paid to guide, implement, and support the policies of the board of the association or society. That's far more complicated than it looks. The members would like to do more of the actual work themselves many times, but they have paid jobs that preclude this. They also want rigid protocol so they can enjoy the perks of serving the association. They want the staff to provide respect, even if they are the most hopelessly crude, under- or uneducated people you've ever met. Executive directors and managers can be called on to raise bail money, get a dunderhead into college, arrange a last-minute dinner at the Four Seasons, keep a fretful wife occupied, virtually anything you can imagine that's legitimate—and in some associations things that aren't. You don't get credit, you give it. Unless you can give yourself strong ego support, this kind of situation can be trying.

A Career in Nonprofits

To advance your career in nonprofits you need to consider four pieces of political advice. These would apply to working in business but not as absolutely.

1. Pick your fights carefully. Don't go after the nonessential. Even if a secretary is clearly unable to do the job, is her nonperformance so grave it's worth making an issue of? If the head of operations has been there twenty-five years but ceased working actively after year fifteen, what hospital function is being endangered? If the convention planning coordinator for the association always picks chicken for formal banquets, is it worth attacking or do you leave the food on your plate and assuage your feelings and palate in a French restaurant later?

You have a limited amount of goodwill built up with co-workers. Since everyone's needs must be considered, you can't afford to offend anyone needlessly. Needlessly really means offend them at all.

2. You must provide all the strokes your ego needs yourself. Your job is to stroke other people's egos. If you know you've done a good job for the organization, tell yourself so. Don't expect others to do so. That reduces the sense of high purpose because you don't seem selfless and dedicated. This is especially important in hospitals and universities if you're in a staff job, wherever perched on the ladder.

3. Negotiate everything. Broker all decisions. Seek consensus on large and small issues. It rarely matters how much time is consumed, because this is an important style issue in nonprofits. The theory is that since people aren't getting full market salaries for their work, we must make them feel important by getting them involved in decision making. We may run things very autocratically but we must sell our decisions. That means that without money as an incentive, you'll also need negotiation as a motivator. You can't promise a hefty raise but you can stroke egos.

4. Support the weak. It's an unbeatable political strategy. It's squarely within the nonprofit tradition and it really builds political capital. You must appear always to have on your mental agenda some ideas to help the poor, the sick, the abused, whatever your cause is. Even if someone is trying to get you, if you've done more for your organization's principles and constituency, you will shine. You don't have to believe in the principles, just get results.

If you decide to work for a nonprofit, keep in mind that reentry into the business world can be tough should you find your grand experiment less than enthralling. You have to keep up both contacts and visibility simply because so many businesses have very low opinions of the people hired by nonprofits. It's probably caused by businesses' allergic and often knee-jerk reaction to both job-security- and seniority-minded people. The idea is to keep your industry co-workers aware that you're getting results. You are in a different ball game but you've still got the bottom line in mind.

◊ WHEN WEAKNESS IS A POLITICAL STRENGTH

In every nonprofit there lurk a few people who force others to take care of them. There is the secretary whose feelings have to be tiptoed around. There is the janitor whose on-the-job tippling has to be ignored. There are the neurotic manager and the temperamental clerk. These people use their personal weaknesses to build power within a system that puts nurturing above productivity. They amass power in proportion to the desire of managers within the system to avoid conflict. As long as a seamless work environment is preferred, they'll have power. For anyone moving from private business to the nonprofit sector, this is the most difficult obstacle to success. Career changers move through three stages, if they don't wipe out and return to business. First is denial. "This can't really be going on." Next is fight. "I'm going to see if I can't get rid of that person." Finally, acceptance. "Let's get on with the job. It's not that big a deal."

Chapter 10. Suing for Peace:
What to Do When You Lose

No one wins 100 percent of the time in the political wars. If this seems obvious, why do so many people, some innocent, some less so, have to be dragged kicking and screaming from the office? It's not necessary. Firing isn't fatal. We've already talked about the importance of selecting a company in which you and they share values, not war over them. Sometimes firing is a very positive thing if it gets you moving in the right direction. You will get another, often better, job. This is particularly true if you've been in the same job five or more years.

Still, being fired or asked to leave is a terrible ego blow. It means somebody actively doesn't like you! We're assuming that you were not fired for insubordination or poor performance but for political reasons. In this chapter we want to look at the whole process involved in leaving a job. This includes being fired, being asked to resign (a distinction without a difference), situations in which you should leave voluntarily, and those in which you shouldn't. We want to explore when the company may compensate you for your pain and their guilt and when that's unlikely. We'll also look at how to leave with style, flags flying. There's no need to adopt the whipped dog look just because you're a political refugee. Finally, we'll look at that all-important question: What do you tell the next employer to explain your departure? A convincing explanation alleviates about 50 percent of the pain and anxiety of forcible separation for most people.

When to Depart

Most people instinctively resist when someone tries to pressure them into leaving. It's probably useful most of the time but may not always be the best strategy. Resistance can use up as much energy as aggression, and it's a wholly negative process. Digging in your heels can retard your career, especially if you should be moving on. How can you tell if this is the case?

1. Your job has been gutted. There's no other explanation for what's happened, despite your efforts to explain it. Your boss has gradually, over a period of three to six months, taken away important segments of your job. You used to be responsible for the company's annual executive retreat. This involved eighty-five top-level people in four divisions. It took about two months of nearly full-time effort and ten hours a month the rest of the year.

One day your boss said, "I've decided to let Harry have a crack at the annual retreat. You've been doing a fine job, but I want someone in the wings who also knows how to do it." You argued that your experience made it more cost-effective for you to do it. You'd found all of the shortcuts, you knew all the people. Your boss was adamant. Harry took over the retreat.

A month later your boss gave Shirley the part of your job that involved planning new employee orientation programs for the department. That involved about ten hours a month. You were also taken off the company-wide task force, which had made you highly visible outside the department.

None of this would be a problem or cause you to suspect you were a potential victim except that you weren't given any replacement assignments. You are now spending about 30 percent of your time sitting on your thumbs, reading trade publications. When you asked your boss for another assignment he said, "There really isn't anything I can give you right now but I'll get back to you."

You can wait until you are diligently working at nothing forty hours a week, or you can recognize what's going on and take action. When a boss reassigns pieces of your job, he or she is giving definite signals that someone, probably the boss, wants you to go. You can access the grapevine for an explanation. You can let everyone know how productive you've been on every assignment. You can fight back by finding other productive work to do. That will make it almost impossible for the boss to fire you immediately, but down the road the whole process of reassignment can be repeated.

This happens most often in service businesses. The reason this tactic is used is twofold. The boss has no remotely legitimate reason to get rid of the employee. Firing would be costly or create political difficulties for the boss. We've explained that in not-for-profits, such as hospitals and universities, people can be left doing nothing for years. It's not particularly stigmatizing either, because other employees know the idle one is a victim. It's most common when a boss is also underemployed and rearranging things is all he or she has to do.

If you find yourself in this spot, you have several possible strategies. You could access the grapevine for information about your boss's past. This may have happened to several other people. It may be a pattern, this boss's preferred way of handling surplus or displeasing people. If the boss is firmly entrenched and his methods have been woven into the company's culture, you should go. He's gotten away with it before, what makes you think you can break his streak?

2. Your ego is being systematically damaged and your view of yourself as a productive worker is threatened. You've been on a string of unsuccessful projects. No blame has been charged to your account, but you can feel the doubts about your performance beginning to mount up.

Two co-workers specifically said they didn't want your help on a project when you offered it. The grapevine is saying you're bad luck. It's Kennedy's second law of political warfare that "they (boss plus public opinion) will get you before you can change their minds." This means that if someone is undermining your professionalism and creating doubts about your competence, it's likely that you'll feel less competent long before you have an opportunity to demonstrate definitively that you are indeed very competent.

It's extremely difficult to prove competence conclusively in a short period of time or with one dramatic act. Your first duty as a worker is to protect your ego and self-confidence. This may sound like psychological eyewash but it's a very practical need. If you begin to feel less sure of your skills, you are likely to make mistakes that under normal circumstances would never occur. Even more important, ego damage can hurt you as a job hunter. You'll come across as very tentative—as if you're not absolutely certain of your own competence. You'll appear to be distressed goods. That certainly won't help you get a top salary.

You can fight back through the grapevine. You can become visible to layers of management above your boss. You can raise visibility outside the company in the industry and make sure your name is associated favorably with your company's. However, if your boss is politically astute, he or she may simply decide to fire you. It's better to avoid that. The best strategy is to leave as soon as you've secured another job.

3. You are feeling rebellious over an issue. It may be the way your job is structured. It may be an incident in which you or someone in your department was treated with blatant unfairness. Your feelings now hamper your ability to do your job well. You find your principles are violated daily. At some point, inexorably and without your conscious participation, you're going to slip over the line from passive resistance to rebellion. When that happens you are likely to be fired.

A woman who'd been with a company as an executive secretary for twenty-six years was removed from her job. Her boss, with whom she'd worked for seven years, left for another job. The person promoted into his position decided he'd be happier with a twenty-seven-year-old. (This goes on routinely.) At this company, policy and culture dictated that once an executive secretary, always one. She, by rights, had a lock on the job. Top management, trapped between the need to let the new executive take control of his job and the need to be true to its values, looked frantically for another executive-level secretarial position. The secretary warmed a chair in the personnel department during the transition. She found a better job on her own and left. End of story? Not at all.

The other executive secretaries were forced to confront a nasty example of the real meaning of job security with that company. Since most were also in their fifties, they saw themselves as vulnerable. They began the sort of small-scale rebellions that would disrupt top management. The vice president's retreat was a nightmare. The wine was tepid and the food was cold. The president's new-employee cocktail party ran out of liquor halfway through. The fallout is still occurring as more potential executive secretaries hear newly embellished versions of the story. The secretary who left also shared with her old cronies the fact that she'd gotten a $200-a-month increase. The level of rebellion increased.

If you can't tolerate the way management is managing, you ought to leave. It's far easier for secretaries to punish their bosses, and be tolerated short-term, than it is for someone on the managerial or professional levels to try it. Executive secretaries are an endangered species and therefore protected. Managers and professionals may not be.

Professionals can find themselves in a similar situation. Top management may cannibalize someone unfairly. If the person seems to suffer more pain or suffers publicly, you may be moved to rebellion. Don't give in to your anger. You can't be sure your motives will be clear to co-workers, much less respected. You'll create insecurity, even frenzy, among the risk avoiders you work with. Besides, as a person of strong principles, don't you think your management has a right to shoot itself in the leg if it wants to?

4. You were hired to do a job that you simply can't do. You have the skills, but not the style or the interpersonal finesse that's called for. For example, you were hired into sales administration as manager of the department. You're technically terrific. Nothing falls through the cracks. Indeed, your boss, the sales vice president, has nothing but praise for those skills. However, an initially underplayed part of your job is spending time jollying the salesmen. You don't just provide administrative support, you're expected to talk with them, broker with them, help them iron out details. Unfortunately, you don't have the comfort level or people skills to do that. You give them an answer to a question and turn away. What they expect is stroking. "Hey, Joe, how are things in the territory? By the way, did your kid get into Stanford? etc." You not only can't, you are quite unwilling to do that. You see it as adult baby-sitting.

You should leave. It can never get any better. The vice president will eventually torture you out of the company if not fire you outright. You are in conflict with a primal instinct in most organizations, which is to keep the salespeople happy at any cost. Your sacrifice is no price at all to pay to do that. The salespeople will eventually begin to complain that you're "cold," or "too technical." Look at it from the company's view. If the salespeople need a warm, friendly sales administrator and that helps them sell more, they'll get them a warm, friendly administrator. They will always believe you chose not to be warm and friendly, which, in a sense, you did. You could have pretended had you wanted to do so.

5. Your boss and his boss are engaged in mortal combat.

However, it's not going to be resolved soon, because both are firmly entrenched. They have decided to use you as a whipping boy. You are being given conflicting assignments from each and told your job is on the line unless you produce. You can be fired since you are junior to both, have not built any kind of protective relationship with either, and haven't solid tenure in the job. You keep trying to broker between them. You work with your boss to whom, presumably, you owe your first loyalty. His boss thinks you should be his ally in the ongoing war to get rid of your boss. You aren't just caught in the middle, your job is being rewritten daily.

You could fight this by slowing everything down and trying to force them to agree whose work is to come first. You could arrange for them to come head to head by refusing to do anything until they agree. Both are high-risk strategies and rarely worth it. Talk about long shots! Would you really be willing to risk money on the probable outcome in such trench warfare? You have nothing to gain from this situation, because it's unlikely you would get your boss's job even if he were vanquished. The reason is that if your boss has enough power to challenge his boss directly, he's got staying power. The war could go on for years. You don't have time. Find a saner environment where getting results is the number one goal—or at least in the top ten.

6. Your work is making you physically ill. You actually asked your doctor for Valium. She told you that the stress of what you're doing is going to shorten your life. You're the best candidate for a heart attack she's seen this month. You've done everything you can to change the way you're doing the job, but situationally it won't work. Your boss has the same kind of pressure. It's just part of the business.

Go. This is the one issue on which we all net out the same way. If your health is at risk, only an overdeveloped desire to self-destruct could keep you there. Get another job immediately, stop tinkering with your present job, and leave. (See the section on "Leaving in Style.")

When Not to Leave

Panic is the enemy of good political analysis and planning. Why should you be put through the trouble and misery of job hunting when you like what you do and the company you do it for? You need to consider when pain outweighs pleasure and rationally decide your next move, not leave abruptly because you feel pressured to do so.

1. Your boss is torturing you for the fun of it. Her career has been seriously compromised and she is on the way out. The black hearse of the outplacement people is practically pulling up to the doorway. She's behaving very spitefully just for fun. She can't fire you but would like to see you driven out, just so you won't get her job. She is making things very unpleasant and you're not at all sure what the company's timetable is. She could be gone in a week or three months.

A different twist on the same situation is that your boss is retiring, under protest, within six months. The person he had wanted as his successor didn't make the cut. You are standing by, having been given solid clues that you'll inherit. Your boss is sure that if you leave, his candidate would be reconsidered. He knows he can't fire you but he can certainly torture you out, providing you agree to be tortured.

You don't leave in either of these situations. Your best strategy is to raise your internal visibility and fight back through the grapevine. Every mistake you've seen your superior make since you've worked together can be dredged up and tossed into the pot. You won't be sorry. This may be your only chance to settle the score before you have to take over. Then you'll be vulnerable because, if you behave badly, your subordinates can do the same thing to you!

2. Your boss and top management are engaged in a struggle to the death but nobody shows any signs of dying! They involve you in the war, make your life miserable, but there's no short-term solution. In fact, the whole contest is so long-standing—it was going on when you arrived, although you didn't know it—the reason they're in conflict has long since left the grapevine. Even the senior secretaries can't remember. You're in no immediate danger unless death by tedium is counted as a danger.

Don't leave unless your actual performance begins to suffer. What you must not do is panic and thrash around. If the grapevine really validates that this situation is normal, you don't move on except on your own timetable and learning curve. If you are enhancing your skills and getting the kind of experience that will allow you to get a higher-level job somewhere else, stick with it. You won't be fired unless you do something that takes the combatants' attention from their war. Remember, they are enjoying themselves tremendously. Otherwise they would have resolved the conflict years ago.

3. A co-worker has developed and is exhibiting an open, vengeful dislike of you. You're not sure why. However, this co-worker has management's ear and even though she's not making any headway now, who can predict the future?

Are you performing? Are your contacts and alliances being fully maintained? Would the grapevine give you notice if top management began to buy her line? If so, don't leave now. Fight back with questions, not statements. Say to another co-worker, "What do you suppose has put Molly's nose out of joint? She seems so touchy." If it's a man who's doing this, ask if he's having marital or financial problems. If the culprit finds out through the grapevine that you intend to fight back, he or she will have a choice. He or she can turn visibly aggressive, giving you something concrete to deal with, or he or she can mute it. The smart money is that he or she will mute it.

A co-worker can't usually do you much damage unless

you go along. Even if you were planning to leave soon, you still should fight back today. Your reputation will follow you—sometimes precede you—to the next job.

4. Your job is making you deeply anxious. It's affecting your family and social life. You never realized until recently how much you like structure. You don't insist on reinforced steel, but it has to be tighter than "Who knows who's responsible for this? Just do what you can."

Are you performing? Is the work getting done appropriately? Is your anxiety caused by fear of failure or fear in general? If you're worried about your performance, but objectively you know things are actually going well, you have several choices. You can begin immediately searching for a different job. You can set a timetable for when you will begin your search. Or you can do nothing.

All of these solutions have risks. Your anxiety may increase. You may adjust to whatever makes you anxious. The most important thing is to keep the job rolling. If you've been very anxious for more than six months, you should consider carefully what you've done to reduce your anxious feelings. If you've simply reacted and done nothing, you shouldn't leave until you take some positive action. If you run away without fighting your feelings, how can you be sure the same thing won't happen on the next job?

5. The problem that's causing you trouble is temporary, although you are worried about its possible forever overtones. You have a particularly difficult assignment that keys right into your boss's insecurities. Your relationship with him is deteriorating. None of the things you've done in the past that pleased him work right now. He's on your back to improve but isn't saying specifically how he wants you to improve.

Many people panic and run when a boss's attitude changes. This generally happens when the source of the difficulty can't be identified. In our example you know the reason. It's not a good idea to leave before the project is completed unless it is a very long-term assignment and you are certain that finishing it won't put things back to normal. Leaving at the wrong time might endanger your reference because you'd be walking out in the middle of a job. You may have to tough it out and suffer the discomfort. Unless you're in danger of being fired for nonperformance, stick it out.

When You're Officially Fired

The war was spirited but brief and you lost. You were called in and told you were out. You may have been offered an explanation, but if the reasons were political, it won't make sense anyway. Even if you were told it was your incompetence, you'll know it was actually a political act if you're told any of the following.

1. "You just didn't fit in around here." That means you're stylistically different from the majority. This is the favorite line in service businesses. It may also mean your boss made a mistake in hiring you and this is how he/she avoids acknowledging it.

2. "You can't get along with people." That means you didn't impress the people who count. Your conclusion should be to screen more carefully the next group you work with. It's possible you don't work well with certain personality types. That's worth knowing so you can make better job choices.

3. "We're restructuring and your job is being eliminated." That's probably true. Truer still is that no one valued you enough to find a new spot for you. Restructuring is a favorite way to eliminate hiring mistakes and the politically impaired.

4. "We're going in a different direction and your skills don't fit in." This is a diplomatic way companies justify getting rid of people they don't like. Unless the firm is changing from an accounting firm to a modeling agency, there's probably going to be someone doing a job similar to yours. It just isn't going to be you.

5. "The customers/clients don't like you." That may be true. What's definite is the company feels it can't afford to back you against those people. Furthermore, there's no compelling need to do so. You are expendable. Reread number 2 in this section. You need to pick more compatible clients/customers next time. You also need to analyze your style. Does it need surgery or just minor alterations?

6. "The other employees find you difficult to work with." Or "The secretaries don't like you." And why don't they? Could it be that most of them haven't done a lick of work in years and you're making everybody uncomfortable with your productivity? A company that is full of people who are violently against work has a long-term problem. Only for the short-term is it your problem.

Developing a Strategy

It's final. There's no way to talk your way back into the job. You've got to go. From a political point of view there are certain things you do and do not do if you want to maximize what they'll do for you as you depart.

1. Forget explanations. There aren't any rational ones. Furthermore, the ones you'll be given won't be particularly helpful, even if you can worm them out of the person who's firing you. Not pressing for a reasonable explanation may be the hardest thing you will ever do. Every part of you cries out for a rational, hardheaded reason for being severed. You'll feel you must have one because you want to improve in the future. Wrong. You have been given a rational, hardheaded, albeit unpleasant, reason. The people with the power to fire you don't want you to stay. It's that simple. It's purely political. Your work is fine and your people skills are good. They simply don't want you on the payroll.

The more you try to pin down your boss or personnel, the more you invite them to look for flaws in your personality, your performance, or the total you. This is not going to help you gear up to get a better job. It will weaken your ego, depress you, give you insomnia, and otherwise mess you up. *Don't do it!* Hearing about an obscure mistake you made in 1980 isn't going to be an uplifting experience. You'll begin arguing, merely convincing them they're making the right choice and helping them erase their guilt. You don't want them to feel less guilty. You want them to feel guilty as hell. To do so you have to appear to be acquiescent and unquestioning. Play the perfect victim. It also will confound them that you aren't arguing or asking for explanations. Do you know something they don't? Contributing to a generalized, rampant insecurity is one of the firee's prerogatives and pleasures.

2. Concentrate on getting as much severance pay as possible. Marianne went to work for a multinational food company as employee communications manager in July. On October 1 her boss announced the communications department was being reorganized. She'd just received an excellent review and a 4 percent salary increase. There was no possible complaint about her work. She was stunned, especially since she'd turned down three other excellent positions to take the job. She'd be on the street again. Her boss, sympathetic and guilty, gave her three months' severance and paid her for three vacation days.

Severance pay is a gift in the form of conscience money from the company. It's a beneficial way in which you will allow them to erase their guilt. You have no legal right to severance pay at all unless you have a labor contract. Many people don't understand that. They think there must be some legal protection for the unjustly fired. Not so. If it's the company's policy to give severance pay, you will get some. If it's not, you won't get a dime. What you can do is use the guilt your boss and management feel because they are firing you unfairly, to maximize your severance. If they ordinarily give a week's pay for each year of service, ask for more. What can it hurt? Say you'd appreciate the extra severance because this was all so "unexpected." Ask them not to contest your applying for unemployment compensation at the state unemployment office. Don't get angry. Don't demand. Show them why it would be better to satisfy you than have the entire ugly story turn up in the industry grapevine. What would it do to their image as a fair-minded organization, a place that's good to work at? (Imply these things, don't state them outright.)

3. Ask for outplacement assistance. Outplacement firms can help you get organized, get your resume in order, and make contacts, shortening your period of unemployment. Most reputable outplacement firms won't take you as a client unless your company hires them and pays the fee. The successful firms charge very high fees. This kind of assistance may be worth giving up severance pay for. Try to negotiate both, but given a choice, outplacement with a good firm is better.

4. Ask for written letters of recommendation from your boss and your boss's boss. Tell them what you want emphasized in terms of your skills and your results. If it seems appropriate, i.e., you won't ruffle feathers, give them a rough draft of what you'd like said. This is important for two reasons. If either is unwilling to recommend you glowingly, it indicates you'll have a problem with reference checks later. You need to know that before you leave the company, so you can circumvent it. If you are not going to get a good reference from your boss, you must get letters from other managers within the company or from clients you've worked with. These will help blunt anything negative your boss might say.

Second, if you get positive letters, it will substantially limit what either boss can say about you in the future. After all, if your boss writes a glowing letter today, when he's anxious for you to leave quietly, it will be hard for him to give a poor reference in three weeks. He will know a written record of his recommendation exists.

5. Ask for photocopying privileges and help from the word processing department. You'll have your resume printed but having it set up on a word processing machine could save you money, especially if your typing is substandard. You'll need photocopies of your job-hunting correspondence, so photocopying privileges will save both time and money.

6. Get your vacation pay and profit sharing when you leave. You want as much cash on hand as possible. Some companies want to wait until the next pay period or the end of the quarter. Get the boss to run interference for you on this with personnel.

7. Ask personnel about the group health insurance. Can you buy an individual bridge policy that will cover you until you get another job? This is important. Remember, a broken arm with a trip to the hospital could bankrupt you. If there's no way to buy a bridge, you'll have to buy health insurance on the open market, but you do need some.

Ask personnel for names of companies they would recommend you contact and names of their counterparts. If you aren't causing them trouble, they may help. At the least, they'll feel obliged to make some suggestions.

What You Don't Want from the Company

1. Don't ask to use your old office and secretary once you're off the payroll. Talk about "forgotten but not gone"! Hanging about the office playing the perfect victim isn't going to do a thing for you. You need total ego strength. Find an entrepreneur with extra space and the yen to fill it short-term if you feel you need an "office." Don't go back to the company. It's OK to solicit former co-workers for job leads by telephone, or meet some of them for a drink, providing you pick a spot other than the favorite company watering hole.

2. Any formal notice to the trade or general media that you're leaving should be coupled with the announcement of your new position. Ask public relations not to crank anything out until you give the word. Letting the world know you're available should be done informally, not in print.

3. You can't give any explanations to fellow employees. This is one situation in which the grapevine will wait breathlessly for explanations. If you've asked for no official publicity, you also need to insure there's no unofficial publicity. While you may be finished with that company's internal network, you're by no means finished with the industry network. You want to position yourself there after you've given your situation some thought, not as you may be gratuitously positioned by gossip and speculation about your departure.

Leaving in Style

Some things you do when you depart cause people to remember you fondly. Some things make you notorious. First, the reputation enhancers.

1. Even if you were brutally fired, write a letter of resignation to your boss emphasizing everything that was positive about the experience. Talk about what you accomplished, what you learned (you don't have to mention the totally negative things you learned), and how much you've enjoyed being associated with the organization. There must have been some good things; try to remember them.

This is blatant flimflam but also necessary. The least sophisticated organization in the world knows how to do one thing—it can file paper. That means that your letter will end up in your personnel file. You want that letter to be positive, not sour grapes. Who knows who may ultimately read it? Your image and reputation depend on not putting into writing anything you wouldn't want someone to read five years from now.

2. Personally thank everyone who's helped you and follow up with a handwritten note. It doesn't have to be on Tiffany stationery. A memo pad will do. Don't include your version of events, any self-justification, or any explanations. You want to leave a trail behind you and you want it to be positive. In this decade you have better than one in three chances of working with at least a few of your former co-workers again. They will remember your professionalism and your style. It will be in sharp contrast, since most people behave like wounded, petulant children.

3. If your co-workers suggest a good-bye party, request that it be held away from the office. You'll be in control there. If everyone waits breathlessly for you to dish the dirt, don't. Reminisce about the great times and spread a positive glow all around. Don't turn the party into a management wake. Everyone else has to return to the tender mercies of those people tomorrow morning. Why compromise their futures?

4. Leave your work in good order. Don't leave any inexplicable messes or unsolvable problems. Leave notes for your successor about work in progress. Leave the office physically clean. This will be remembered because so many people, once fired, just walk out. That's not professional.

5. Offer to talk to or train a successor. It's unlikely your assistance will be wanted, but it's still important to make the offer. One woman did this with no hope her boss would be interested. He asked her to spend one day with her replacement and as a reward gave her three extra weeks' severance pay and made phone calls to several of his pals in her behalf. She was employed in four weeks.

6. If you have a secretary, give her a plant for her desk to show your appreciation and, incidentally, to remind her of you. She'll feed it and the grapevine very positively.

There are some things you never do. You may be tempted because they'd be such fun. Again, don't.

1. Never discuss any of the juicy details surrounding your departure with personnel during an exit interview. If your accusations—and that's what they'd have to be—get back to your boss, it could compromise your reference in the future. So far, the boss may be neutral or even positive. If you give personnel a chance to cause him/her trouble, you're the one who'll pay. This is why that might happen. Personnel soaks up rumors like a sponge. They lack real power in many companies and will run to management with negative feedback because it makes them appear to be "in the know." Don't give them a tidbit or shard worth running with.

2. Don't settle any old scores before you leave. Don't give anyone a piece of your mind or any controversial advice. Go quietly. You don't know what you might set in motion by telling a co-worker what the boss really thinks of him. And what purpose would it serve? Let him find out on his own, if he wants to know. He may be blissful in his ignorance.

3. Don't threaten to spill the beans to everyone in the industry. How could that help your career? There's a loser as well as a winner in every political game. You'll be downgraded for your lack of style and sportsmanship, and it could hurt your job search.

Unemployment Compensation

Run, do not walk, to the nearest state unemployment compensation office as soon as you leave. Don't put this off. It takes them time to do the paperwork and interview you. You don't know for sure how long you'll be out of work, and your company has paid taxes so you would have this resource. In most states you can still get unemployment even if you were fired. Get the facts. Don't worry about filling out applications that ask if you've ever been on unemployment. That question is there to trap lower-level people who work six months and go on unemployment six months. As one personnel director said, "We don't worry too much about professional people becoming addicted to unemployment. If you're earning forty thousand, you will not be happy with a hundred and twenty-five a week."

Explanations

What every firee worries about most is not leaving or being out of work. Some are secretly relieved and joyous in spite of all the complaining they do. The real hidden agenda questions are "How can I explain that I was fired?" and "Do I have to tell a prospective employer I was fired?" One woman working for a company recently taken over by a company with a terrible reputation worried about the "stigma" of being fired. Since the company's new management was legendary for its excesses, being fired from that company was an honor. Other people in the industry worried about the values and competence of those who hadn't been fired! This is an extreme, but real, example of the purely situational nature of firing. The answer to these questions is simple. You only have to say what the company is saying. If the company said you resigned, that's what happened. That means you must check before you leave to see what they intend to say. Ask personnel and ask your boss.

Because of the recent flurry of slander and wrongful discharge cases, companies are extremely reluctant to tell reference checks that a person was fired. In many large companies it's a firm policy to give only dates of employment. They won't even say whether they'd rehire the person. That's driven reference checkers to try to contact former bosses rather than personnel. In many companies a boss who gives an informal reference can be fired. Top management is that worried about lawsuits! In medium- and smaller-sized companies, top management is less concerned. They may report whatever they truly believe.

Your best strategy is to find out what your company policy is and make sure everyone will give the same story. You want them to say you resigned. If there is one hard-nosed person, his minority opinion won't carry much weight.

To a new employer, your explanation can be one of two simple reasons. If you were on the job less than six months, you left because you realized that you'd made a mistake in choosing that job. Once you knew the job wasn't going to work out, the only honorable thing was to correct your error. That is what you are doing. If you'd been there more than six months, the reason was lack of opportunity to advance.

Personnel people are hopeless voyeurs. If you mention, hint at, or whisper the word *politics* in a job interview, they'll be off and running. It's a taboo subject. If you are asked if you've ever had political troubles, answer with a question: "What kind of problems did you have in mind?" Don't denounce your former boss, his/her boss, or the company. You performed, you left. End of your story.

Revenge

All workers who have ever been fired for political reasons share a common dream. The scenario goes like this. You go to a new company where your star ascends. Back at the old shop management recovers its purpose and sanity and your former boss is fired. He turns up at your new company, asking for a job. You have a choice. You can hire him and make his life unbearable, doing everything to him that he did to you plus using all the torture techniques you've since learned. Or you can say, "You must be nuts! I wouldn't hire an incompetent boob like you if you were the last person on earth." (Naturally in your fantasy you don't sugarcoat your response.) How delicious, but remember it's a fantasy!

The fact is, you can't afford large-scale and public revenge as long as you intend to work anywhere in the civilized world. You really can't, because your career is not a crazy quilt of a job here, a job there. After you've been working five or ten years, you will have a reputation. And you want it to be good. You can't afford, even for the supreme pleasure it would give you, to take revenge. Even if your ethics dictate "an eye for an eye," it's not good business. The tables could turn again. You could get enough bad publicity to make your name anathema in circles where you want to be a star. You could seriously compromise your future.

This is especially true higher up the ladder. Getting even is seen as the antithesis of team play. Even incompetent top managements believe it. They also fear that if they hire you, it might turn out that you have developed a taste for the pleasures of revenge. Who knows who your next victim might be or what might provoke you? Revenge is the highest risk game in the working world.

However, there are some legitimate things you can do that will make you feel that justice (remember, that's an inappropriate thing to hope for in business anyway) was served in some small way.

1. You can get a much better job. You won't need to say a thing to anyone but your former colleagues. They'll set the grapevine abuzz with the news that Patrick, so despised by their management, has just moved two steps up the ladder and gotten a 30 percent increase in salary at a competitive company. Such knowledge implies that maybe your former boss has problems in making sober judgments. Could it be he's not much of a judge of character or competence? As you keep advancing, keep in touch. You can make your former boss squirm for years!

2. You can warn off job hunters you meet who are considering your former company. You don't bad-mouth it, but you raise questions. Ask a prospect, "How good are you at political games? Can you handle deliberate misdirection?" (Or management secrecy or whatever the problem was.) You need only leave the impression that whatever they do there is not always healthy for employees. The savvy job hunter will look elsewhere. Most people are taught to ask about turnover. If you mention casually that turnover was very high, especially among professional and managerial people, the questioner will get the point.

One firm in Chicago has gotten such a bad reputation that it has begun to use out-of-town recruiters, because everyone who's been in town very long has heard from former employees it's a good place to stay away from. Since its alums outnumber employees about ten to one, there has been quite a lot of revenge. The alums have annual cocktail parties and congratulate each other on subsequent successes.

Finally, try to keep in mind that firing is often a positive, career-affirming event. One woman, fired after a short-term nightmare on a job, went into business for herself. The first year she doubled her former salary. Three years down the road, she was earning five times her previous salary and loving it. Is she bitter? She laughs all the way to the bank and has even made a small contribution to her former boss's favorite charity in his name!

◊ WHEN'S THE BEST TIME FOR SEVERING?

Personnel professionals have long debated when the best time to fire someone is. Should it be Friday afternoon at 4:30? How about Friday before someone leaves on a two-week vacation? The object is to get the person out, humanely if possible, with the least disruption in the office. Friday at 4:30 tends to be popular but has some detractors. Before a vacation is just plain cruel. What does tend to minimize the political fallout in the office is offering no explanations at all. Management pretends that the departed has been kidnapped or fallen into a well. The people who care about the departed tend to feel less anger when the grapevine doesn't carry any atrocity stories. It also allows those who feel justice was done to ignore the unpleasantness entirely.

Chapter 11. Sex and Warfare

For something that is usually so enjoyable, sex in the office turns out to be about as much fun as having someone do the flamenco on your spine after disk surgery. Office sex isn't fun but political dynamite. The problem is that nobody who gets involved anticipates that! Experience seems to be the only convincing teacher.

Otherwise sensible, sophisticated workers, eyes wide open, will get involved with a co-worker and wonder why their careers begin to flag. After all, they're still performing. Nothing has changed. They're being very discreet. Of all the miscalculations that people involved in an office romance make, the worst is that they believe nobody knows what is going on. In the early stages they may believe no one knows they're attracted. Wrong. If two people who work for the same company get involved, everybody who has any interest in soap opera (100 percent of the people in the company) knows. Before you get involved, or if you're already involved, you need to consider the political problems likely to plague you. An office romance may be thrilling in theory, but in practice it presents tremendous career and political problems.

Why People Get Involved

We talked in the first few chapters about the intensity and character of the baby boomers' relationships with work. They tend to expect work and the workplace to fulfill a cross section of personal, as well as professional, needs.

One of these is romance. The rallying cry of the twenty-five- to forty-year-old crowd, especially women, is "How can I meet people to date if I don't meet them at work? Look at the alternatives! Singles groups!! Singles bars!!!" They get a lot of sympathy because even the most conservative critic in the office has to agree the office is infinitely preferable to many other alternatives. What nobody says, of course, is that top management's attitude toward office romance usually makes Queen Victoria look like a libertine. Individually and collectively, they are not amused. They emphatically do not approve.

If the person in the next office causes your temperature to rise and you'd like to pursue—or are pursuing—that relationship, you need to think about the information in this chapter. A great deal is at risk—your career, your image both internally and in the industry, and, most important, your internal political alliances which ultimately affect your ability to do your job. "All the world loves a lover," but in the office it also can and usually does cause him, her, or them a tremendous amount of grief.

People of all ages who get involved in office romances think something unique has happened to them. They've met someone they can really care for. There's a rapport. They share the same interests. They're compatible. That's a fairly superficial analysis because, although true, it's not because of any unique attributes these people bring to the workplace. They're practically preconditioned to be comfortable with co-workers of both sexes. They were selected by the same management, to work within the same value structure, in a similar political environment. Of course they get along—they're practically clones! What's surprising is that more people don't get involved, not that so many do. There is a taboo against involvement just as there is one against two employees marrying. Some banks are especially strong on this, so their officers don't get married, they just live together.

People get involved in the workplace because they get

acquainted without the pain and artifice of the usual dating relationship. The relationship has time to develop a solid base of shared experience before anyone does anything overt. They become friends first. Is it any wonder that more than 80 percent of office romances end in marriage or very long-term relationships? These people have weeks, months, even years, to learn about each other under many different conditions. There aren't that many surprises left and those seem quite minor.

Since, at least initially, few are actively looking for lovers, the people who get together are fairly honest. You can't hoodwink someone you've worked closely with forty or fifty hours a week. That person has seen your warts, your anxieties, your vulnerabilities, and your prejudices. Overall, he or she has a fairly well-rounded view. These relationships may be dormant for years, and one day the participants raise the level of involvement. That's when what we call "love" begins. It's also the beginning of political trouble.

Never misjudge the intent of the people you watch get involved. They do literally fall into love. They are innocent. It wasn't their conscious intent. Therefore, feeling innocent, they tend to misunderstand the consternation others feel about their involvement. They're not hurting anybody. Only one in ten is married and cheating on a spouse. Usually that's a man and he's building his ego with secretaries. (Incidentally, he's also a candidate for a sexual harassment suit if the romance ends badly from her point of view.) Most who engage in serial office affairs choose partners outside their office in case top management has latent Puritan tendencies. Why feed the grapevine unnecessarily?

What about gays? Surprisingly, their romances, unless they are observed necking at the Christmas party, hardly cause a political ripple. This is especially true with men. Lesbians have more problems because both sexes seem offended. Gay men seem to be liked and respected by most women. The women certainly don't feel threatened. Many straight men, however, are still deeply ambivalent and

sometimes threatened by gay relationships. These men refuse to acknowledge that any such thing is going on and
actively work to build and keep good political relationships
with the lovers. For everyone it tends to be business as
usual. Think of the power this gives gays! Others will ignore every signal, bend over backward to be scrupulously
fair, just so they won't have to confront any unpleasant
truths. The same is not true in heterosexual relationships.
Everybody gets involved.

People who have casual affairs at trade shows, corporate retreats, training programs, etc., rarely have a political
problem. Even if they only indulge when out of town and
it's with the same person year after year, there is little
political effect. Does that mean we're endorsing casual
sex? Not at all. It's simply a fact. Casual sex, as long as it's
not done in the conference room with the boss's secretary
during a directors' meeting, doesn't disturb the power
structure or the politics. "Everyone is entitled to an occasional aberration" sums up management's attitude. It's
long-term relationships we need to look at.

Top Management's View

Top management's attitudes, confused as they sometimes seem to be about the business, are fairly straightfor-
ward about love affairs between co-workers. They're
against it. Even if they've been involved or are involved
themselves, they're against it for the troops. The reasoning
is simple. Love affairs make the working relationships that
surround the lovers unstable. They have a profound effect
on the power structure. They undermine some alliances
and bring into being new ones. They raise anxiety and
jealousy. They also cause management to review and frequently change its collective opinion of the participants.
This reevaluation is almost never positive. What can anyone expect? If you force top management to rethink its

opinion of you professionally, based on your personal relationships, you've preconditioned a negative response.

Top management has three issues to deal with. Generally they aren't talked about in boardrooms. They might be called the hidden agenda.

1. Will one or both of the lovers alter his/her business judgment or perspective because of the involvement? The lovers would vehemently deny this was even a possibility. "We're consummate professionals," they bleat. Yes, but management can't be sure. They are in a netherworld of the unmeasurable impact on an unfathomable problem. How can anyone be sure? Management has megaproblems when trying to measure results and productivity under normal circumstances. How do they measure such things under less tangible circumstances? No wonder top management prefers to avoid such problems.

2. What if the lovers break up? What will that do to the working relationships they've had? Will the business be affected? The lovers in question don't have to be key decision makers. Top management is always cynical, sometimes from experience and sometimes from observation. They know anyone on the professional staff or in middle management can cause near chaos if the romance takes a left turn, because virtually everyone will feel the need to side with one of the combatants. People who say, "Leave me out of this. I have no opinion," don't really mean it. They mean they don't want you to know what their opinion is.

3. Are these people concentrating on business? Of course, other employees fall in love, out of love, marry and divorce, and top management gives these peregrinations only a passing thought, unless whatever has happened is unspeakably messy. There's a simple reason for this. Whatever is happening is not happening in the cafeteria. It's not going on under their noses nor are their secretaries serving up the latest episode with the morning's coffee and the *Wall Street Journal.* A secretary agog over some news about Janice and Roger is going to mention it to her boss. The accounting people are going to scrutinize Roger's expense forms and may remind top management it's time to put out a new memo on the hazards of expense account cheating.

Top management judges men and women differently in such affairs. Are you surprised? Don't be. Top management is into rampant, sexist stereotyping. Men, despite liberation and the advent of the new sensitive man, are seen as weak if they're involved in love affairs that are serious. It's the Samson complex. Top management, even if their own pasts are not unblemished, believes that men who get involved emotionally with a co-worker are not as strong as the stoic, Gary Cooper types they hoped they had hired. The memory of this perceived weakness lingers after the romance has ended.

Women are still prey to the double standard. "Boys will be boys," top management reasons, but "the girls should say, 'No!'" Whatever equality women think they've achieved is purely imaginary when it comes to office romance. Their illusions certainly aren't shared by management. Women may also be branded as adventuresses. Usually this is not remotely true, especially if the romance is clearly one with strong feelings on both sides. However, it is what management would like to believe. Otherwise, they have to confront not only the disruptive effects of the relationship, but the fact that it may go on indefinitely.

What does top management want? They want to preserve the political relationships between people so they will cooperate but not become involved, possibly to the company's detriment. They don't want to have anything known publicly that would hurt the company. Remember the Mary Cunningham/Bill Agee scandal at Bendix Corporation? Agee was top management but it's a virtual guarantee the other directors didn't share Agee's sanguine, eagerly optimistic view of his relationship with Cunningham.

Speaking of Cunningham and Agee, it's clear that outright love affairs aren't the only thing top management feels negatively about. Cunningham and Agee swear they weren't lovers at the time they worked together at Bendix. That completely misses the point and begs the issue. Top management is against any intimate relationship, including very close friendships. If two workers, at whatever level, become very close, soul persons as it were, they are going to cause problems just as knotty and disruptive as if they were lovers. A deep friendship is, if anything, even more difficult to fight, because how can any company be officially against friendship?

Middle Management's Agenda

When Jack Z., a production manager, and Ruth N., the assistant director of personnel, really got acquainted, a great and enduring love was born. They were both hard-working, serious, intensely work-oriented people. Even after they began dating that didn't change. What did change was their relationships with co-workers. Within six months they were both thinking of changing jobs. How did that happen? Jack and Ruth originally got together because Jack had several openings to fill in the plant. They became interested in each other, quite literally, discussing job descriptions. When this hit the grapevine—Ruth's secretary totally lacked discretion, besides this was *news*—two other production managers began to wonder if now they'd get the dregs from the application pool when they had spots to fill.

After all, wouldn't Ruth send Jack, her lover, the pick of the availables? Each acknowledged that that's what he'd do in Ruth's spot. The fact that Ruth wouldn't and didn't was difficult to prove conclusively. The grapevine duly noted the other managers' concern.

Ruth went blithely about her tasks for a full two months, totally unaware that any question had been raised about her work. Imagine her surprise when her boss, the personnel director, called her in and began to question her about her evaluations of various candidates.

Why had Jack been sent candidate A to interview rather than candidate B? Was Rob, another production manager, getting a crack at the same quality—and quantity—of candidates? Hurt and angry, she asked why her judgment had come into question. Had someone been dissatisfied? Her boss, risk avoider par excellence that he was, said, "No, I just want to be sure everything is kosher."

That was not true. What he wanted was to cover himself with the other production people, not to mention their bosses. Ruth's behavior, although completely professional, was causing him political problems. People looked at him knowingly and asked him about the lovers, to his acute embarrassment. His peers asked unnecessary, anxious, barely polite questions.

You may think Jack's fellow managers were mean-minded, stuffy misogynists but their concerns were and are valid. Each person at the middle management level who hopes not to languish there forever has one agenda item. No one must be allowed to move ahead by any "unfair" (there's that word again) advantage. Having a lover screening the candidates is patently an unfair advantage. One hundred percent of those who've been in the position of Jack's competitors would concede that it's unlikely someone in Ruth's position would overtly help her lover. Why should she, when there are so many other things she could do that would not be traced back to her and still would give her lover a boost? What were those untraceable things she might be doing? Nobody had specifics and that's what really worried people.

Co-workers worry that Ruth will make embarrassing mistakes that involve them, because they realize she's being systematically cut out of internal networks by people who don't approve of such relationships, not to mention the pure hypocrites. Ruth's coffee group is censoring the news. They're mildly on her side, and they don't want her to hear anything about Jack that could upset her. The fact that his boss is not terribly keen on Jack's new enthusiasm ought to be passed on to Ruth. It won't be. They have a great deal invested in their relationship with Ruth. Romance may pass but they'll still be seeing her every morning for coffee unless someone changes jobs.

Paranoia may grip some of Ruth's contacts, especially those who work regularly with Jack. What news is being passed on in the heat of passion? Is she still a reliable confidante? They worry. Their solution is to gradually lessen their contact with Ruth. Radiantly happy with recent events, it may take months or a major crisis before Ruth wakes up.

The more solid Ruth's relationship with Jack, the more likely it is to damage both of their careers. As we said, a passing affair isn't very disturbing. It could happen to anyone. Nobody has to take a stand about a momentary fling. But once two people become a couple, everything changes. They cease to be independent individuals whose independence can be counted on. The joining is terribly important. It creates a new force in the politics because these people have a permanent ally in each other. It may not be totally permanent, but it rests on a very different base, and is a much stronger bond, than the usual alliance. This is also true of really close friendships.

Most middle management people are feeling the competitive heat right now. Peter Drucker, the guru of management, continues to wage war about "middle management glut," and other writers have taken up the cry. With that kind of pressure, even the sexually liberated resist office romances.

The Subordinate's View

Most subordinates, willingly or not, look to their managers for leadership. More than that, they look for clues as to how those above them should behave. They want role models. They want clues to top management's values. Any relationship or any event that makes the manager a less credible source, such as participation in a love affair that has the grapevine electrified, makes subordinates harder to manage. It can't help but work that way. Anything that undermines the manager's credibility presents a problem.

Subordinates watch for signs of changes in values or judgments. They are sensitive to mood swings. In the past if a man had a bad day it was because the day was objectively bad. Now, people speculate. "Do you think George and Rhoda had a fight? He's really upset. It must have been heavy, because he hasn't done a thing all morning!" The love affair is thought to have some impact on every judgment. Since no one can comfortably (and few would try to) ask the manager how the affair is going, speculation from the wild to the probable sweeps through the office in waves.

Loyal subordinates worry, and sometimes become resentful, that others in the company are laughing at the manager, and by extension, at them. They begin to explain things more fully, adding more detail on what's going on within the department to outsiders. This fuels the speculation already moving through the grapevine. Something must be going on! It must be bigger than originally thought! People outside the department begin asking questions. What is hardest on subordinates is to find that every other department has heard about the affair, but they've been totally in the dark. They dislike the boss intensely, if momentarily, for having let them be the last to know and thus embarrassed before their peers.

Subordinates have only one agenda item when any sort

of change is in the air. They want guarantees of stability. They want to be dead certain the manager isn't going to change—not vis-à-vis them, not in values, not in the direction the department is moving. Unfortunately, just when it's most important to stonewall and provide stability, the manager is changing, however subtly. But it's not subtle enough to escape his underlings. He's worked until 6:30 every night for years. He now leaves at 6:00. He always came in at 9:00 A.M. on Saturday. He's arriving at 10:15. Could it possibly be he now hates getting out of bed? All this adds fuel to their belief that things are changing, and subordinates who've been happy aren't pleased with any change, especially since they see this as "senseless" change. Literally! Eavesdrop on some loyal subordinate and hear him/her savage the manager who's gotten publicly involved. It's enough to bring tears to the victim's eyes.

By now you're probably looking at your subordinates with a withering glance. Don't. They haven't been bitten by the love bug. They're still worried about the mortgage.

Affairs with Clients and Customers

Men, as well as women, may develop an acute interest in someone who's a client or customer. This happens most frequently in service businesses. You are an advertising copywriter and you and the product manager at the client company meet and fall in love. What is the political fallout? That depends on how secure that business is and how discreet you are. If the business is shaky, top management will go out of its mind. You thought they were flaky before, you haven't even seen the tip of what's coming. Your involvement with a key decision maker, or just a decision influencer, changes your relationship to your own employer dramatically. Is your lover likely to have you fired from the account or switch suppliers? Suddenly you have more power than you did when you were simply doing the job. You also have far more risk. If something happens and the account is lost, for any reason, you are through. It will always be believed subliminally that you were responsible.

Top managements divide right down the middle on whether client/customer romances hurt or help hold the business. What all agree on is that such affairs are unpredictable and tend to be uncontrollable. Both companies feel they are totally at the mercy of the two individuals who are center stage. It doesn't help you move up to have been involved, however benignly, in such a relationship.

Has Your Judgment Been Affected?

You're involved in an office romance and you've spent some time toe-to-toe with the world, swearing on your mother's life that your romance has changed nothing. Your judgment is sound. The work ethic is intact. You are, if anything, working harder. You know other people in the office who are having affairs outside the office and they are the ones who've changed. Here's a quiz, just for fun, that may give you a better fix on the problem. Answer true or false.

1. You have greater enthusiasm for your work.

2. You want to get into the office earlier so you'll be free in the evening.

3. You've shown patience and forbearance with subordinates you've been short with in the past.

4. You've gone along with your boss on most of the big issues.

5. People think you seem happier.

6. Your productivity has increased. You have new energy.

7. You've cut out those boondoggles to other plants you used to take.

8. You smile more, and difficult problems don't make you flare up as quickly.

9. You've bought an attractive new suit, had your hair restyled, and polished your shoes.

10. You're dieting and getting noticeable results.

If you answered true to any of these, you've changed. No wonder your subordinates are worried! No wonder your boss and co-workers are thinking up ways to either lead you back to the fold (doubtful) or torture you back to reality.

That wouldn't be so bad except that the old irascible you was more serious about details. What you call an improvement everyone else calls change, and they don't like it. Can you fight this? Can you make sure no change takes place? Absolutely. If you're a professional, you will. The problem is other people's perceptions. They aren't buying the program. The unfair wretches are watching another manager having an affair outside the office, and he's getting off scot-free. You are paying.

Even if you don't like to admit it, you may have less will to fight their opinions. You can be lulled into thinking it won't matter long-term anyway. The problem is that it will. You need an objective outside opinion from a peer who's been through the same thing. If you can't find someone who is far enough removed not to cause you political problems, consider a friend who lives out of town.

The Politics of Sex

Totally without your intent, certainly without your acquiescence, your love affair is disturbing the relationships you've built up over the years that allow you to do your job. Your boss, peers, and subordinates are uneasy. That means their working relationship with you is changing. The safety nets you've put in place are weakening. Your coffee group is censoring the news so that you won't hear anything bad about the Loved One or about yourself. How long can it go on?

Here's the key political element: Unable to say to you through the official structure, "Thou shall not," your boss and peers are left with only one weapon. They have got to apply informal pressure on you in order to convince you to reestablish normal, uncolored relationships with them. They do this in a variety of ways.

1. Your boss isolates you. She doesn't say anything, you just get the news much later. This gives you less time to prepare for meetings, respond to memos, and review position papers and other data that you're expected to have considered opinions about. The reason this can unhorse you is that it forces you to respond in too short a period of time. It also forces you to play someone else's game. You are totally working from your boss's time frame. The outcome is predictably unpleasant.

2. Your co-workers question simple judgments. They want to know why. They want reassurance that you've made a rational decision. "Why did you pick that supplier? Last year we used Roberts and Associates." "Why are we going with that campaign? Last month you liked the other strategy better." This is terribly irritating, especially when the reasons for your judgments are clear—to you. If you show even the faintest trace of irritation, they'll feel attacked. Again, you've changed. "Watch out for Cheryl, she's on a tear." Whatever superhuman effort it takes to remain unperturbed, you have no choice but to muster it.

3. People question your long-term plans and commitment. Sometimes this takes the form of reasonably subtle questions over a drink. "Do you think you'll really be here five years from now?" It may be very unsubtle. "You're not planning to blow out, are you?" If your romance weren't public knowledge, people would never ask these questions.

This is torture because it diverts your attention from the job and causes you to question the quality and staying power of your assiduously cultivated political relationships. You may begin to think about leaving your job, even before the new romance that's causing the problem is stabilized. Talk about having your life in flux!

Your best strategy to combat torture is to wait it out. Unless you and the Loved One are hanging over each other at the watercooler and the water is beginning to boil, you can always stonewall. What are these people talking about? As long as you aren't constantly meeting your lover in the local watering hole or doing something overt, the grapevine will eventually turn to other issues, because it needs constant fueling to keep one subject out front.

Confronting the Rumormongers

Sooner or later—sooner is always better—you'll have to confront the platoon leaders in the informal war. You do this by asking them some blunt questions. Why are they talking about you and Harry? Is something going on you should know about? Have they complaints about your work? The latter is especially important, because they haven't any specific complaints. Your strategy is to silence them by shifting ground and redefining the game. The new game is they aren't supposed to talk unless they talk in specifics. This won't work forever. It won't work at all if you've done anything really public; for instance, you and Harry danced at the Christmas party and the lightbulbs on the Christmas tree shorted out.

You raise the issue of how much your cooperation has meant to them in the past. You're still available to help out supporters. Other people, unfortunately, will find your cooperation lacking, especially if they persist in passing these absurd rumors about you. (Don't say they are untrue. Absurd is not the same as untrue.) You haven't changed, why are others overreacting? This will work occasionally. It works best with people who long for nothing so much as a return to the status quo.

When the Romance Ends Badly

It's over. You and the Loved One have severed all ties. It wasn't a particularly pleasant process. You haven't even had time to move through the grieving period. Faced with the need to hold on to your job while you regroup, you're trying to reintegrate into the political process. This won't be as difficult as you might suppose. It even has some pluses, provided you don't do two things: Never acknowledge the affair happened, and since it didn't occur, you naturally can't and don't give any details of the ending. Remember that you've been operating entirely within the informal system. The formal system has ignored your alleged indiscretions. You can make this work for you, even go so far as pretending the entire flap was a puff of smoke, providing you don't say so much as one word about your departed lover to anyone. If you stonewall, at least some of your colleagues will begin to think the entire affair was overblown. Maybe the two of you really were just pals. That's what people want to believe. You tell them differently, and you are now speaking officially in the formal system. If you and the Loved One are still speaking, you might make your final act as a couple to swear eternally never to discuss what happened with anyone even remotely, much less directly, connected with the office.

Men have an easier time at the end of an affair because male co-workers aren't as likely to ask each other about affairs of the heart. Not that a man isn't dying to know and won't listen to the gory details, he just won't ask for them directly. (The stress of not asking probably accounts for a few heart attacks and the fact that women generally outlive men.) Women have a problem. Part of women being supportive of other women is rallying to help and comfort a sister when something goes badly. If you're a woman, let your mother, your other female relatives, or your college roommate in Des Moines play that role. Long-distance telephone calls, even on AT&T, are cheap compared with the damage you can do your career if people get the details.

Why is this unnatural secrecy important? If this had happened with someone outside the office, your co-workers would have been most sympathetic. Inside the office, someone has to be tagged with the blame. Remember, the grapevine isn't going to transmit just details of your affair, it's going to be judge and jury.

It's virtually impossible for the troops in general to agree that you did it to each other and both of you were equally at fault in the breakup. First, that's probably not true. Few things are perfectly equal. One of you precipitated the ending, and that's probably the person the grapevine would like to identify and savage. Second, fine distinctions, if it was almost mutual consent, are neither interesting to pass along nor the grapevine's forte. You may seek revenge, long to make the former lover miserable, wish he'd come down with a painful, lingering illness, but you don't do it in the grapevine. You'll pay politically if you do.

Suppose you've tried to be rational and think about the political consequences, but love has turned to hate. You want blood. You want revenge. You'd do anything to get even with your former lover, even at considerable risk, even outright damage, to your career. Get help from a competent therapist. The desire for revenge is normal. Acting it out is not. It means you need help. To repeat, it's not just your reputation at this company we're protecting, it's your reputation within the industry. Your colleagues in other companies will find the details of thrust and counterthrust every bit as entrancing as your co-workers do. You could lose some of the credibility you've built up over the years. Furthermore, your credibility would be undercut for a totally non-work-related reason. Imagine, all your years of productive work undercut by a short-term indiscretion.

Should you leave your job because the affair ended badly? If it's with someone in your immediate work area so that the two of you will meet every day, you may want to consider that option, depending on how uncomfortable you are. One man, involved for more than a year with his secretary, left within a few weeks after they broke up. His reason: It made him break out in hives to think of handing her work every day while she looked at him with sad, accusing eyes. Who needs that?

Leaving as a matter of principle (whatever that is) is something else entirely. You didn't do anything official. The official system, now that things are back to normal, can easily pretend nothing ever happened. If you and the Loved One can reestablish a professional relationship that's properly cordial and businesslike, the regular rules for leaving a job apply. You move on your own timetable and when it's good for your career.

What if your boss thinks you should leave, considering your recent "disgrace"? That depends on whether your working relationship with the boss has been seriously damaged. It may be the boss is just anxious that she or he will get flack from higher up. As long as nothing overt happens and the grapevine quiets down, stick it out. A few weeks of absolute calm may soothe the boss. If not, you will have to think about leaving. Honest discussions don't help. You're bound to be asked what went wrong. Get into the nitty-gritty and you'll hurt, not help, your relationship with the boss. He or she may have had only the vaguest notion of what was going on. Fill in the blanks and the boss will worry retroactively.

The Romance Doesn't End

You and your lover have been a happy duo for several years. The grapevine has ceased to talk about it and gone on to other topics. If you maintain the status quo, you should be safe, right? Wrong. You'll never have protection from career damage, because neither job is static. Let one of you get into a bind and the relationship will again be the topic of general gossip. You have to accept this and not appear dismayed. This is the price of a continuing relationship. Only you can decide whether it's worth it. Changing jobs may be the best solution for one or both.

Will your relationship keep you from getting promoted? If you're female, probably. If your lover is critical to the management team, you may be asked to leave. The company may feel it's got to have him; you they'd like to keep, but not as much. If you're male, the outcome is less clear-cut. Everything depends on how carefully you've cultivated and maintained your relationship with your boss. In some instances you can sound out your subordinates. Top management may want to give you another chance but will seriously consider whether you still have grass roots support. If top management thinks you aren't 100 percent focused on business, you're dead. Let any of your subordinates point out any aberrations in your habits and that's what management will think.

Love and Good Politics

It's possible to have a love affair and good politics under two circumstances. Your company is in a small town that, for a variety of reasons, is an undesirable place for single people to be. They talk a lot about the "quality of life," which usually means they have trouble recruiting stars who, despite protests that wouldn't fool a neophyte recruiter, really prefer large metropolitan areas. For top management, then, it's a trade-off. They have to put up with behavior they dislike on principle in order to keep a rising star. They'll be more flexible because they have to be. They hope you'll get married and "settle down," becoming a credit to the community. Such things do happen.

The second instance applies to scientists and engineers. For some reason, a romance in the lab has a far less disruptive effect than a romance in the front office. Two engineers can get involved with less backlash. The explanation is probably that top management, at least, considers scientists and engineers a breed apart, even if they are managers. Their work is long-term and more measurable. They appear to be isolated even though this is probably an illusion. Scientists can be very political but management, conditioned by its own provincialism, doesn't usually recognize this.

Are we suggesting that if you meet the love of your life, someone you're dead certain is the right one for you, you should sacrifice all for your career? Certainly not. Nobody is that political! All we care about is that you think about the possible outcomes up front. Is it worth it to you to put your career at risk? Have you soberly considered the risks? Can you survive attempts at torture by co-workers? It's also important that, eyes wide open, you acknowledge at gut level that everyone will know. As Dorothy Sayers observed in her novel *Gaudy Night*, "Love and a cough cannot be hidden." You might want to think about that.

◊ JEALOUSY AND OFFICE POLITICS

How much is the extreme censure of office romances attributable to jealousy? Haven't you ever wondered about that? You're spending warm, pleasant evenings with someone you care deeply about, and your co-workers are depending on Fido or Muffin to warm up the bed. It would be nice to think they're just jealous, but it's simply not true. Most people's response to romance isn't mean-minded, just wary. After all, you can see better stuff on television any night and if you get cable television, much better stuff! Maybe one coworker in twenty is jealous. The rest just have a clearer picture of the political wars that are about to start than you do.

Chapter 12. Managing Office Warfare

Sam M., manager of the claims department for a large insurance company, was called into his boss's office one Friday afternoon. Leo, Sam's boss, closed the door. "Sam," he said, "there are going to be big changes in the next three months. We've been acquired by our major competitor. I'm out in sixty days. You'll probably be kept—although I'm not sure you'll want to stay." Sam wasn't surprised. The grapevine had been alive with rumors that something big was about to happen, and he'd surmised it could only be an acquisition. What concerned him—as it does most managers—was how to manage during a major transition, especially one with so unpredictable an outcome.

Acquisitions and mergers aren't the only times of turmoil in companies. In chapter 2 we talked about both chronic and crisis situations that create company war zones and how you personally should react. What we need to address now is how you manage your job and your people when unpredictable change is all you and they have to look forward to.

Managing Your Job

What are any manager's priorities during periods of change? What should he or she be doing? We asked people who've been through it and here's what they said.

Uncovering Top Management's Priorities

Our example of how middle management's problems begin makes it clear—and this is typical—that Sam isn't being given a clue as to what present management wants. His boss indicates that his only concern is that he's out. He doesn't indicate what Sam is supposed to do. The most difficult task any manager has when change is imminent is trying to find out what top management expects middle management to do during the transition. That information won't be easy to get either, because top management, individually and collectively, probably doesn't know. If asked, they invariably reply, "It's business as usual for now," which given the upheaval in the power structure is impossible. They assume their subordinates will somehow get the work out. The question is, what work? Which projects are to be finished and which allowed to die? Here's how to get any information that is available. In the end, most of your answers will come from your own assessment of the situation and your judgment. That's why it's so important to look for information. Get all the guidance that's available.

1. Ask your immediate boss what he thinks your department's priorities should be. What does he want done? Ordinarily you'd get some straight responses. Now, you may not, depending on how your boss feels he's being treated. Nothing might give him greater pleasure than letting all his areas fall apart—an act of revenge for what's happened to him! That may be OK for him but it has significant political problems for you. Your job may not be on the hit list. This happened to an account executive with an advertising firm during a crisis over the loss of a major client. His boss, furious at his treatment, gave his subordinate totally wrong information. The subordinate, trusting his boss, carried out his instructions until he realized that what he was doing totally violated common sense. This happened early on so he managed to recoup. He's been an ardent internal networker ever since this close call. He was saved by the supervisor in accounting.

Unless the possibility your boss might use you as an instrument of his revenge occurs to you, you can be caught in a double bind. Your strategy with your boss should be to follow his direction but not turn off your brain. If you feel you're getting bad direction, and you know he will be out in sixty days. you'll have to stall. Above all, you don't want to go down with him because you failed to realize what was happening.

By the way, get a letter of recommendation from him before he leaves. Who knows where he may end up, or how much trouble you might have six months from now, tracking him down. Give him a good-bye party, off-site, with style. He's as much a victim as anybody can be. If you respected him, be sure to send him a letter stressing how much you respect him and how much you've learned from him. Offer two or three examples of what you've admired about his leadership. This is a kind, thoroughly decent thing to do. It shows you are fair-minded and you care about his troubles. Just because companies have no mandate to be fair doesn't let you off the hook. You do. Most important, your boss, if he's on the way out, is being shunned by survivors at his own level. For some inexplicable reason people behave as if they thought unemployment was catching. Your decency will be remembered. You will get a glowing reference from that man ten years from now. Even if you hated your boss, you owe him a written letter of appreciation. Stress the positive even if you have to tickle the truth to do so.

2. Ask your boss's boss what her priorities are. This is one time that breaking the chain of command isn't forbidden, especially if your boss is on the way out. If your boss isn't leaving, you can't do it overtly but you might, on purpose, run into your boss's boss in the hall and find out what he or she is thinking. This isn't the art of covering your anterior parts. If there's a contradiction between your superiors, clear it up now. You'll have enough to manage with your own people without your bosses getting into a fray. These are not ordinary times and different rules apply. You can't afford to go off in a direction that may create problems for you later even further up the chain of command or with the new company.

The administrative manager in a law firm in turmoil over the bankruptcy of its largest client assumed it was business as usual as the partners scrambled for new business. He didn't ask his boss's boss even though his own boss had resigned. Imagine his wholly preventable embarrassment on learning that what top management really wanted was for him to start interviewing outplacement firms, not secretaries and staff support people!

3. Consult with top management's secretaries. Sift their opinions for any clues as to what direction the changes are taking, and look for traces of consensus. What are they saying might happen? The longer they've been in the company, the more you should listen to and seriously consider their speculations. All that stroking you've done is going to pay off. If the secretaries don't agree with either or both of your bosses, listen to the secretaries! Don't assume that the pecking order means anything. The secretaries are uniquely positioned to give you advice. This was pointed up during major turmoil at a company careening toward Chapter Eleven. The operations manager, frantic as to which products to schedule for the next production run and unable to get an answer—much less a straight one— from his bosses, asked the CEO's secretary. She told him. She knew from her boss which things were likely to be jettisoned in the coming reorganization. Her predictions were 95 percent correct. Top management might not have done as well!

4. Find industry colleagues who've been through whatever has caused your current turmoil and get advice. Fellow sufferers and veterans are your soul brothers. What would they advise you to do with your bosses? If you can find your counterpart in a troubled company, the two of you can help each other. Don't take advice from anyone who hasn't been through whatever you're going through. The last thing you need is theory. That you can supply yourself without help. Networking involves sustained support and advice, not just trading hot job leads at association meetings.

Staying Plugged In

Your first impulse in a crisis may be to put your eyes on your work and never look up. That's a terrible strategy. You've got to spend more time accessing internal and external networks, even if you're working overtime as a result. Since massive change is in the offing, only the grapevine will be current. Any announcements the company issues to the press will be long after the fact, sometimes absurdly so. When Continental Bank was going through its financial crisis, they grabbed headlines one day by issuing a year-old report on who'd been responsible for the problem. Everyone at the bank was nonplussed because this was such old information as to be nonnews.

You need breaking news so you can improve your performance practically every day to meet a changing agenda. For instance, if you don't hear for ten days that the marketing vice president who liked your ideas has resigned, you may not find her successor and begin selling your ideas to her quickly enough. You also need to adjust your game plan. If the company is going to lop off a division, and you're part of that group, you'll probably be dropping some projects and initiating others. Nobody is going to really manage you as you might have been directed in the past. That's why you need to know as much as you can about what's happening everywhere.

Internally your strategy should be to listen to, but not join in, the speculation, even if asked. Pass it back by say ing, "I'm not sure what's going on. What do you think?" This is no trick, because most of the people speculating are dying to give you their pet theories, not listen to yours. Frequently they're just asking if you have any to be polite. It's universal that people talk far too much and too personally in a crisis. Speculation is best done by oneself far from the workplace.

Get information from people in widely differing jobs. What do the janitors think? What do the food service people think? Don't network just with peers and secretaries. You need an overall picture of what's going on, and that's acquired by putting together the jigsaw puzzle piece by piece. It's not a process of searching for The Word. In unstable situations there may be no definitive word.

Externally you want to talk to competitors, suppliers, and customers. Most important are the company's competitors. One of the ways you gauge how serious the problems in your company are is by finding out how many of your management people have resumes out to competitors. The panic reaction during any crisis is to send a resume to a competitor. If the majority of your top and upper-middle management people have resumes on the street and are eagerly calling executive recruiters, you can be sure they don't think things are likely to get better soon. If they are optimistic, they'll be promising resumes but letting the delivery slide.

Executive recruiters are a lot like vultures. The least hint of blood brings them out en masse. Call some you know and test their knowledge of what's going on. If they are geting a lot of calls from companies who hope to get one of your people at a fire-sale price, that's worth knowing. You may change your plans or adjust your timetable depending on how you analyze the situation. If people are talking but few are leaving, you can worry less about your immediate situation. Don't start job hunting today. If every Friday there's a going-away party for someone, you might want to call some headhunters.

Researching the New Management

Who are the people who are taking over? Where did they come from? What have they done in the past? Most people important enough to be acquiring companies or to be brought in as white knights have been highly visible. Spend an evening at the library finding out as much as you can about the company and the people who are likely to impact your job. This will do two things. You'll learn something about the company's style. If it's one individual, you'll learn a lot about his or her style. This will help you gauge your long-term viability should the worst happen. Second, you may need to reassure your people in order to keep them working. Facts are far preferable and far more effective than speculation.

Ask your industry sources for names of people who've left the new company. Track them down and make a date for lunch or drinks. You can do this long-distance and with foreign companies; it just requires a bit more diligence. Don't ask for their opinion on the company or an individual, ask questions about management style. You don't need to know if the new people were liked; being likable is hardly a top management priority, and the answer won't help one way or the other. What is important are questions about how the company does things, the background of its top management, company philosophy and hiring policies, etc.

One woman, carefully doing her homework at lunch with a friend from the acquiring company, found out that they had promoted far more women into management than her own company had. She left the restaurant considerably cheered! It's not going to be all bad news. That's another reason to do your homework with an open mind. You may find it's worth making an effort to perform well through the transition with thoughts of promotion opportunities firmly in mind.

Speaking of promotions, had you considered how the instability at your company might create career-advancing opportunities? If your boss leaves, you may have a shot at succeeding him. If not, you're not worse off. As the reorganization gets underway and the crisis begins to wind down, you may find you're acquiring new and valuable expertise. Think how difficult it would be to get the same level of experience in a stable company!

Retaining the Troops

You're not the only one who's concerned. When there is a major change or financial crisis, your employees are going to become concerned and you'll see it in their work. If they all begin job hunting, all pretense of productivity will cease. You need to confront each one and ask for a commitment to stay for a certain period of time. It may be difficult to get a commitment, but you must put people on notice that you'll be unhappy if they try to sneak off in the night. Your unhappiness could be acted out in notes in their personnel files and references.

Updating Your Resume

There comes a time when you'll have to grapple with your own job tenure. When do you update your resume? When do you begin job hunting? You update your resume immediately because you'll feel better knowing you've done it. You are ready for the worst case scenario and, being prepared, can get on with the job. You shouldn't feel compelled to send your resume to anyone who asks for it or to anyone who, in moments of panic, you think should want it. Stop and think. Just as you know who in your company has resumes out, someone will know yours is circulating. Unless you want it known, don't circulate it.

During takeovers, especially, this could be a problem, as the acquiring company may have its feelers out to see who's looking. Unless you have made up your mind you'll leave no matter what, why ruffle the new management? You don't begin job hunting until you've determined that you no longer can—or want to—stay with the company.

You don't begin job hunting as a matter of principle. Why allow yourself to be prematurely forced out? The company may give extra severance pay, outplacement, or other kinds of aid to those who help during the transition. When it becomes known that people will be cut, find out what kind of job hunting help they'll be given.

Job hunt only when you're serious. Why be scheduling interviews months before you're sure you need or want to go? It's silly and could make some people you'd like to impress angry. From a career planning point of view, you won't impress people positively if you're sending out waves of tentativeness and "should I or shouldn't I?"

Managing Your People

Sam might have problems with his disgruntled boss and the general malaise sure to fall over the executive suite, but they are small compared to keeping his troops going during the crisis. As any manager knows who's been through an acquisition, Chapter Eleven, or a reorganization, what management may try to tolerate, the troops try to fight. To get the job done, a manager has to keep people moving. The first casualty of massive change is productivity. Even if logic would dictate that everyone should be working at top speed to impress whoever should be impressed, it doesn't happen. The troops do two things. They spend inordinate amounts of time gossiping in a vacuum, and they assume the work can wait. Who cares anyway? The assumption is that management is scrambling for political gain and won't be scrutinizing what and how well work is being handled. As a manager, you'll have to combat these tendencies.

Keeping Up Output

The hardest job in a crisis, as we've said, is keeping the troops working productively. Even if that isn't your assignment from the company and in spite of how you may feel about what's happening, this has got to be top priority for several reasons. (1) Your life will be easier if everyone is working at top speed. Even if you have to come up with additional assignments, it's important to give them a sense of accomplishment and to prevent them from spending time exchanging destructive rumors. Your goal is to keep people so busy they don't have time to agitate each other with idle speculation and destructive gossip. (2) Destructive political games must be prevented and, if some occur, dealt with. If you allow the troops to think that all the rules of office politics have been somehow suspended, you'll have chaos. During normal times they know they have to work together and get along. In bad times they may assume they can now give co-workers their "real" opinions. Keeping them busy helps prevent some of this. (3) Work is cathartic. For everybody's mental health it's better to be busy. The uncertainty won't make people as anxious if they don't have time to sit and think. They may not even realize things are as bad as they are until the situation has been resolved.

One manager whose department seemed to be dissolving in infighting put up $100 of his own money for a productivity contest. He offered four $25 prizes, each to be awarded to the employee who most improved his productivity, and could prove it, in any one week. Suddenly his people had something to look forward to. Everyone, from clerks to supervisors, began looking for ways to win one of the prizes. As the rest of the company stumbled along, his people concentrated on winning. The scheme was so effective the new management offered to reimburse him!

Keeping the Troops Informed

One of a manager's most ticklish problems is deciding what and how much to tell subordinates about what's going on. Clearly, a general panic and exodus would create a problem for you. You can't and don't want to train an entire new staff just because your previous one bolted. How do you gauge what to tell them?

1. Stick to the facts. They are getting the same stuff from the grapevine as you are. They may even have heard things you haven't. Don't speculate or give assurances that everything is OK or say anything you don't know is absolutely true. Your credibility is on the line. Your relationship with your boss may be affected if there's too much agitation in your department. You have to think through the implications of even hinting at an untruth before you say anything.

A lot of executives think that it will calm the ranks if they are told nothing is going on. That never fooled a child. People know when something is going on even if they haven't a clue as to what it is. Remember, people hate change. The lower in the organization they are, the more they hate it, because they feel like helpless victims with no control over their own lives at all. Therefore, it's useless to try to reassure people with platitudes.

What is calming is facts. Even if you get no guidelines at all from above, you should stick to the facts. The company either has or has not been sold. Someone either has or has not resigned. Scrupulously avoid any speculation about who may be next or who may buy the company. If the company is having financial problems that appear especially grave, stick to how much money was lost. Don't speculate about how much the company can lose before going belly-up.

2. Don't lie for anybody. If your boss tells you to tell the troops something, and you know it's not true, attribute the statement to the boss. Don't let anyone think you're the source. If the troops ask if you agree, you can say, "No, I don't." You were ordered to pass something on, not to agree with it. If the troops can't distinguish between what you think and what you're paid to say, you've recruited some genuine losers.

3. Don't promise anybody anything. That won't help you keep people and it will seriously undercut your ability to manage. You must not promise anyone anything you can't personally do for him or her. Managers panic when someone hints he or she may leave and may promise something that isn't remotely possible—such as that the person's job will be saved. That manager's credibility just took a nosedive. Whatever is said to one employee will be repeated to all.

Intervention

Is there a veteran manager who hasn't been driven to near hysteria during a major crisis by his or her troops choosing just that moment to start a war among themselves? Probably not. Suppose, despite your yeoman efforts to keep them busy, the troops have started a squabble. Even though it's usually better to let them work things out, when there's a generalized crisis hanging cloudlike over the environment, you don't have time to let them inch toward a solution.

When a small manufacturing company's new product failed, the company took a nosedive. The manager of the financial department found that her subordinates actually began looking for things to fall out over. One secretary got into a shouting match with the CEO's secretary over which of them was supposed to clean the refrigerator that week. The accounts receivable clerk and the accounts payable clerk chose that moment to demand more help, even though they, more than anyone else in the company, should have seen the financial problems. Finally, desperate to get on with her paperwork for a bank loan, she called them all together, read them the riot act, and actually threatened to replace everyone, innocent as well as guilty. Things didn't return to normal but people muted their disputes.

A better way is to haul the culprits into your office and get the facts. Propose a solution. Tell them you want them

working smoothly within an hour. Get apologies, conces-
sions, whatever's necessary on the spot. This is not the
time to let people sort things out. You have to keep the
environment as harmonious as possible even if that means
twisting arms rather vigorously. Why the need for such
dispatch? The troops are already distracted. Give them
something really juicy, like an internal scandal, and nothing will get done.

Intervention should be done even when nothing "official" has come to your attention. You have to monitor the
atmosphere twice as carefully during crises as during normal times. If you sense hostility, check it out. Don't wait
for a flare-up. With the entire political system in flux, with
power beginning to drift in new directions, some stability
has to be maintained and that's part of your job.

Paul managed the sales force for a medical supply company. The company had been experiencing some difficulty
and the salespeople seemed restless. He decided to call a
meeting. What he found out was that several people had
been squabbling for three months over a particular account
and that, as a result, two big customers had been neglected. Paul had heard from one of the secretaries six
weeks before which salespeople were involved but he had
thought it minor. As a result he'd lost three months' worth
of extra orders, waiting for someone to mention the problem officially.

Crystal-Ball Gazing

If you and your subordinates have gotten along well
and have a mutually supportive relationship, they can't
help but look to you for some speculation as to the ultimate
outcome of whatever crisis is occurring. You wouldn't be
human if you didn't want to offer some of your own opinions. You've got to resist. This isn't a credibility issue as
much as it is the need to prevent the grapevine from positioning you as a guru. You can make the troops swear they
won't repeat a thing you've said, but that's a waste of time.

The entire company is as permeable as Swiss cheese right now.

Hiring and Firing

What do you tell an applicant you're trying to hire? If you let a new hire walk into a highly volatile situation with no warning, you are asking for a resentment problem down the road. Anyone foolish enough not to have checked on the company's health before applying there probably lacks star qualities anyway, but we can't be a curmudgeon on this point. Stick to the facts. Make no attempt to pat them into shape. If you do, the new employee will have an attitude problem before you can blink. A blink is the exact length of time it will take co-workers to fill him or her in. After you've explained that the company is going through a reorganization, say you can't predict the outcome. Answer specific questions but stonewall any requests for opinions.

Firing someone during a crisis often means you won't be able to replace him or her immediately, because a hiring freeze has been imposed. Should you fire, even if it will mean more work for others? Definitely. Politically speaking, the last thing you need is a shark or a dedicated nonperformer hanging around. He or she demoralizes everyone else—already under stress from the uncertainty —and gives them a license to goldbrick. The bottom line is this: Nobody cares what you say; what you do influences the troops.

Helping People Out

If you can see clearly that your department is going to be eliminated and you have good people who will need jobs, it's time for informal outplacement. Give your subordinates some help with their resumes if you believe they need it. The company has the right to keep people as long as they are wanted, but the troops have some informal rights as well. Some will job hunt immediately. Don't make it hard for them. Remember, you may work with these people again sometime. Think long-term. What are they going to remember about you as a manager? That you helped them when things turned mean? That you wrote good letters of recommendation when they needed them? That you made telephone calls? Or will they remember that like the fable of the dog in the manger, you barked at them even when you knew you couldn't keep them? Tacky, mean-minded, and self-defeating!

There is a difference between management and leadership. Management is the process of using leadership to reach goals. It's better to be known everywhere as a leader. Your subordinates won't forget what you did for them, and if you were a true leader, who knows who might hear about you? You might be job hunting soon yourself and good publicity never hurts!

◊ EXTRA HELP FOR YOU

Now that you've dealt with top management and placated your subordinates, what about you? You need to pamper yourself during the crisis as well. Two things veterans recommend. You need to exercise more than is normal. If you don't exercise at all, start! You are going to have great stress during the transition, and nothing helps alleviate that or helps you keep your cool better than three fifty-minute periods of a racket sport. It allows you to beat out your frustration in a socially acceptable way and it gets your heart going. Check with your doctor. He or she will confirm this.

We've mentioned this before but it's worth repeating. You've got to give yourself strokes and special treats for all you're doing. Don't be a stoic good soldier. It's not good for your mental health. No matter how anxious you are or how much extra work you're doing, there has got to be some relaxation and some time to put your work-related problems aside. After all, if your effectiveness is impaired, that won't do you or the company any good.

Finally, for what it's worth, every one of the veterans we talked to felt he or she gained enormously from the company's crisis. This was true even if he or she experienced a period of unemployment. All felt they'd learned management techniques they could use again. None would have chosen that method of learning, but all felt the positives far outweighed the negatives.

Epilogue: Political Ethics

Have you ever thought why you, and most other people, hate office politics? It's not difficult to become a good politician. Politics is absolutely a part of every work situation. If two people work together, there will be some jockeying for position, i.e., politics. Some people are very good at politics and they still hate it. The reason is that ninety-nine out of every hundred people believe that office politics is necessary but unethical! Even those (the majority) who can't even define ethics believe good politicians are by definition unethical.

Generally speaking, ethics refers to a code of conduct developed to guide behavior. Professions have written Codes of Ethics. Trade associations also have them. Violation of the code by a member of the group can be grounds for expulsion or censure. Codes exist because the group believes people won't behave ethically unless what is ethical is spelled out. The code also serves to alleviate any difficulty members may have in making choices.

The codes usually cover two types of situations: what members in good standing will do, such as provide good service and live up to terms of the contracts; and what members will not do, such as steal one another's clients or violate confidentiality.

Personal codes of ethics are highly subjective and open to interpretation by the individual. A bank robber might not countenance purse snatching. To him, robbing old ladies is highly unethical, if not immoral. Personal ethics, at best, are firmly rooted in an individual's acculturation. That leaves you, the individual, on the spot. What are your political ethics? Have you ever thought about it, or have you avoided the whole question? If you're ducking, you've got problems. Most of the material in this book requires you to make ethical choices. Would you outplace a boss? Would you force out a subordinate? Could you live with yourself if you did? The time to think about your code of ethics is now, not when you're up to your eyeballs in choices.

What do you owe the organization that pays your salary? A full day's work would seem to be a minimum. However, what is a full day's work? There's no universal definition. How about that old shibboleth, loyalty? What is that? Is outplacing an unproductive subordinate who can't be rehabbed an act of loyalty to the company?

What do you owe your boss? When do you decide you've covered up his drinking problem for the last time? When do you undercut him with his boss in order to save an important project or keep the company from losing money?

What do you owe your co-workers? Do you protect a pal even though you know he's ripping off the company? Do you confront the nonproducer? Do you confront the person who spreads harmful rumors even if they aren't about you?

What do you owe your subordinates? Do you have to be fair? What is fair? Is it ethical to fire someone because you don't like him or her?

All of these unpleasant questions demand that you develop your own code. You can work forty years and never confront your own ethics. If a clear ethical issue comes up, you can duck. However, you'll know you're ducking. Ultimately, what other people think isn't nearly as important as what you think. Although you should know that CEOs surveyed on what they look for in managers, to a man, mentioned personal integrity, i.e., high standards and a personal code of ethics.

You can avoid years on the couch, trying to figure out why you're unhappy and your life isn't what you wanted or expected, if you decide what principles are going to guide your decisions. Once you've decided, you will discover one thing. You are at your most vulnerable, politically, when you violate your personal code. Even the semiconscious co-worker can practically smell when you're ethically overextended. It comes across like an unusual tentativeness. Without a code you're vulnerable all of the time. Even you can't predict your own response.

A word of advice: A good test of whether you have written your code of ethics to reflect your real values is whether or not you like living with the person you see in the mirror each morning. If not, you need to examine your code and your actions.